Creating A Home
Designing and Planning Room by Room

First published in the UK 1996
by Ward Lock
Wellington House
125 The Strand
London WC2R OBB

This edition published by Index 1997

Copyright © Eaglemoss Publications Ltd 1996

Based on *Creating a Home*

Front cover: (t) Richard Paul, (bl) IPC Magazines/RHS, (br) Smallbone of Devizes
Back cover: Elizabeth Whiting Associates; *illustration*: Ross Wardle/Portland Artists
Title page: Eurostudio; *imprint page*: Dorma; *contents page*: Ross Wardle/Portland Artists:
Introduction: IPC Magazines/Robert Harding Syndication

A British Library Cataloguing-in-Publication Data block for this book may be obtained from the
British Library

ISBN 0 7063 7563 7

Printed in Spain by Cayfosa Industria Grafica

CONTENTS

INTRODUCTION

Creating a home is one of the most exciting, challenging and rewarding occupations in life. Exciting because colour, pattern and lighting can transform a room out of all proportion to cost. Challenging because you have to visualize how you want it to look, then carry out things in the right order – and to a budget. Rewarding, because as you work towards getting it right, you'll have a place to come home to that's welcoming, comfortable and personal.

Whether you intend just to redecorate one room, are re-assessing your existing home, or are about to start from scratch with a completely new property, this book will provide a comprehensive and practical guide. Here, in one volume, is all the basic design and planning knowledge you need to enable you to give your home a facelift with the minimum of trouble. Straightforward instructions and clear line drawings show you how to draw up the type of plans used by professional interior designers, and the five chapters cover the most important aspects of the home: the living room, kitchen and dining areas, bedrooms and bathrooms.

Before getting down to details, there are some general points to consider. If you can possibly manage to, don't rush. When thinking about improving your home, be prepared to be flexible. Consider all the possibilities carefully and remember that the best solution is often the simplest. Re-think room use – there is no reason why you shouldn't turn the room you sleep in into the living room if it affords the best daytime view. Re-organize a room by changing the position of a door, for example. Think about adding on or converting an attic or garage. Rather than moving house, it may well be cheaper and more satisfactory.

With lavish photography throughout to help and inspire you, here is the best place to start to create the home you have always wanted.

THE LIVING ROOM

The living room is the most important room of your home to plan and design. A well thought out living room is the focal point – and the showcase – of the entire house.

In the past, most houses had a separate parlour kept for special occasions and entertaining guests. The family lived in the kitchen, and ate there if they were not prosperous enough to have a separate dining room. But today, living rooms work much harder than any other part of the home. You may want to relax there after a hard day, and entertain guests in an uncluttered, welcoming atmosphere, but this competes with the family's demands for somewhere they can watch television, listen to music, study, plan and eat. It is these conflicting demands that make designing the living room such a satisfying challenge.

As the chapter unfolds past the important planning stages, you will find out how to accommodate all the functions of the living room without sacrificing style and comfort – whether you plan to knock down walls to increase the size of the living area or simply want to re-arrange the furniture to make better use of the space.

Helpful advice on choosing living room furniture from the bewildering range of styles available today is provided, and lighting also gets special attention – vital for creating the right ambience as well as for specific tasks.

MEASURE THE LIVING ROOM

Knowing the measurements of a room helps you estimate quantities and plan the layout accurately and easily.

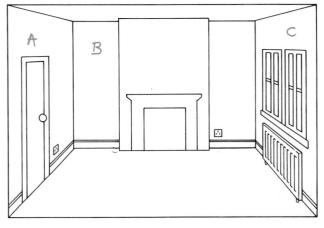

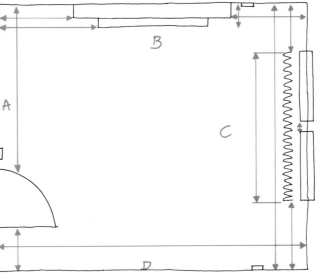

Top: view of room. Above: rough sketch of floor plan.

Plans of floors and walls are invaluable when you start to design a room from scratch or wish to give a new look to a room by rearranging the furniture.

☐ When you are redecorating, plans are essential to estimate quantities of materials accurately.

☐ If you are moving house, a floor plan for each room in your new home will help you work out what will fit where and also show the furniture removers exactly where to position the pieces.

☐ If you are making any alterations to your home you can work out ideas to discuss with an architect, and produce plans to show your builder, plumber or electrician exactly what you want.

METRES OR FEET?

Generally, it is best to use metric measurements these days. But although the metric system was introduced some years ago, many people (and a few manufacturers) still think in imperial yards, feet and inches. If you are measuring up for something specific – such as an alcove cupboard, floor tiles or wallpaper – find out which system the manufacturer of your chosen product uses.

Avoid measuring up in one system, then converting to another. A yard is less than a metre, for example, and if something needs to fit exactly, being a few millimetres out can be disastrous.

DRAWING A FLOOR PLAN

The sketch (top right) shows a typical room in an older house or flat, but measuring up is the same for any room. (The letters A, B and C indicate the walls in the floor plan below.)

Making a rough sketch Start by making a rough outline sketch of the room on which to jot down your measurements. Don't worry if it looks out of proportion.

Mark the position of doors, windows, radiators, plug sockets, light switches, fireplaces and other permanent features on the rough sketch. Show which way the doors open, and also the windows if they swivel or pivot.

It is customary to mark in windows, radiators, switches, and so on, on floor plans even if they are not at floor level.

Filling in the measurements It's much easier to measure up if you work with a partner. Work around the room systematically; start at one corner and run the tape along the floor, keeping it straight and parallel to the wall you are measuring (if the tape is angled, the measurements will be inaccurate). As you take each measurement, mark it on the sketch.

If there is a feature jutting out from the wall, run the tape from wall to wall in front of the feature, and then mark on your plan the measurements:

☐ from first wall to fireplace
☐ the width of the fireplace
☐ from fireplace to second wall
☐ from wall to wall

Then check that the individual measurements add up to the wall-to-wall total.

Remember, too, to measure the width of the doors, door frames, windows and window frames.

Measuring accurately For most purposes rooms can be assumed to have right-angled corners and parallel walls that are equal in length and height, though this is rarely the case. If the measurements are only slightly different it is not worth worrying about, but if you are measuring up for fitted furniture, such as a cupboard to be built into an alcove, you will need a much more accurate plan.

EQUIPMENT CHECKLIST

☐ A4 pad of large-scale squared (5mm) paper *or* standard (2, 10 & 20mm) graph paper plus some scrap paper.

☐ Retractable steel measuring tape. The longer the tape the better – the fewer times you move it, the more accurate the measurements.

☐ HB pencil, eraser and ruler.

☐ Sturdy chair or stepladder, plus two 2m/6ft straight poles (dowels or garden canes), strong adhesive tape and chalk for measuring heights.

☐ Pocket torch for lighting dark corners.

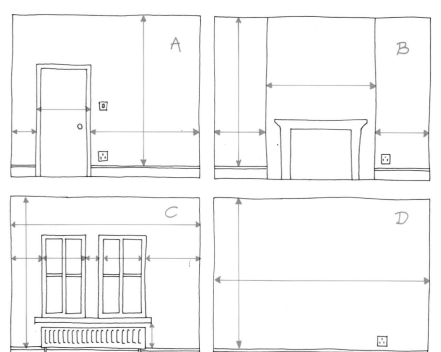

DRAWING ELEVATIONS

The floor sketch gives you the basic dimensions of the room; the next step is to do a plan of each wall, called an elevation. Make a rough sketch of the wall. You already have the widths of each wall from your floor plan; now, measure the height of each wall and the height of features such as doors, windows and picture rails.

Trick of the trade If you're on your own, use a couple of 2m/6ft canes or dowels to measure elevations. Stand on a chair and hold the poles against the walls; slide them apart to the full height of the room and then tape them together firmly.

Now mark the height of each feature – curtain track, mantelpiece, window and door-frame etc – on the taped-together poles. Place the poles on the floor, read off the measurements and then transfer them to your elevation sketch.

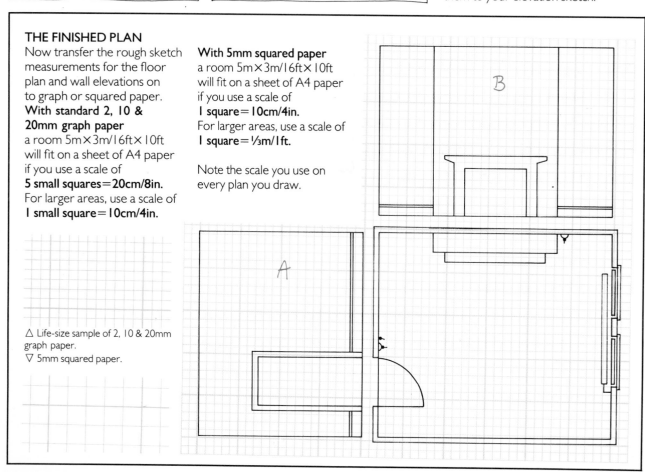

THE FINISHED PLAN

Now transfer the rough sketch measurements for the floor plan and wall elevations on to graph or squared paper.
With standard 2, 10 & 20mm graph paper
a room 5m×3m/16ft×10ft will fit on a sheet of A4 paper if you use a scale of
5 small squares=20cm/8in.
For larger areas, use a scale of
1 small square=10cm/4in.

With 5mm squared paper
a room 5m×3m/16ft×10ft will fit on a sheet of A4 paper if you use a scale of
1 square=10cm/4in.
For larger areas, use a scale of
1 square=⅓m/1ft.

Note the scale you use on every plan you draw.

△ Life-size sample of 2, 10 & 20mm graph paper.
▽ 5mm squared paper.

CALCULATING QUANTITIES

How much paint, tiles, wallpaper, etc, to buy depends on the area they are intended to cover. So you need to work out the area of the floor, walls and ceiling before you set about ordering any materials.
Use the elevation drawings to find the area of the walls in a room: multiply the height by the width of each wall in turn and add the totals together.

Use the floor plan to help you estimate both the floor and ceiling areas. To find the area of the floor or ceiling, multiply the length of the room by its width.
If the room is L-shaped, simply divide the floor plan into two rectangles, multiply the width and length of each rectangle and then add them together for the area of the whole room. Use this method for any recess or bay.

SYMBOL SENSE

These are the most common of the standard symbols used on plans drawn up by professionals.

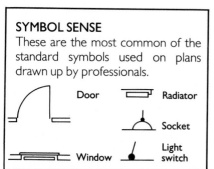

PLANNING YOUR LIVING ROOM

With the pressure on space in today's homes, living rooms often have to accommodate a variety of activities.

Nowadays, living rooms are the place for doing all kinds of things, from entertaining guests to reading; from watching television to doing homework. But at the same time, the living room is the showcase of your home, somewhere you can express your tastes and display treasured possessions. The way to reconcile these two aspects is through good organization and planning.

ALTERING THE STRUCTURE

Any changes to the basic structure of the living room must be carried out well before you start to decorate. Alterations vary from simple work you can do yourself to major, expensive changes for which you will need professional help. Common alterations requiring building work include:
☐ blocking or opening up a fireplace
☐ blocking or opening up a doorway
☐ knocking two rooms into one
☐ moving a partition wall
☐ enlarging or putting in a new window – for example, making french windows
☐ extending the living room – for example, building on a conservatory.

Consider whether the changes are worth the cost and disruption. If you are only planning to stay in your home a couple of years, a cosmetic solution might be a wiser alternative. For instance, instead of blocking up an unused doorway, you could simply disguise it by placing a large piece of furniture in front, or turning it into a display alcove.

SERVICES

Installing central heating, new wiring or new socket outlets is also work that should be carried out at an early stage. Don't finish decorating and then discover that you need more electrical points. If you are already engaged in building work, think about adding more points at the same time. This will provide you with flexibility when it comes to planning seating and TV and hi-fi arrangements, and also prevent trailing flexes ruining the appearance of the room. You might also consider wiring all the lighting to a central switch by the door, regulated by a dimmer.

LIGHTING

Before you begin to decorate is also the time to decide whether you need to make any changes to the existing lighting set-up. Avoid glaring overhead fittings; instead create atmospheric pools of light with table lamps, uplighters and spots. Provide a concentrated light source for a work area if you need one. If you want wall-mounted fixtures or concealed downlighters, you should also install these before you start to decorate.

▽ Lighting plan

A ceiling track with three spotlights provides general illumination in this squarish room. The two table lamps and standard lamp make pools of light for reading, while the picture light and concealed display lights either side of the fireplace give indirect light.

BEFORE YOU BEGIN
Start by listing all the activities you expect to take place in the living room, now or in the foreseeable future. These may include:
☐ watching television; listening to records
☐ entertaining guests; parties
☐ putting visitors up for the night
☐ reading; quiet study or other hobbies
☐ dining
☐ children's play.
Now look carefully at existing features, furniture, lighting and decoration to decide what you would like to retain and what needs replacing.
☐ Is there a special feature you would like to emphasize?
☐ Would some structural work improve the layout?
☐ Is the furniture right for the room?
☐ Does the lighting work well?
☐ Are there enough electric sockets – in the right place?
☐ Does the decoration suit your taste and belongings?
☐ Do you need more shelves or cupboard space?

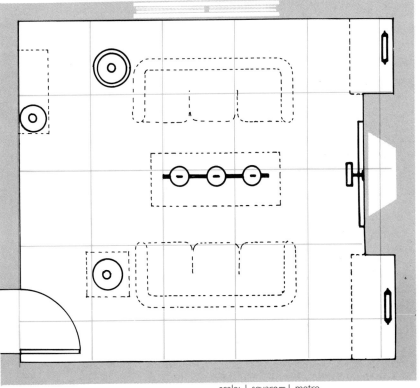

scale: 1 square = 1 metre

KEY		
⊢⊣ wall mounted picture light		▭ concealed display light
◎ standard lamp		⊸◯⊷ track mounted spotlight
		◉ table lamp

FURNISHING

Living rooms are all about seating arrangements. There are several guidelines to bear in mind when devising a layout. The first is to identify a focal point. This can be a fireplace, coffee table or a good view. If your room lacks a focus, think about creating one: a group of plants lit by an uplighter; a strategically placed mirror to reflect light or a view; a painting, a beautiful object or fine piece of furniture.

Seating plan Now work out your seating around the focal point. Draw up a scale plan of the room, marking on doors, windows, electric sockets and switches, lighting fixtures, radiators and any features, such as a fireplace or alcove. Measure the furniture you own or would like to buy and draw the shapes to scale on a piece of card. Cut them out and arrange them on the plan of the room and move about until you arrive at the best layout.

Symmetrical or L-shaped arrangements suit most rooms, provided the size and style of the furniture is right. Take a good look at the furniture you have. One piece that is too large or overbearing can ruin the feel of the whole room. Be firm with yourself, if something doesn't look right it might be best to sell it or lend it to friends or family.

Bear in mind that a three-seater sofa can be a waste of space. Although it may seat two people comfortably, no one likes to sit in the middle. A sofa placed directly in front of a fireplace will block the heat and the view, and create a dead area behind.

Flexibility If you entertain regularly, ensure at least some of your furniture can be moved about easily, and provide upholstered stools for extra seating, and side tables for glasses and plates.

Arranging seating so that everyone can watch TV in comfort, but without the blank screen dominating the room when you are entertaining is often a problem. Try to plan your layout so that chairs and sofas can be turned around or moved so that the emphasis is changed. Another solution is to keep the TV on a wheeled base or trolley that can be pulled out for viewing.

Dining area If your living room must provide space for dining, arrange the furniture so there is a degree of separation between the different areas. A partition or screen might help and an extending table and folding chairs will save on space.

Finishing touches are important. Make room for your treasured possessions, whether they are pictures, objects or a special chair. Your living room should say something about yourself, not be a sterile display of 'good taste'.

A DECORATIVE SCHEME

The best starting point for a decorative scheme is often the floor. This is likely to be the most expensive item and will have a dominating effect because of the sheer surface area involved. It will also outlast the paintwork, so if you are choosing a carpet, for example, opt for a shade that will suit several different colour schemes.

Always plan the decoration for the room as a whole. Don't find your options strictly limited because you have picked out a particularly vivid pattern for the curtains and then can't find anything to go with it. Take your time, especially if you are decorating from scratch. Most mistakes are made when everything is chosen and bought in a hurry.

Collect samples of the colours, patterns and materials you would like to use for curtains, blinds, upholstery, flooring, walls, ceilings and woodwork. Assemble them on a single sheet of paper or card to see how they look together.

STORAGE

If your living room caters for several different activities, maintaining the overall style and atmosphere without sacrificing practicality is largely a question of providing adequate storage. Books, records and ornaments can be displayed on open shelves; other items are best concealed in cupboards.

Built-in cupboards or free-standing units can be used to stow electronic equipment, sewing materials, games or hobbies – anything you don't want on view. A sideboard in a dining area can be an attractive way of storing table linen, cutlery, drinks and glasses.

A trolley is also very useful – as a mobile drinks cabinet or to carry the TV or video equipment. When not required, it can simply be wheeled out of sight. And if your living room is also the children's play area, a deep wicker basket with a lid, or a wooden chest would make a stylish home for toys at the end of the day.

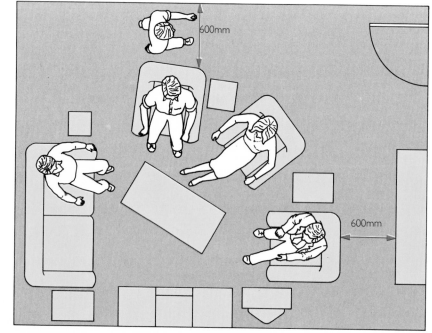

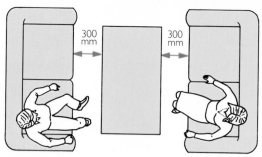

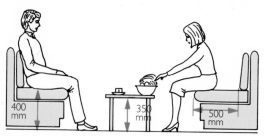

△ **Space to pass**
Allow a minimum of 600mm for someone to walk into or around a room without having to squeeze past people already seated.

◁ **Knee room**
Make sure there is at least 300mm between the edges of seats and the coffee table so that people can stand up and sit comfortably.

◁ **Standard seating**
These measurements are the typical height of a coffee table and the depth and height of an armchair.

THE HEART OF THE LIVING ROOM

The key to creating a welcoming living room is to have a focal point – something which invites people to gather round and relax.

A living room without a focal point is a room without life. Family and friends need something to gather round when they're sitting down, otherwise they tend to feel uneasy and 'lost' – even in a modest-sized room.

Without a focal point, it is almost impossible to plan the rest of a room successfully. A well-planned room has nothing to do with the quantity of furniture. It is easy to make the mistake of cramming a room full of tables and chairs but still not manage to give it a focal point. More often, it is a question of planning your layout to make the most of the room's good points and minimize the bad ones. Simply by rearranging the furniture and rethinking the lighting, you can give a room a 'heart'.

The appeal of a fire In the past, the hearth was always the heart of the living room. There's something about the warm, flickering light of a fire that draws you towards it – even if you're not too cold.

But many modern houses don't have a traditional log or coal fire. Instead, they rely on gas or electric fires which by themselves can look uninviting, particularly when switched off. And some homes have no fireplace at all – only central heating.

The temptation is just to turn to the TV set as the source of life and interest, then arrange things accordingly. But although this is fine when the TV is on and everyone wants to watch it, the results are unsettling when it's switched off, and the blank screen sits there watching you.

Home is where the hearth is
Traditionally, the fireplace has always been the focal point of the living room – few things compare with the inviting glow of flickering flames.

ALTERNATIVE FOCAL POINTS

If there is no fireplace, you need to look carefully at what else the room has to offer, then decide where to place the emphasis. Two favourite alternatives are coffee tables and picture windows, but before you consider their pros and cons, do remember that often a combination of focal points works best. For example, the focus can change easily to a coffee table when the fire is unlit or the curtains are drawn.

Coffee tables The classic focal point for an otherwise featureless room, a coffee table serves as the centre around which seating can be clustered. You've probably already got one somewhere but ask yourself if it is large enough to do the job – can the family really gather round it? If you can't find one the right size consider butting together two square or oblong tables.

The beauty of coffee tables is that they are easy to decorate. Make sure yours is interesting and eyecatching – use flowers or houseplants, books, candles, collections of seashells, a bowl of fruit or attractive ashtrays – and change it whenever the mood takes you.

Try to make the table display a personal one, to avoid the anonymous, 'waiting-room' style of decoration. (Try to keep it from becoming a permanent depository for children's bits and bobs, and dirty cups. It is the one piece of furniture that attracts attention – and inspection!)

Windows A wonderful view is too precious to ignore. You may decide to plan the seating so that the outdoors is part of everyone's view when seated, and so that your visitors' attention is drawn to it the moment they enter the room.

Set-off the view with pull-up blinds if

BRIGHT IDEA

A floor socket lets you plug in a table or standard lamp almost anywhere without having to put up with a trailing flex. Fitted with a child-proof hinged cover plate, with a satin brass or matt chrome finish, it can be stood on safely when not in use.

◁ *Coffee table centre piece*
When a room lacks a 'natural' focal point, create your own with a coffee table and arrange the seating around it. Notice here how the basket of fruit and flowers help to attract the eye.

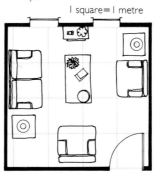

I square= I metre

▽ *Creating a pool of light*
This alternative arrangement based on a three-piece suite makes more use of the window view as a focal point. By night the coffee table becomes the main centre of interest – lit by a ceiling downlighter instead of a lamp, with a recessed eyeball downlighter making the painting a secondary focal point.

the windows are narrow – or pretty curtains tied back to each side if they are wide.

Whatever the focal point, don't forget to make your furniture arrangement inviting. Often there isn't enough room to do this successfully with a three-piece suite so, if you are thinking of changing your furniture, consider the alternative scheme of two sofas placed at right angles or facing each other. Research shows that the right-angle arrangement puts everyone at ease straight away and creates the perfect place for a coffee table within everyone's reach.

A ROOM FOR ALL SEASONS

Like a garden, the truly comfortable living room can change with the seasons.

In summer In a room where the fire is the natural focal point, you need to think about those long summer days (and evenings) when it won't be lit. If you want the general atmosphere to be light and airy, pull your furniture back from the fireplace and aim to make better use of the room as a whole. A coffee table makes an excellent alternative focal point when illuminated by a gentle pool of light from a downlighter set into the ceiling.

To stop the fireplace itself from looking dull and gloomy, surround it with plants, fill the grate with pine-cones or place a treasured item – such as a decorative screen – in front. Here the TV has been moved out of picture to the wall where the camera is positioned so it can be watched from both sofas but doesn't dominate the room.

In winter Cosiness and warmth are the main considerations, so group your sofas and chairs around the fire, with the coffee table playing a secondary role.

Now you can move the TV to one side of the fireplace so both focal points are close together and you can watch in comfort in front of the warm, flickering glow of the fire.

I square= I metre

Summer freshness, winter warmth
In summer (top), the fireplace plays more of a background role. Open up your seating plan to give people air and space, grouping them around a pleasantly decorated coffee table. But don't forget the empty hearth – plants or dried flowers will stop it looking gloomy.

In winter (above), cosiness becomes the order of the day (floor plan right). Re-group seating around the fire and move the TV to this side of the room.

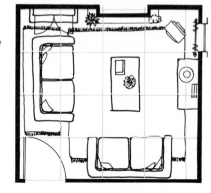

A ROOM WITH A VIEW

An attractive view can provide a satisfying focal point by day, particularly if you choose a simple, undistracting curtain treatment. But don't forget that at night you will no longer be able to see the view and need to make some other arrangement.

Night and day

At night (right) plants are lit up, both indoors and out, to become the focus of interest.

By day (below) the owner of this flat can enjoy the view, while the indoor plants provide foreground interest and a visual link. The TV set is placed to one side so it does not spoil the view or reflect the daylight.

I square= I metre

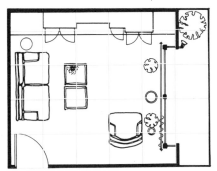

Here, the room is planned by day to make the best of the group of large plants, the balcony and the view beyond. The sofa faces outwards and the swivel chair can face in or out.

By night, clever lighting emphasizes the indoor plants, while a light on the balcony creates a 'view' outside. A floor uplighter – rather like a tin can with a bulb in it – is placed below the main group of plants to focus attention on them, and cast dramatic, leafy shadows over the ceiling. Another plant outside is picked out with a weatherproof spotlight mounted above the doors, making the balcony part of the night time focal point.

◁ **Television centre**
In this attic room the emphasis is on the TV which forms part of a purpose-built shelving system. When the rafters were boarded in, a recess was created above the bookshelves for a video, and it also provides attractive windowsills for plants and ornaments – alternative viewpoints when the set is switched off.

The L-shaped seating arrangement in this rather narrow room offers an inviting corner to curl up with a book under the lamp.

▷ **Behind closed doors**
Here, the problem of what to do with the TV was overcome by filling one wall with shop-bought wooden shelves, drawers and cupboards; the centre section houses both TV and video behind a pair of doors. The formality of the units is emphasized by the arrangement of pictures.

When the doors are closed on the TV, the focal point changes. The seating is grouped to make the most of the enclosed fireplace and gives a glimpse of the outside to those sitting on the sofa. From the chair there is a 'borrowed' view in the mirror.

◁ **Effective paint**
This corner used to house a large TV in a nasty imitation wood finish, a video and masses of tangled flex. The inexpensive solution was to build low cupboards between the fireplace and window wall, angled at the window end to make a deeper shelf. The video is now hidden in the cupboards; the TV, minus its legs, sits above. The TV and cupboards were all painted pale grey and then rag rolled and sponged in blue and yellow, picking up the colours in the room.

DOUBLE RECEPTION ROOMS

A traditional part of many homes, double reception rooms can remain two rooms or be combined into one.

In many homes, double reception rooms are divided by doors which can be folded back on themselves to combine the two rooms into a single larger space. These dividing doors have the advantage of allowing great flexibility since, with the doors open, the two rooms can be combined almost instantly – for a Christmas party, perhaps. In most houses, however, the front and back rooms remain entirely separate.

Traditionally, one reception room was set aside for 'best' use, a room in which to receive visitors. The second room served as a family living area; in small homes, this was often a combined kitchen/diner.

With today's more informal lifestyles – and the ease with which large rooms can now be kept warm – many people find that a single, large living area is more appropriate to their needs.

Where doors were part of the original design, this is fairly easily achieved. The doors can be removed entirely – or a compromise reached whereby solid doors are replaced by glazed ones that make the division seem less complete.

Two small, separate reception rooms are often best combined by removing the dividing wall – but remember to check whether the wall is loadbearing before it is removed or altered. A squared-off or arched opening, dividing doors, or some form of temporary or removable partition, could be installed to enable you to enjoy the best of both worlds: separate rooms or a single one.

Traditional elegance
Large, well-proportioned double reception rooms lend themselves to a traditional style of decoration. Here one room is used as a living room while the other serves as a dining room. A decorative opening divides the two.

◁ ▽ *On a formal note*
With only an elegant arch to divide them, the double reception rooms in this home serve as a through living room. By positioning the television in one end of the room (left), the front part (below) becomes a more formal living room.

Both 'ends' of the room are simply decorated, with a mixture of traditional and antique furniture set against plain walls, carpeting and upholstery. The sole exception is the window dressing where patterned fabric forms full, rich curtains, topped by pinch-pleated pelmets.

The single decorative theme creates a feeling of unity between the elaborate windows at each end.

MAKING CHOICES

The way you make use of double reception rooms is governed by your lifestyle, the size of your home and, of course, the way the house was built.

What are your needs? If you have a large, naturally untidy family, would it be a good idea to keep one half reserved for 'best' use? That way, the arrival of unexpected guests won't throw the entire household into a state of panic as a frantic rush begins to make the living room look presentable. If this is the case, it's best to ensure that the front room is entirely separate, so that family clutter doesn't gradually creep over the boundaries. If necessary, install a partition (perhaps a movable one) where there was none before.

Is there a dining room elsewhere in the house? If not, you may want to use one of the reception rooms for eating. On the other hand, you may not want a separate dining room – a table in the kitchen may well suffice.

Does the house pose any limitations? If the front and back rooms are very small, combining them into a single larger space may be the only option that makes sense. In contrast, bigger double reception rooms which have been combined may feel too large for comfort.

You may feel that you need to maintain a division in order to keep the functions of the rooms separate. If you like formal entertaining, for example, a small dining room and an equally small living room may be much more useful than a single room, however much more spacious it may be.

Considering your options It is important to ascertain whether a dividing wall is loadbearing or not. If it is, removing it entirely (or partially) is problematic since a supporting beam must be installed to carry the load. Consider your options carefully, and bear in mind the original layout envisaged by the builders of your home – a gently-

△ *Decorative arch*
By removing as much of the original dividing wall as possible, a squared-off opening has been made in this double reception room. The angular shape is softened by a decorative corbel at each corner.

curved arch may be more in keeping with the style of the room than a squared-off opening. Decorative mouldings, architraves, or corbels not only enhance the look of the arch: they also protect if from accidental damage. Erecting a partition where none existed before is, obviously, less difficult.

A useful compromise may be to arrange matters so that the two reception rooms can be temporarily divided (by means of a movable screen or curtain), or partially divided (perhaps by arranging a piece of furniture across the opening). However, in some situations – that of a messy family, for instance – this may be self-defeating.

THE BEST OF BOTH WORLDS

Apart from completely removable divisions, there are many ways of separating the two parts of a double reception room so that, when necessary, they can still be combined into one.

Folding doors were often installed for this reason and can be replaced fairly easily if they have been removed – as can conventional doors which hang from side hinges. Folding, concertina and sliding doors all save on floor space – but remember to allow sufficient wall space for sliding doors to open.

Doors are available in a great variety of styles and finishes. Fully or partially glazed types allow both rooms to benefit from an extended view and make small rooms appear larger. Panelled doors suit period homes; flush doors are better suited to more modern houses.

△ *Through room*
It's often best to decorate two combined reception rooms similarly. The floor and wall treatments unite these rooms and the ornate mirror in the foreground echoes that in the dining room.

▽ *Flexible division*
If rooms are not to be permanently divided, thick curtains hung across an opening can be drawn when required. A pair of armchairs placed so that they form a barrier reinforce the division.

Scale: 1 square = 1 metre square

◁ **Vertical blinds**
In a modern setting, streamlined vertical blinds can be used both as a flexible room divider and as a covering for large windows. In order to ensure that they hang well, each of the vertical louvres that make up the blind can incorporate an individual weight in a sealed pocket – or the weights can be linked by a continuous chain.

▽ **Letting the light through**
A partition constructed entirely (or partially) of doors allows double reception rooms to be opened up and closed off in a matter of seconds. If solid doors would cut out too much light, fully or partially-glazed types can be used.
  Cut glass stars add an individual touch to the mahogany doors shown here.

A radiator shelf provides extra shelf space and protects the wall above from staining. A self-fixing shelf such as the one shown here easily slots securely into place behind the radiator.

△ **Traditional feel**
In order to produce an extremely spacious living room, almost all traces of the divider between the original rooms has been removed; all that remains is a narrow supporting beam at ceiling height.
  Although the colour scheme, furniture and soft furnishings do not change, a pair of armchairs visually divides the living area.

◁ **Plain and pale**
Knocking double reception rooms into one can produce a long, thin shape in which it can be difficult to arrange furniture successfully. Here, several sofas are placed round the walls, and a large wall mirror makes the room seem wider. Pale colours throughout enhance the sense of space.

OPEN-PLAN LIVING

If they are to work successfully, open-plan rooms need careful thought and planning.

Although open-plan living may not be to everyone's taste, many of today's homes are built with such a layout. Because of the relatively small size of many new houses, the living and dining rooms are often combined, and sometimes the hall, stairs and kitchen are also part of the same layout. The absence of dividing walls allows a limited floor area to appear roomier so that the inhabitants of an open-plan home feel less cramped.

On the other hand, large modern houses can also be open-plan in layout, and dividing walls on the ground floor of many older homes have been removed in order to combine one or more rooms into a single, spacious living area.

The pros and cons Open-plan living has several distinct advantages. In the first place, it is particularly suited to an informal lifestyle, where different activities are not confined to separate rooms. If, for example, you and your family are not keen on formal entertaining, but like guests to mingle with the entire family and, perhaps, its clutter, then an open-plan layout creates a relaxed feel.

In a small space, the absence of clearly-defined rooms produces an illusion of spaciousness – and it is also true that walls do take up valuable floor space. In a larger home, a layout which is not sectioned-off creates a luxurious feeling of unlimited space with unlimited possibilities.

In contrast, though, open-plan living implies a sacrifice of privacy as well as peace and quiet. It is more difficult for members of the family to pursue different activities if they cannot physically separate themselves from each other. Teenagers, for instance, may want to listen to loud music while their parents would prefer somewhere quiet! In addition, decor and furniture are more difficult to arrange so that the space is functional and visually unified.

A clever compromise
Partitions create distinct activity areas in this open-plan attic flat. The living area is cut off from the bedroom by sliding doors, and from the kitchen by shelves. A peninsular unit used for meals separates kitchen and work area.

△ A modern home

A single decorative scheme unites this open-plan living/dining room. The same wallpaper and carpet are used throughout, and the curtain fabric and tablecloth link the two ends of the room. A large rug ties the seating together, and the clear coffee table allows the geometric lines of the rug to show through.

Scale: 1 square = 1 metre square (approx)

◁ An open-plan living area

In many newly-built houses, the entire ground floor has an open-plan layout. In this example, the living and dining rooms are combined into a single living space. However, a wall separates the front door and the living area, thus creating a small but useful hallway. The small kitchen is either a separate room or it is separated from the main living area by kitchen units.

BRIGHT IDEA

Vertical poles can divide rooms without entirely blocking them off. Here, an elegant vertical radiator serves a dual function.

A FEELING OF SPACE

An open-plan layout can be successfully created even if this was not what the architect originally intended. Knocking down a non-load-bearing wall can be a relatively simple matter, although it's always best to seek professional advice. All traces of the wall can be removed, and the rooms totally united.

However, a load-bearing wall is essential to the structure of the house and cannot be removed entirely. A reinforced joist or beam must be installed to carry the weight of the floor or roof above. Since the joist and the side pillars on which it rests will be visible, some traces of the obsolete wall have to remain. An arch is often installed in such an opening, so that the room appears long and thin, with a 'waist' in the middle.

Before taking any action, though, consider the character and proportions of the rooms. Period houses can be ruined if interior walls are indiscriminately knocked down. So long as it is done with sensitivity, an eye to proportion and respect for the original structure of the house, however, there is no reason why some rooms, at least, cannot be combined.

UNITY OF STYLE

Planning the decor of an open-plan space can be complicated, since you need to combine an overall impression of unity with a suitable atmosphere for each activity area.

Overall cohesion is best created by the use of the same (or similar) wall and floorcoverings throughout the room. Use lighting, furniture and accent colours in accessories and furnishings to alter subtly the mood in, say, the living and dining areas.

If the room has a natural break (for example, along the line of a wall which has been removed), it is easier to change the colour scheme and flooring in the two parts and still avoid a bitty and disjointed end result.

Where you decide to place items of furniture needs special attention. There must be enough space to allow people to move around easily, but without creating 'dead', unused areas in the middle of the room or in one leg of an L-shape. List all the activities that are likely to take place in the room and group the furniture to form relatively separate activity areas. Rugs can form effective focal points and furniture can be positioned to section-off areas.

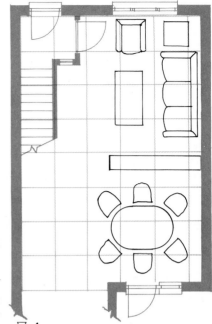

Scale: 1 square = 1 metre square (approx)

▽ **A new arrangement**
Since space is limited in this open-plan room, a see-through shelving unit serves both to display plants and ornaments and as a room divider. This separates the dining area to some extent but at the same time ensures that the two sections of the room do not feel uncomfortably claustrophobic.

DIVIDING THE SPACE

If you are unhappy with an existing open-plan living area, a large space can be sub-divided into two smaller ones.

A partition not only increases privacy in the newly-created rooms; it also makes decoration easier as the new rooms can be tailored for their intended use.

Before you forge ahead and build a permanent divider, or buy a freestanding partition which may not fit the bill, experiment with an improvised divider to make certain that the new arrangement will be to your liking. The dividing line needs to be carefully placed so that it does not cut across a window, make a room disagreeably dark, slice an elegant plastered ceiling in two or obstruct movement about the room.

◁ *An open divider*
Shelves and half-height doors visually separate and hide any mess in the kitchen without totally cutting off the kitchen from the dining area.

▽ *Partial division*
Although several walls have been removed in this modern home, part of one wall has been left intact so as to screen cooking activity from the sitting area.

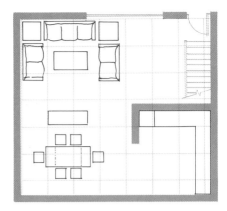

Scale: I square = I metre square (approx)

▽ Furniture as a room divider

Arranging furniture in an open-plan living area can be difficult. Here, a long, low sideboard has been positioned along a line separating the dining and living areas. The seating has also been rearranged to form an L-shape with a two-seater sofa screening the hall area and front door.

Boxing-in the radiators to match the dining table and chairs makes them part of the overall decor rather than necessary evils.

CHOOSING A PARTITION

The least permanent way of dividing up a living area is by arranging the furniture – a sofa, sideboard or shelving unit – so that it forms a barrier. The only proviso here is that the back of the piece of furniture must be presentable – and this is often not the case with furniture designed to be placed along a wall.

Floor-to-ceiling curtains can muffle sound and create a soft look. Because they will be seen from both sides, use either a double thickness or a sheer fabric. Another possibility is to hang vertical or roller blinds from the ceiling. (Since roller blinds are not made in large widths, you may have to hang two or three next to each other.) Finally, folding or sliding screens are available in many different styles – or you can make your own. They are easily moved around to suit the occasion.

A permanent dividing wall is not difficult to build since it need be no more substantial than a timber frame covered with plasterboard. A half-height wall may be the answer in a smallish room, providing privacy without complete division. Sliding doors can form an entire partition in themselves, or they can be incorporated in a partition wall.

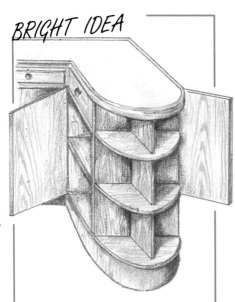

BRIGHT IDEA

Two-way access A double set of doors on kitchen units between an open-plan kitchen/dining room means that crockery and cutlery are easily reached from both rooms, making setting the table and emptying the dishwasher quicker and easier. One side – preferably the one opening on to the kitchen – can be left open for even easier access.

◁ One-room living
The strategic use of sofa beds and fitted storage units turns this room into a complete living space.

Scatter cushions disguise the main bed, which is framed by fitted storage units. The sofa converts into a second bed; such units often incorporate floor-level storage space.

A table and strip light divide the space. As well as providing a work space, they can also be used for dining.

▽ Light and airy
Plain white walls enhance the spaciousness of this combined living and dining room. The two areas are also brought together visually by white and off-white furniture and common floorcovering.

USING ROOM DIVIDERS

A room divider can help to make the most of any living room, whether large or small.

Room dividers come in a great variety of shapes and sizes and can be useful in the smallest or largest of living rooms. They range from temporary to more permanent structures and you can either purchase one ready-made or improvise your own arrangement.

The type you choose will obviously depend on the function it has to perform, as well as the size and decorative style of the room. So begin by carefully considering your reasons for wanting one. Do you want to create different activity areas within a single, perhaps relatively small, room? Or do you have a large living space which would become more inviting and cosy if it were sectioned off into relatively private corners?

Do you want the divider to be a permanent structure in the room – or should it be movable to allow flexibility if, for example, you want to use the whole room for a party or family gathering?

How completely should it divide the room? In some instances, particularly in smaller spaces, it is often best to choose a style which is open so that it is still possible to see through from one part of the room to another.

Total division
Floor-to-ceiling bookcases divide a narrow room into a seating and office area and provide useful storage space. The wood matches the door, writing desk and fitted cupboard.

MAKING CHOICES

Partitions can be very dominant features in a room. So before going ahead with major building projects or purchases, it's a good idea to try out a makeshift screening arrangement to check it is comfortable to live with.

Permanent dividers Fixed bookshelves can have a solid back for a total division; open shelves naturally create a more open partition. A low wall, or kitchen base units, divide a room up to waist level. And although they are permanent features, folding and sliding doors are extremely flexible.

Temporary dividers are flexible and need not be expensive. As well as a huge range of screens, consider the simple solution of arranging furniture to create a division. Curtains or blinds can be hung from the ceiling to be drawn when needed.

▷ Vertical blinds

Like sliding or folding doors, vertical louvre blinds can be closed or opened to suit the occasion. In a living/dining room, this allows you to hide the debris of a meal while enjoying an after-dinner cup of coffee.

The louvres can also be angled to allow a partial view into the other half of the room.

▽ Open partition

A combined kitchen/living room often benefits from some form of division. Although this need be no more than a kitchen base unit between the two areas, a more substantial divider is often preferable.

Here, a combination of open shelves and cupboards reach from floor to ceiling. An integral fold-down table makes a practical addition.

△ Open-plan

Dividers create distinct activity areas in this large living area. A low wall is backed by a sofa to form a dining area, and a sideboard in front of the second sofa defines the other side of the seating area.

◁ More complete division

To create greater privacy, floor-to-ceiling partitions have been installed above the existing dividers.

The low wall has been topped by framed panels of perforated hardboard screening, while open shelving and cupboards have been added to low cupboards in the foreground.

SCREEN PLAY

A freestanding screen is one of the most flexible types of room divider in terms of style, size and portability.

Because they are not usually fixed to the wall, floor, or ceiling, screens can be easily moved around. In addition, of course, most screens can be folded back against a wall when not required. And since the individual panels which make up a screen are generally clipped, hinged, or bolted together, you can create a partition as large or small as you need.

Many different shapes and styles are available, and you can also make your own to co-ordinate exactly with the style of the room. Apart from antique screens, there are many modern versions made from solid or slatted wood or cane, or plastic or metal for high-tech designs. Japanese-style screens, where paper is attached to a wooden frame, are widely available; for a romantic, translucent effect, consider stretching a lacy or sheer fabric over a frame.

▽ *Colour co-ordination*
By making a screen yourself, you can choose a colour and shape to match your decorating scheme.

Here, a three-panel screen with an elegant arched top has been covered with the same fabric used for the upholstery. As a result, the screen becomes an integral part of the room's overall colour scheme.

By placing furniture on both sides of the screen, any possibility of knocking it over is drastically reduced – an important consideration in a household which includes elderly people or boisterous young children or pets.

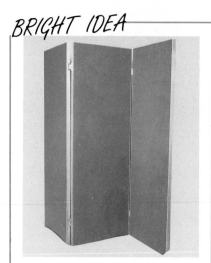

BRIGHT IDEA

Making a screen need not be difficult. This screen was made by hinging together three hardboard-faced doors (available from DIY outlets). Such a simple screen can be decorated to match it to the decor.

THREE STAGES TO A PERFECT LIVING ROOM

Build up gradually so that at every stage you have a pleasant living room.

It is a rare event indeed if you can move into a new home, look at your bare surroundings and go straight out to buy furniture, furnishings and accessories in one fell swoop. Most people are restricted by their budget – and you may have children and feel it's not worth having 'good' furniture until they've grown up.

Nevertheless, you have to start with some furniture, and there are two ways to approach this, depending on your circumstances. First consider how long you plan to stay in your new home. If you are a first-time buyer, statistics point to you moving within five years. If, on the other hand, it is your second (or third) move – to a real family home –

you'll probably be there for much longer. No matter which of these two pictures fits you, planning a staged development is a practical approach to achieving the room scheme you want, whether over a short, medium, or long time span.

SHORT TERM

Stage 1 If it's your first home, go for the basics and keep things simple. You'll need a coffee table – choose one big enough to serve all your seating – and a sofa – buy the best you can afford, as they take a lot of wear. For extra seating look for something inexpensive yet stylish, such as director's chairs.

Storage is vital – as much as you can afford. Adjustable shelving that's part of a modular system will fit in with a planned scheme. Paint the walls white or creamy beige; at the window drape inexpensive fabric or fix a blind. Perhaps sand and varnish floorboards.

Stage 2 Within nine months, review the flooring – either replace old carpet or buy a rug. Review window coverings again, replace or buy curtains or blinds. Consider your walls and perhaps liven them up with some colour – either sponged or marbled paint, or a wallpaper. Plan a lighting scheme and make a start on it.

Stage 3 Within 18 months, complete your lighting scheme and add those extras that dress the room: perhaps another small table, a comfortable chair and more storage units. Hang a few prints, or make a display of favourite items.

First-stage style

This city flat is furnished with basic necessities – a comfortable sofa and stylish table and lamp. The next step would be flooring – either a fitted carpet or a large rug – and lighting, possibly wallwashers. Some extra chairs would be a logical addition, too.

Wood design A simple and inexpensive way to give real character to a sanded floor is to use different shades of varnish.

For a chequered pattern, apply several coats of pale varnish to give a good covering over the whole floor. Then mark off the walls into equal divisions about 30cm apart and join up the marks on opposite walls to form a square grid. You can do this easily by stretching a length of string which has been rubbed in chalk between the marks: flick the taut string to get a chalk line. Brush on darker varnish to create a chequerboard effect.

LONG-TERM PLANNING

When you move into your second or third home, your planning considerations are bound to be very different from those that were paramount in your first home.

First, you probably have quite a lot of furniture which has to be housed. Then there may very well be more people to be accommodated: children of various ages and their attendant clutter can take up a lot of space.

On the other hand, time is on your side. So – don't rush, but plan over as much as five or six years to arrive at your ideal room scheme.

Stage 1 If you can't stand the walls, strip the paper if necessary and paint them a warm neutral shade. Spend your money on flooring – either fitted carpet or perhaps sanding and staining the floorboards and using a large rug.

You'll almost certainly have to invest in new curtains or blinds, so that is perhaps the point to start your new colour scheme. And if your new scheme clashes with the remainders of your old one – perhaps the upholstery fabric – improvise. If you can, make some new toning loose covers, or use inexpensive soft fabric as a throwover – a rug or Indian bedspread would be good choices. Look for natural, undyed fabric that can be wrapped over and tucked into the seating. It can look surprisingly effective.

Stage 2 After a couple of years, gradually withdraw some of the old furniture – use it elsewhere – and replace it with some new pieces.

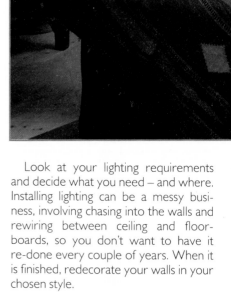

Look at your lighting requirements and decide what you need – and where. Installing lighting can be a messy business, involving chasing into the walls and rewiring between ceiling and floorboards, so you don't want to have it re-done every couple of years. When it is finished, redecorate your walls in your chosen style.

Stage 3 After four to six years, buy anything you feel is still missing in the way of furniture and make a point of putting together your finishing touches. Take a hard look at the decorations and freshen up anything that looks rather tired. In particular, if you installed blinds or simple curtains when you first moved in, now is perhaps the time to dress the windows rather more elaborately.

Family progression

The sunny family room shown on this and the opposite page looks comfortable at each of its progressive stages. In the first stage (far left) simple yellow curtains hang from poles. Off-white painted walls provide an inexpensive neutral backdrop that can be easily touched up if it gets scuffed and scraped by unruly children. Main seating is a chesterfield: director's chairs are a carry-over from flat-dwelling days.

In Stage 2 (left) chairs have been replaced by a relatively inexpensive sofa. A rug under the new coffee table and soft primrose walls add cosiness, while a good mirror has found a home over the fireplace. A table lamp is more in keeping with the room than the replaced standard lamp.

The third stage (below) has achieved a pleasing symmetry with upholstered chesterfields placed either side of the fireplace. Elegant swags and tails top the windows where the curtains are held with co-ordinated tiebacks. The two alcoves have matching cupboards and shelves.

△ ◁ *City slick*

The pictures on this page show how a slick city style lends itself especially well to advancing by stages. Modular furniture can be bought by degrees, as the budget allows.

The second stage (above) is already a thoroughly comfortable room. Storage in the alcove houses a growing amount of city-living essentials, and has been painted to match the coffee table that was one of the first purchases. Carpeting, a first-stage buy, has been refined by the addition of the rug used to define the working area. First steps in the lighting scheme provide the work area with its own overhead light.

By the time Stage 3 (shown on the left) is reached, the whole scheme takes on a more permanent air. Solid, built-in furniture fills the alcoves on both sides of the chimney breast; one unit serves as a desk area, replacing the table shown in Stage 2. The carpet – possibly showing signs of wear – has been removed to a bedroom and the floorboards sanded and attractively stained and sealed. A sleek glass coffee table allows an uninterrupted view of the stylish rug lying in front of the re-covered sofa. The window has been dressed with a smart roman blind.

▷ ▽ *Growing points*

Progressing through to a totally adult and sophisticated living room can take quite a time – and careful planning. Stage 2 (right) retains a practical family eating area and easily-vacuumed wall-to-wall carpeting. The new sofa and chair are upholstered in a hard-wearing weave. Scatter cushions tie in the new acquisitions with the existing curtains. Stylish modern nesting tables replace a previous coffee table – and provide more resting places, too.

The move to Stage 3 (below) looks quite a jump, but there are links with the room's past. The same dining table is still in use, completely hidden by an extravagant swathe of cream chintz. The apricot tones of Stage 2 have moved to the windows which are dressed with sheer austrian blinds and translucent curtains that echo the rich pattern on the re-covered seating. There's plenty of wood in evidence – from the rich woodstrip floor to smart display units. A new cornice reinforces the richness. The overall result is warm, chic and very sophisticated.

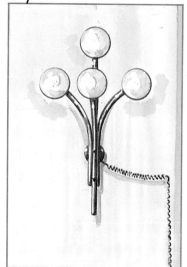

Light work This wall-mounted light with attractive curly cable is handsome enough to be given a permanent place in a living room. It's also a flexible choice when you are advancing in stages as it can be plugged in anywhere, allowing you time to think about a final lighting scheme.

TRICKS AND TREATS

There are several quite simple 'tricks of the trade' that can help you make the transition through the various stages. Use paint to link diverse pieces of furniture together – either as solid colour or, more subtly, marbled or sponged in two or three different shades. Alternatively, you could stencil a design in one or two corners of a chest, a cupboard door, or an old table. Paint techniques work equally well on small accessories, too.

A serviceable but unexciting carpet – or perhaps one that's worn in a few places – will be enhanced if you treat yourself to the best rug you can afford and let its colours lead naturally into the next stage of your room scheme.

If you'd like elaborately dressed curtains but find that you can't afford the real thing, look out for inexpensive fabrics such as muslin or curtain lining. Seconds or ends of rolls of voiles or light cottons are other budget buys well worth considering. Drape generous quantities of the low-cost fabric you have chosen over a pole, using Velcro to hold in it place.

Give worn furniture new life by throwing a length of co-ordinating fabric over it – perhaps an Indian-style cloth or even a soft rug. These measures all help to create a comfortable room to live in while you progress through different stages.

△ *Marbling style*
Maximum co-ordination can be achieved at minimum cost by employing a special paint technique. Here, marbling has been used on everything from the fire surround to the picture frames, subtly enhancing the wallpaper.

▽ *Paint extras*
Thin painted red lines emphasize the horizontals on both furniture and architectural detailing that are otherwise a gentle cream. Red and green stencil designs are reinforced by touches of green in accessories.

SEATING IN THE LIVING ROOM

The sitting area forms the heart of any living room and needs careful planning to make it work successfully.

The seating in a living room needs to be comfortable and flexible, so that it can be re-arranged to suit a variety of activities. In winter it is cosier to face into the room – perhaps towards a blazing fire. In summer you'll probably want to make the most of the light and the view outside the window.

Conversation circle A group of people naturally form themselves into a circle around a focal point such as a fireplace and/or a coffee table.

This circle needs to be self-contained and should not be crossed by others passing through to reach the kitchen or the hall, for instance. If the living room contains a dining section, the ideal is to keep the two areas separate and well-defined.

In addition to the main seating area, an isolated corner where one or two people can talk or read away from the main group works well, especially in a large household.

Furniture Sofas and chairs are the most noticeable pieces of furniture in a living room. They affect the character of the room and the mood you wish to create.

Scale is an important consideration. Giant sofas look wonderful in big rooms but you'll be forever climbing over them in small ones. Likewise, dainty furniture can easily look lost in a very spacious room.

The shape of the room will have a bearing on whether you can achieve the exact arrangement you want. Make the best possible use of the space in which you have to work; you may be able to turn an apparent disadvantage into an asset.

A long narrow room, for example, often ends up with a wasted area at one end. It is better to create two, separate, intimate groups of seating, each for four people, than a large, spread-out arrangement.

Three-piece classic
With no fireplace in this room it is easier to re-arrange the three-piece suite. The sofa could face the view with a chair on either side.

SEATING ARRANGEMENTS

The three-piece suite was the most popular combination of living room furniture for many years; it was almost impossible to buy sofas and chairs separately. But nowadays you don't have to have a three-seater sofa and two matching armchairs unless you really choose to.

The problem with such a set is that it is not very flexible. The logical way to place the pieces is with the sofa in the centre and a chair on either side. And although the sofa is called a three-seater, three people sitting in a row is not ideal for conversation.

An arrangement of two roomy, two-seater sofas plus an armchair gives the same number of places but is much more versatile. The two sofas can face each other, or they can work equally well placed at right angles to each other. The armchair can be moved into or out of the circle as required.

Other flexible alternatives are three chairs and a two-seater sofa; or a group of four or five armchairs. If you decide on the latter, be careful with your choice of shapes or you could get a bitty effect. One way to avoid this is to have at least two chairs in matching fabric.

A chaise longue is a wonderful indulgence if you have the space. To achieve a similar effect, choose a chair with a matching run-up stool.

Coverings Whatever arrangement you opt for, you don't need to have all your seating covered with the same fabric. It is more chic to mix plains with a pattern or patterns of different scales or closely related colours.

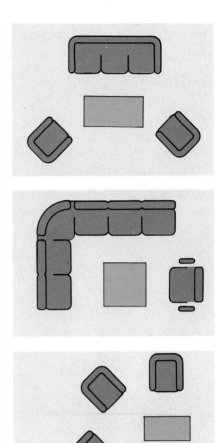

△ **Seating circles** Top to bottom:
☐ A three-seater sofa and two armchairs are a traditional choice.
☐ Add a chair to unit seating to complete the circle.
☐ A two-seater plus three chairs is a flexible choice.

△ **Convivial plan**
Two sofas placed one on either side of a fireplace is a good layout for conversation. A table between them is useful for coffee or drinks and helps to 'anchor' the seating.

◁ **Ringing the changes**
An alternative set-up for the same room has two sofas at right angles to each other, plus an armchair.

▷ **Tailored look**
A three-seater and small two-seater are a neat option in a small room. The clean geometric lines of the seating are echoed by the rectangular rug and square coffee table; a glass topped table appears to take up less of the floor space than a solid one.

OTHER CHOICES

Living room seating does not have to consist entirely of conventional sofas and armchairs.

Informal style You may prefer to mix a traditional sofa with less formal cane chairs, giving a less crowded look to a small room. Another option is a fully upholstered sofa and chair plus a chair with a wooden frame. In either case, you should give the pieces a sense of unity by linking them via the patterns or colours used in the covering.

Modern setting Modular seating made up of some armless chairs and corner units can be used to fit a larger number of people into an area than could be accommodated more conventionally.

Units can be put together to make an L- or U-shape, depending on the space available. In many ranges, the corner unit can be replaced by a small table. A right or left arm can usually be fitted as appropriate to end a run. This kind of seating works well combined with one or two chairs that can be drawn up to complete the circle when needed.

△ *Conservatory mood*
A sofa and two cane chairs gives a less crowded look to a room which also has to house a piano. The same summery fabric is used on all seating; the theme is carried through with pale walls and plants.

▽ *Spacious attic*
Modular units make a neat L-shape in this attic and, with an extra chair, are a good layout for conversation. The uncluttered feel is enhanced by keeping everything pale except the seating which is in strong greys.

SEATING FOR COMFORT

Take the time to plan seating to suit your needs, your home and lifestyle.

Comfortable seating for reading, watching television, listening to music, knitting, sewing, eating or simply relaxing is the first big furniture buy most home owners make. Seating is so important to comfortable living that it is worth buying the very best you can afford – and taking time to make sure the furniture suits your needs and is a pleasure to use.

MAKE A ROOM PLAN

Once you have assessed your needs, make a plan of the room in which you are going to install the seating. This seems unnecessarily fussy but is well worthwhile. Sofas and chairs may look a reasonable size in a large furniture showroom, but can be much too large for a domestic living or dining room.

The basic plan Draw the shape of the room on graph paper, allowing one square per centimetre. Mark windows, doors, and permanent fittings in colour. Draw the shapes of existing furniture which is going to remain in the room on graph paper, using the same scale as the main plan, and cut them out. If you have an existing dining table but want to buy new chairs, measure the space from the underside of the table edge to the floor and mark it on your plan. This helps you to choose chairs to fit comfortably under the table.

First steps Armed with your checklist, go through manufacturers' brochures and cut out chairs and sofas you like the look of and which suit your needs. Draw the shapes up on graph paper, using manufacturer's measurements as a guide. Cut the shapes out and colour them in so that they stand out from the main room plan. Write the name of the model on the back of each piece.

Traffic flow Take into account the traffic flow through the room when arranging furniture pieces on your plan. Lightly mark in the flow patterns from one door to another to make sure that seating won't cross any of the main pathways through the room. In a small or awkwardly shaped room, unit seating, where pieces can be pushed together or separated as needed, are probably more flexible than two sofas or a sofa and two chairs. Folding chairs are extremely useful in a small room.

Space Remember to allow enough space in front of furniture for people to stand up and sit down easily. It is important to allow a minimum of 600mm for someone to walk into or around a room without having to squeeze past furniture. When dining chairs are grouped around a table, each chair needs 12-15cm of space on either side to allow diners to get in and out easily, and to eat without jostling elbows.

ASSESS YOUR NEEDS

Before you buy seating, sit down and assess your needs, using the checklist shown here.

Who will use the seating?
☐ Children
☐ Adults
☐ Elderly people
If an elderly person uses the room on a regular basis, you need a chair designed to suit his or her needs. If children and pets use the room, you need washable, hard wearing upholstery.

How many people use the room regularly?
☐ 2-4
☐ 4-6
☐ 6-8

How do they use the room?
☐ Watching TV
☐ Homework
☐ Reading
☐ Hobbies
☐ Play
☐ Eating
☐ Listening to music
Think about the selection of chairs needed for these activities. Two recliners mounted on a swivel base might, for instance, be more useful than two armchairs when one person wants to read or listen to music (using headphones) and the other wants to watch television.

Will extra seating be needed?
☐ Not often
☐ Often (weekly)
Consider flexible unit seating if you regularly need extra chairs.

RELAXING SEATING

Your assessment and plan show what type of seating to look for but it is only by sitting in a chair that you can find out whether or not it is comfortable. Upholstered relaxing seating can be a combination of chairs and sofas, two or more sofas, or unit furniture that can be pushed together to make sofas or separated into chairs as needed. There are several important characteristics which affect the comfort of seating.

Seat slope The seat should slope slightly from front to back so that your body is in a relaxed position. Avoid seating with a pronounced slope – it curves the spine at an angle that is too acute for comfort.

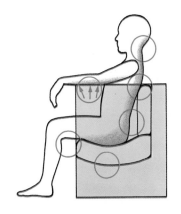

△ *The wrong chair*
This chair has no support for the head, neck or spine. The seat is too low and the arms too high.

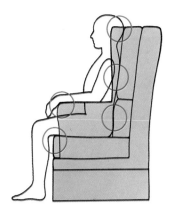

△ *The right chair*
A high back supports the head, neck and spine. The arms and seat are the right height for relaxation.

Seat height The front part of the seat should be at a height which does not apply pressure to the back of your legs. If there is an adult in the family above or below average height, look for a chair a little higher or lower to suit them. Avoid very low chairs or sofas which apply pressure to the back of the legs and are difficult to get in and out of. An elderly or disabled person needs a chair with a fairly high seat for ease of movement.

Seat width The seat should be wide enough to allow freedom of movement. If your legs or ribs press against the sides of the seat, it is too narrow.

Softness A very soft chair may seem appealing but isn't as comfortable to sit in long-term as a well-sprung seat which supports your body. Good springing usually means a high price but is worthwhile as cushions keep their shape (cheap cushions stuffed with foam chips compress at the front, go lumpy and become uncomfortable) and the chair is more resistant to hard wear.

Back height Low-backed seating where support ends below shoulder level is very uncomfortable. If you want low-backed seating, look for a design where the back reaches shoulder level. High-backed seating gives extra support to the back as well as your neck and shoulders. Head rests add to comfort but should be adjustable. Thick, fixed headrests are often positioned so that the centre of the head is supported but the neck isn't, which can be uncomfortable.

Arms Chair and sofa arms should be wide enough and at the right height for you to rest your arms in comfort.

▽ *For the elderly*
This chair is the perfect shape for an elderly person. It has a high seat and back with a headrest.

▽ *Stressless seating*
The ultimate relaxer reclines with you, has an adjustable headrest, swivels with a smooth action and offers a comfortable footstool.

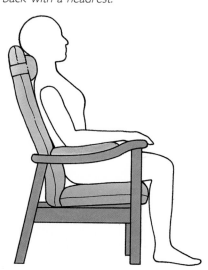

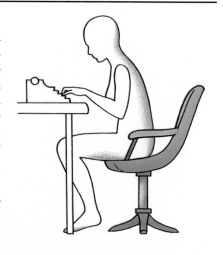

◁ *Pressure points*
A dining chair which is too high will press uncomfortably against the back of your knees and thighs.

EATING CHAIRS
Dining chairs must be considered with the dining table. If you are buying chairs to match an existing table, remember to take the measurements for the size of the table and its height from the floor with you. If you are buying a new table and chairs, try the two together.

Height If a dining chair is too high, your legs tend to press against both the underside of the table and the front edge of the chair. If it is too low, eating is difficult. A gap of about 30cm between the top of the table and your knees is right for most adults.

Arms The arms on carver chairs should be at the right height to rest elbows in comfort. Seat width is important on dining chairs with arms – if the seat is too narrow, the arms will press against the ribs and thighs of the person sitting in the chair.

Back height Look for chairs which give support up to shoulder level. Stooping over food gives most people indigestion, so avoid very low-backed dining chairs which encourage this.

WORKING CHAIRS
An upright dining chair is not suitable for use during long periods of study or typing. If a member of your family works at home on a regular basis, it is worth buying a special typist's chair or a Scandinavian posture chair designed to hold the spine in the right position. Sitting on the wrong type of chair to use a keyboard can lead to backache.

▷ *Working comfortably*
This is the wrong chair for a typist as it offers no back support and slopes badly.

SEATING FOR THE ELDERLY
When buying seating for an elderly person, look for the following:

Seat height The seat should be high enough to allow the user to get in and out of the chair easily.

Back height Most older people find a high-backed chair comfortable.

Seat slope Don't buy a chair which slopes acutely – an old person may find it difficult to get in and out of.

CHOOSING A SOFA

Buying a sofa is a major investment so it pays to consider the options carefully

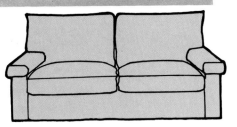

△ CURVED-ARMED LOVE SEAT
Style This shape fits well into any traditional or modern scheme.
In use Good for small rooms or as an extra sofa, but it only seats two at close quarters – hence the term love seat – and it is not good for 'sprawlers'.
Watchpoint Arms get dirty quickly: choose dark or patterned covers, or a light fabric which has been treated.

There's a strong trend today towards having one or two sofas and a few occasional chairs instead of the traditional three-piece suite. If your living room can accommodate two sofas there are many design options. The sofas can be identical – a classic approach – or different – a more adventurous choice.

Either way, sofas are major investments, and you should know what is available before making your choice. Seating capacity, versatility, practicality, style and cost are all considerations. A compromise is usually necessary and it should be the best possible for you.

Size and style The terms 'two' and 'three' seater are misleading: most two seaters only take two adults at a squash. For comfort, two people need a three seater. Make sure that a large three seater really does seat three adults comfortably.

Consider external dimensions in relation to room size as well as internal ones such as seat height and depth, back height and length. Bear in mind that:
☐ low seats are difficult for older people to get up from,
☐ tall people with long legs need a deeper seat,
☐ very soft sofas don't support you properly,
☐ a low back will not support your head and shoulders,
☐ the arm rests are at a comfortable height.

The style you choose can complement an existing scheme: a Victorian-type chesterfield in a Victorian-style living room is a safe bet. A sofa's style can also contrast with its surroundings: the same chesterfield can look superb in a stark modern room. There are also many timeless styles that are 'at home' in a wide range of schemes.

Comfort and cost A sofa is a major purchase so don't rush into it. To a certain extent you get what you pay for. The price is likely to reflect both the construction – a really comfortable spring system – and the quality of the covering fabric. Bear in mind that an upholstered sofa is usually covered in

△ LOW-ARMED TWO SEATER
Style Its simple modern shape can also be used in any sort of scheme.
In use Though compact, the low arms make the sofa easier for lounging in than the love seat.
Watchpoint Check on quality of upholstery. Cheap foam can easily lose its shape.

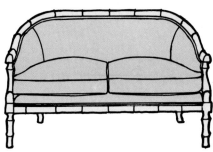

△ WOOD-FRAMED SOFA
Style Elegantly traditional, good in a classically decorated sitting room or large bedroom.
In use Not for lounging. This is definitely formal seating.
Watchpoint Plain or small-scale geometric print fabric, such as velvet or damask, is in keeping with its formal shape. Avoid chintz.

△ BAMBOO SOFA
Style A light-looking sofa for sun rooms, Oriental or conservatory-style rooms.
In use The bamboo frame may not stand up to long, hard wear.
Watchpoint Cushions must be well filled, as the frame is not upholstered. Covers should unzip for easy cleaning.

▽ HIGH-BACKED THREE SEATER
Style An old-fashioned sofa with the emphasis on comfort.
In use A good lounging, relaxing sofa. Can be covered in any fabric, patterned or plain.
Watchpoint Can be oppressive as part of a three-piece suite, especially in a small room.

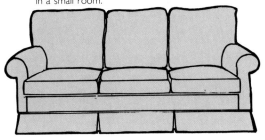

△ CURVED THREE SEATER
Style Traditional, comfortable and plump.
In use The informal, curved shape makes it easy for three people to sit and converse.
Watchpoint Upholstered base could get dirty quickly. Avoid light fabrics unless treated. Not suitable for loose covers.

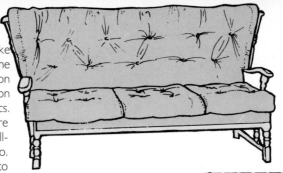

the fabric of your choice, so it will take at least 6-8 weeks to deliver. (The chapter on upholstered furniture on pages 55-56 gives more information on sofa construction and upholstery fabrics.

On a tight budget, it is best to ignore the cheapest models and buy a well-constructed sofa covered in calico. Cover it in a washable loose cover to start with and then when funds permit, you can replace the loose cover with a more luxurious fabric . . . or make your own with the help of Creative DIY.

◁ 'SETTLE' HIGH-BACK
Style Definitely traditional.
In use High back and curved sides make this ideal for a draughty room. Not for sprawling or lounging; good as an extra sofa.
Watchpoint The frame should be steady enough to support the topheavy superstructure.

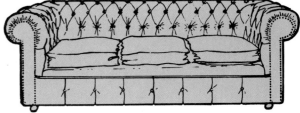

△ CHESTERFIELD
Style This design fits into both traditional and contemporary schemes. Leather-covered versions are particularly versatile, though expensive.
In use Comfortable both to sit and lounge on, and worth considering for the 'one-sofa' room.
Watchpoint If 'button-back', buttons should be securely attached. Loose covers spoil the line.

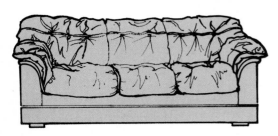

△ MODERN COUCH
Style Generally leather covered, this shaped sofa is definitely for a modern room.
In use Suitable for informal sprawling and lounging.
Watchpoint Not good for back problems, as there is minimal support. Check that buttons are firmly sewn.

▽ CAMEL-BACKED THREE SEATER
Style Definitely traditional.
In use As good for curling up in as for stretching out.
Watchpoint Can dominate a small room, and often better on its own than as part of a three-piece suite.

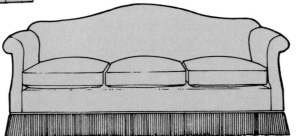

▽ TUBULAR TWO SEATER
Style Modern enough for a contemporary setting, though would provide a note of contrast in a traditional scheme.
In use Adequate seating but not especially comfortable. Usually covered in plain fabric or leather.
Watchpoint Check cushion filling: lumps and bumps spoil the line.

◁ DUVET SOFA
Style A leather or fabric covered bag with a soft filling is draped over a firm base and attached on the underside. Suits modern and uncluttered rooms.
In use Leather covered sofas 'mature' with age and acquire an attractive patina.
Watchpoint Make sure the base is firm enough and a good support. .

▷ ARMLESS COUCH
Style Modern seating for a modern room.
In use Great for lounging, but no corners to curl up in. Usually upholstered in a plain fabric.
Watchpoint Unsuitable for loose covers. Get extra fabric for a few scatter cushions, if possible.

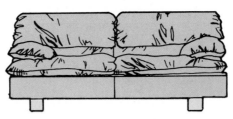

▽ MODULAR UNIT SEATING
Style Best for large-scale modern rooms.
In use Theoretically, modular seating offers maximum flexibility, as seats can either be pushed together or used separately.
Watchpoint Can look somewhat impersonal in large doses. Not very comfortable if armless, awkward to use separately if one-armed.

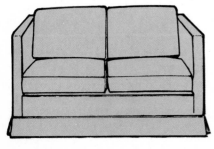

◁ SQUARED-UP LOVE SEAT
Style Good for small rooms, modern or traditional, or as second sofa. Good, also, in pairs.
In use For sitting only. More comfortable for one person than for two.
Watchpoint Tight-fitting cushions essential.

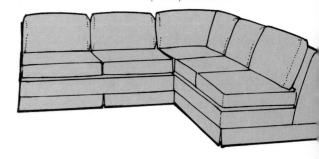

CHOOSING AN ARMCHAIR

Choose an armchair to suit your room and your needs – something to curl up in or give your back support.

The traditional three-piece suite consists of a sofa and two matching armchairs. Today, living room furniture is much more flexible and you can have a variety of seating options depending on the size of your room and the style of the furnishings.

The sofa and armchair don't have to be the same style or even be covered in the same fabric, so you can buy them at different times and spread the cost.

Most of the considerations outlined in Choosing a Sofa, on the previous two pages, apply to armchairs too. Cost is usually directly related to the type of construction used and the quality of the fabric covering. If you spend more on the construction and less on the fabric the chair will last longer and you can always re-cover it later in a better fabric when funds permit. When you choose the fabric for upholstery buy enough to make up arm and head covers which can be removed for cleaning as these areas get dirty and worn first.

There is no substitute for actually sitting in the chair itself for a reasonable length of time to find out if it suits you. If support for your head and shoulders is important avoid low backed chairs but make sure that the back is at the right height for you and does not push your head forward. Arms should be positioned so that yours rest comfortably and the seat should not be so low that getting up is difficult.

TRADITIONAL ARMCHAIR STYLES

CURVED TUB
Style The arms curve round and up to form the back. Lightweight versions have show wood legs and no seat cushion; more solid versions have an upholstered or valanced base with a fitted seat cushion.
In use Ideal for additional seating or in a room where space is limited.
Watchpoint The low back does not give much support.

CHESTERFIELD
Style Essentially a miniature version of the chesterfield sofa – medium height with deep buttoning and solid arms. Upholstered in fabric or leather.
In use High arms restrict sprawling but make a cosy corner to curl up in.
Watchpoint They take up a lot of room – check external measurements – and the style can look heavy unless there is plenty of space. Loose covers spoil the line.

WING BACK
Style This traditional high backed style with scroll arms has carved cabriole front legs. Variations in the design include a buttoned back and a slightly less padded version with show wood arm supports, and straight front legs. Available upholstered in both fabric and leather.
In use Most models are lightweight, both to move around and to look at. The high back gives good support to back and head and is ideal for use in a draughty room.
Watchpoints Firmly upholstered over a rigid frame, this is not a chair to lounge in. Not all shapes are suitable for loose covers although the seat cushion cover may be removable. If button backed, pull on the buttons to check they are sewn on firmly.

BEDROOM CHAIR
Style Small low chair without arms. The high back can be curved or straight, buttoned or plain, with an attractively shaped top edge.
In use Originally designed for bedrooms but ideal as additional seating particularly in a small living room.

HIGH BACK SCROLL ARM
Style A high backed chair with scroll arms angled outwards and a generous seat.
In use A cushion or two adds comfort to the deep square seat. Suitable for fitted loose covers.
Watchpoint A solid piece of furniture which takes up space and looks as though it does.

CURVED ARM
Style An elegant chair with tapering arms that curve outwards, and shaped back and deep seat cushions.
In use The formal style looks good in modern and traditional rooms.
Watchpoint Check the covers are removable for cleaning.

CURVED BACK
Style A traditional design with generous curves and a deep comfy seat.
In use The curved back looks softer than square backed versions.
Watchpoint Not very good for posture – the low back encourages sprawling.

MODERN STYLES

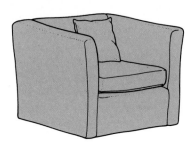  

SQUARED UP
Style A low backed chair with high slim arms and a square seat cushion. Neat and compact, it suits both modern and traditional rooms.
In use Like the chesterfield this squared up shape is not suitable for sprawling but makes a comfy seat. The cover is loose for easy cleaning.
Watchpoint Check there is sufficient density of foam covering the wooden frame.

BAMBOO
Style A lightweight bamboo frame (usually made from steamed beech and treated to look like bamboo) holds deep comfy cushions. Styles include many classic armchair shapes including the squared up and tub.
In use Ideal for conservatory or oriental style rooms.
Watchpoint Not so strong or long lasting as chairs with a conventional solid construction.

WOOD FRAME
Style These lightweight chairs are not upholstered, simply a show wood frame supporting a pair of covered cushions. Suit a country style room.
In use Not chairs for lounging in, but the firm back gives good support. The back can be high or low and a rocking chair version is also available.
Watchpoint Check the density of the cushions and make sure the frame joints are strong.

 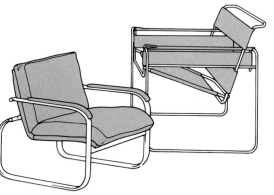 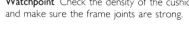 

SWIVEL RECLINER
Style Modern in style and made from chrome and upholstered in leather or fabric. Usually on a pedestal base, this office chair is often now seen in the home.
In use Can be adjusted to any angle right to the horizontal. Some designs also have an extending leg rest.
Watchpoint Expensive.

LEATHER AND CHROME
Style Definitely for a modern room style. A variety of designs – the seat and back can be upholstered or simply leather slung across the frame something like a deckchair.
In use Not a lounging chair but lightweight to look at and to move around.
Watchpoint Leather wears in beautifully but greasy marks and scratches are impossible to remove.

SQUARE LOW ARMED
Style A high backed chair with feather or foam filled cushions and broad comfy arms. Suitable for most traditionally furnished rooms.
In use The low arms make this an ideal chair for lounging. The seat and back cushion covers can be removed for cleaning.
Watchpoint Check the density of the foam covering the frame.

ARMLESS MODERN
Style Usually covered in leather or a heavy textured plain fabric. Some styles look as though an upholstered duvet has been draped over the frame. Most suitable for a modern style of furnishing.
In use An informal chair which encourages sprawling.
Watchpoint Little support for backs.

MODULAR UNITS
Style Fabric covered sculptured foam blocks. Look for corner units, and end units with arms, for versatility.
In use Can be put together to form a run or fit into awkward space. Relatively cheap to buy and the covers are removable for easy cleaning.
Watchpoint Low backs mean little support for head and shoulders and encourage lounging. Not very comfortable if armless and difficult to use separately if one armed.

SAG BAG
Style Colourful canvas or leather bags filled with polystyrene granules.
In use Versatile additional seating, ideal for a first home or children's rooms.
Watchpoint Check whether the granules are in a lining bag which is easy to remove when washing the outer cover. The granules will compact in time and may need topping up.

LIGHTING YOUR LIVING ROOM

The way you light your living room is as important as how you decorate it, so the subject merits serious thought.

Good lighting is a vital ingredient in any room and particularly a living room. There is more to it than hanging a single pendant in the middle of the room and leaving it at that. But it can be quite difficult to decide what you need and how to achieve a pleasing and practical result.

There's really no point in spending a lot of time and cash on decoration, furniture and furnishings and ignoring the lighting. After all, you probably spend as much, possibly more, of your time seeing the room by artificial lighting than you do by natural light.

You can change the whole look of the room with clever lighting – and it may be a much cheaper option than redecorating. Use it to create atmosphere with light and shade, for specific tasks such as reading, and to make the best of your decoration.

Lighting is about fittings too. Floor and table lamps, wall lights and ceiling pendants all contribute to the style of the room – choose lights for their looks as well as the quality of light they produce.

Versatility A living room is where a variety of different activities take place. So plan the lighting to be as versatile as possible.

Dimmer switches, which allow you to adjust the level of lighting to suit the mood and the activities taking place, are an excellent investment. You can turn the lights right up for all-over illumination, or down for a cosy feel, with perhaps table lamps giving intimate pools of light.

Several table and floor lamps are a flexible way of providing a variety of lighting options – different combinations producing different effects.

Think of your living room as a stage – bathe it in light when you want a bright effect, turn the lighting down to create a mood, use table lamps to light specific areas where activities such as reading, doing homework or watching TV take place.

Flexible arrangement
Decorative matching wall lights and low-hung pendant in this living room can be used together for overall illumination or to give separate pools of light. Dimmers add to the possibilities. For instance, you can lower the wall lights to bring the table into prominence or vice versa. The adjustable floor task lamp can be positioned for reading in any part of the room, while the large table lamp creates another cosy oasis.

CREATING A MOOD

When planning living room lighting, think about how you use the room and choose the lighting with function very much in mind – reading and entertaining, for instance, require very different light levels. Do you entertain here a lot, use it for general family life – or a combination of the two? If you read, work or watch TV in it, where are the lights in relation to the furniture? Are there pictures or objects you want to highlight?

Another consideration is atmosphere. Do you want the living room to be intimate and cosy, bright and efficient, or have different moods for different occasions? Remember to use shadow as well as light to create atmosphere.

Different areas of a room can be lit in different ways and brought into prominence according to the activities at the time. So several sources of adjustable lighting are invaluable. For instance, when you are alone in the room reading, then the area you are in can be lit by a table lamp or possibly a standard lamp, with or without general background lighting. When entertaining, the standard lamp can be moved to behind the sofa, putting the occupants

Shelf light A shelf for ornaments becomes more interesting if illuminated. Mount a small strip light behind a batten, under the front of the shelf above the one you want to display. Run the flex down one of the back corners and plug into an electric socket.

◁ *Low light*
This night-time living room is geared more towards conversation than reading or working.
  The candlestick wall lights with low wattage bulbs (between 15 and 60w) provide a little general light but not enough to destroy the gentle atmosphere. The fire is the centre of life around which the furniture is grouped; table lamps cast pools of light, creating interesting shadows and leaving the rest of the richly painted room gently out of focus.

▽ *High lights*
The same room given a different treatment; one more suited to reading or hobbies such as sewing.
  Recessed eyeball fittings in the ceiling highlight the pictures in the corner by the fireplace while the table lamp at the other end of the sofa provides light for reading.
  Two separate lighting circuits – each controlled by a dimmer switch – are wired in to give versatility. One controls the eyeballs directed towards the pictures; the other deals with the table lights and the eyeball which is trained on the chimney breast.

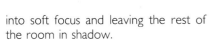

into soft focus and leaving the rest of the room in shadow.
  While lighting levels are very important in creating a mood, a simple but often forgotten way of providing atmospheric light is with candles. An ordinary room can be transformed into something quite mysterious, bathed in the soft, warm light of some flickering candles.

LIGHTING POINTS

While flexibility is the key to good living room lighting, your choices will, of course, be determined by cost and by how easy they are to fit.

Plug-in fittings – table and standard lamps, uplighters, and so on – are the easiest from an installation point of view, as long as you have enough electric sockets.

If you want to install a completely new system, inevitably there will be some rewiring to be done. Wall lights can be installed wherever you like, although you will have to redecorate over the new plasterwork where wires have been chased in. Floor and table lamp sockets can be wired to a single switch by the door, so that they can all be turned on and off easily.

Fittings such as downlighters and directional eyeballs are often recessed into the ceiling. You may not be able to do this, however, because of the type of ceiling – there may not be enough space above it, for instance. And some people, quite rightly, are unwilling to cut into a fine period ceiling.

Surface mounted downlighters or directional spots are alternatives; the latter are, on the whole, much more attractive than they used to be.

Electrified tracks are another good idea for a living room; they provide a flexible system, enabling you to use a mixture of fittings. Tracks come in a variety of styles and finishes – the best approach is to choose an unobtrusive one, unless you deliberately want to make a feature out of it.

Finally, don't forget dimmers. They're easy to install and are invaluable because you can brighten or darken the room at the turn of a switch.

▷ *Overall illumination*
Downlighters in the ceiling provide good overall light in this living room. The table lamps, which create separate pools of light, are used to create a warm atmosphere. Floor-to-ceiling mirrors on either side of the fireplace double the effect of whatever lights are on.

▽ *Clever disguise*
Here, background lighting is provided by wall uplighters either side of the chimney breast; they bounce light off the ceiling and the mirror above the fireplace. These wall lights are made from plaster and can be painted to blend with the walls. There is also a reading lamp on one side table and a standard lamp which can be moved wherever it is needed.

◁ *Unclutterred attic*
An attic living room with streamlined lighting to complement an airy, unclutterred decorative scheme.

Recessed adjustable eyeballs direct light just where it is needed – on to the painting, to wash the walls, to highlight the coffee table or towards the seating.

▽ *Mixed media*
Another room with a similar airy feel has a mixture of wired-in and free-standing lighting.

Light for reading or working is provided by a stylish desk light and adjustable standard lamps. A recessed downlighter in the ceiling (out of picture) highlights the sofa and rug when wanted.

▷ Highlights and shadows

A good example of how a carefully chosen modern floor lamp can perfectly complement period architecture. The tall chrome uplighter throws light on to the gloss-painted wall above it, leaving the rest of the room fairly shadowy. The lamp subtly emphasizes the height and features of the room, without distracting attention from the glow of candles and firelight.

▽ Standard direction

The generous wide-angled shades on these standard lamps direct light down on to the sofa. The classically modern style of the lamps is very much in keeping with the plain room and streamlined furniture.

◁ Background for viewing

A series of glass shelves for books and ornaments is bathed in light from above, giving the display a warm attractive glow.

As well as creating an interesting focal point, this practical solution makes the shelves a subtle light source when the TV is on, and the round ball light turned off.

LIVING ROOM STORAGE

The living room needs generous storage to keep clutter at bay and maintain a stylish and streamlined appearance.

Storage furniture is a major investment in any home and, in the living room in particular, it needs to be organized to cope with the diverse nature of its contents. Finding a place for everything you need within reach is an enormous help in keeping the room looking smart and comfortable for both entertaining and everyday family life.

Every family's storage needs are different so the kind of storage furniture you ultimately choose depends on your budget, lifestyle and type of home. Refer to the checklist above to make sure that you don't forget any essentials at the planning stage.

A well-chosen storage system can enhance the atmosphere of your living room. So while it's important to keep clutter behind closed doors, an element of display to allow you to show off treasured possessions is also essential.

Practical and decorative
Living room storage usually includes both open and closed areas. Modular units such as these allow the minutiae of everyday life to be kept safely hidden away, leaving only a charming collection of china and pottery – and the television – on display.

FREESTANDING STORAGE

Freestanding storage units have the obvious advantage of being easy to rearrange and, if you plan to move home in the future, you can simply take them with you when you go.

Self-assembly systems are often cheaper than their ready-made counterparts; if you intend to install a storage system to cover an entire wall, a flat-pack which you can assemble yourself is much easier to get through the front door! Conversely, flat-pack furniture can usually also be dismantled with relative ease if necessary.

Modular systems are well suited to a modest budget and the limited size of many modern living rooms. As well as offering a combination of open and closed modules, they allow you to start off in a small way and add to them as your funds allow or your needs grow. This way, you can tailor your storage to the possessions you already have and the ones you are likely to accumulate.

Single items As well as streamlined storage systems, some rooms look best with a classic combination of freestanding furniture: a roll-top or knee-hole desk for personal effects; a sideboard for drinks, crockery and glass; and a bookcase or glass-fronted cabinet to house books and treasured objects.

Small pieces of specialized furniture – such as coffee tables that include a drinks cabinet underneath, TV and video cabinets, and hi-fi units with space for an amplifier, cassette deck, records or tapes – can be extremely useful.

▷ **Ample storage**
It is possible to provide plenty of storage without spoiling the atmosphere of a room in which you entertain guests.

Here, storage which almost completely covers an entire wall is broken up by a wall mirror and low table.

A CUMULATIVE APPROACH

Storage furniture need not be purchased all at once – modular systems can 'grow' as needed. Remember to check with the manufacturer that the range will remain on the market.

▽ **Starting off**
At first, only a few units need be purchased. Sensibly these have been chosen to include both closed cupboards and open shelves. Arranged along the wall of the room, they provide a sturdy shelf to hold the television.

▽ ▷ **Adding on**
As, perhaps, the family's budget and storage needs grow, extra units can be added. Here, a table top and chair provide a useful work place while taller glass-fronted cupboards allow precious items to remain safe while on show.

▽ ▷ ▷ **The final stage**
Here, the storage system has grown to almost ceiling height. Several of the units have been rearranged to produce a symmetrical arrangement which flanks a large mirror and coffee table.

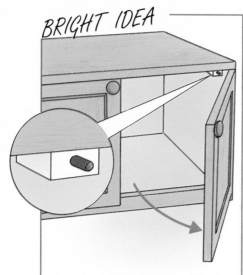

BRIGHT IDEA

A cupboard light It can be difficult to see into a cupboard, especially one at floor level. A door-operated switch will turn on a light inside the cupboard when the door is opened and can easily be screwed in place under the top of the cupboard; position it so that the closed door depresses the button sufficiently to switch off the light.

BUILT-IN SOLUTIONS

Built-in storage can be as simple as shelving fixed to the walls, or as complex as custom-built units. Either way, building-in represents a long-term investment as the furniture becomes a permanent part of the room.

A 'working wall' of built-in storage can be made to your own specifications, allowing you to choose the shape (perhaps to fill an awkward gap or disguise an eyesore). You can also decide what combination of shelves, closed or glass-fronted cupboard space and special features you want. Built-in units can be traditional, with moulded or panelled doors to complement the architectural detail of a period home, or ultra-modern to set the style in a modern room.

Open shelving A living room without shelves can appear rather bare. Family heirlooms, books, photographs and clocks, flowers and plants all need a home where they can be seen and enjoyed, and their colour and character make an important contribution to the atmosphere of a room. Open shelving is also extremely versatile because the contents can be altered as the family's

needs change, and easily rearranged to create a fresh new look.

Pre-cut shelves and brackets suitable for DIY installation are available in many different materials, finishes and sizes. Group a number of shelves together for the best effect and keep an eye on proportions – top shelves need to be accessible; narrow shelves are more efficient for display; deeper, well-supported ones are necessary for books, a television, sound system or drinks cupboard. Records need special racks or the support of full-width uprights to prevent them from falling over when just one is removed.

Glass shelving, enhanced by subtle lighting from above, is ideal for showing off delicate collections of china and glass. Resist the temptation to overcrowd as your collections grow.

▽ *Custom-built*
Building-in represents sound, long-term investment so long as you plan to remain in the same home for some time.

This custom-built combination of open shelving and cupboards has been specially painted to blend in with the decor of this elegant living room.

△ A working wall

In an open plan living area, a wall storage system can help to create a useful room divider. A plain white finish allows the shelving to merge with the wall behind giving pride of place to the decorative knick-knacks and small rug.

It's a good idea to place cupboards rather than open shelving at floor level. Although their contents may be slightly more accessible, low-level open shelving tends to gather dirt and is difficult to keep neat.

▷ Specialized storage

Not everyone possesses a large enough library to merit an entire wall of bookshelves. This alternative arrangement has been designed to incorporate a drinks' cabinet with a pull-down door which can double as a serving surface. In addition, this system has been designed to include frequent full-width uprights to prevent all the records falling over if only one is removed. Similarly, shallow shelves provide a home for a cassette collection.

△ **Cheap and cheerful**
In a first home, the budget does not
always stretch to the luxury of an
elaborate storage system.

Furnished on a shoestring, this living
room is nevertheless bright and cheery.
The bright red, black and white colours
in the Mondrian poster are echoed in
simple modular storage cubes which
can easily be added to, and high tech
shelving in black metal forms an
interesting feature, even if it is not
crammed full of possessions.

▷ **Stylish storage**
Although it looks like a single piece of
furniture, this stylish oak-veneered
storage system is actually made up of
modular units which can be put
together in many different
combinations. Here a tall glass-fronted
central unit flanked by shorter shelves
and cupboards makes the storage itself,
as well as the items displayed on it, the
centre of attention.

CHOOSING BOOKCASES AND DISPLAY CABINETS

It pays to choose the right furniture to house books and cherished ornaments.

One advantage which single bookcases and display cabinets have over modular storage furniture, consisting of basic matching shapes, is that they are more likely to fit into other rooms in your home should your requirements change or should you move house. Basically, single pieces are easier to move about because they are less complicated and not tailor-made for a specific length of wall or a certain ceiling height. Also, they can usually be moved without having to be dismantled.

Minus points However, the disadvantage of single pieces compared to modular storage furniture is that for the amount of space taken up in a room there is less actual storage/shelf/display area. You can offset this by choosing pieces of furniture which have a definite decorative value in their own right and

therefore deserve the space which they take up.

Buying old You may be able to find suitable items second hand, through classified advertisements in newspapers, in junk shops or at furniture auctions. Older items may require renovation work, but can be relatively cheap to buy and should repay any time and money spent on restoration handsomely.

Old furniture tends to have a character which is difficult to find in new items, and especially suits older houses or period-style decoration.

Safety Whether you buy new or second hand, always remember that bookcases and display cabinets must be stable. This is particularly important if you have small children who could be badly hurt should such pieces of furniture fall over while full of heavy books

or laden with fragile china and glassware.

Materials and styles Bookcases and display cabinets are mostly made from wood – either solid wood or plywood, chipboard or fibreboard covered with a thin layer of wood veneer. Alternatively some modern designs are covered with man-made laminated finishes. They come in a variety of shapes and sizes from traditional to more off-beat designs. Whatever you buy, it should fit in with your room decor.

STYLES OF BOOKCASE

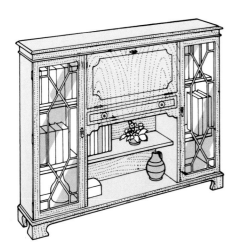

BOOK/DRINKS CUPBOARD
Style Shelves at each end of this wooden bookcase are fully adjustable and enclosed by Gothic-style beaded glass doors. The inner section contains a cocktail cabinet which has a mirrored back and a fall-front door. Below this, there is a drawer and two open shelves.
In use Versatile and functional, the cupboard is 146mm wide × 32cm deep × 184cm high.

LIBRARY-STYLE
Style Floorstanding wooden bookcase comprises a base unit of cupboard and drawers and a top unit of adjustable shelves with glazed doors.
In use This style can create a traditional 'library' look in any living room or study. It stands 193cm high, 99cm wide and 37cm deep. For the relatively small amount of floor space it takes up, it provides a lot of storage room.

MODERN SLIDING
Style Compact, wood-veneered bookcase which incorporates shelves and drawers behind sliding glass doors. The middle shelf is adjustable, so most sizes of book can be accommodated.
In use Slimline enough (30cm deep, 100cm wide, 105cm high) to be unobtrusive in any room.
Watchpoint Each time the doors are opened or even touched, fingerprints will mark the glass.

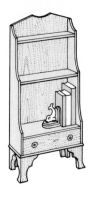

WATERFALL

Style This is called a waterfall book/display shelf because of its attractive appearance – it's narrower at the top than at the bottom.

In use Open wooden shelves suitable for housing books, ornaments or other knick-knacks. It stands 115cm high making it the right height to double up as a bedside cabinet.

BOOKTROUGH

Style Simple open wooden shelving. Shelves are angled so that book spines face upwards slightly. This means you can see, at a glance, all the book titles and their authors – handy for older or disabled people as it saves on bending.

In use This booktrough measures 80cm wide × 30cm deep × 75cm high.

REVOLVER

Style Revolving wooden bookcase.

In use Such a bookcase should not be placed flush against a wall as it needs room to revolve. This makes books easily accessible from both sides (front and back) of the bookcase. It stands 82cm high, 47cm wide and 47cm deep.

STYLES OF DISPLAY CABINET

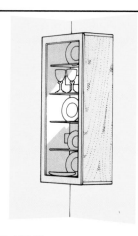

MODERN DISPLAY SHELVES

Style This modern open shelving unit in fashionable stained or lacquered wood is suitable for displaying ornaments, china or books.

In use As well as storage shelves, it can also serve as a low room divider. It measures 180cm wide × 30cm deep × 78cm high, but is available in a larger size. Its shape makes it easy to clean.

REPRODUCTION QUEEN ANNE

Style Reproduction wood-veneered display case with Queen Anne-style cabriole legs. The doors are glass, as are the sides of the cabinet and the shelves (which are mirror-backed).

In use An abundance of glass shows off prized pieces to the full. It is 90cm wide, 45cm deep and 150cm high. Drawer is ideal for cutlery.

WALL-HUNG

Style Wall-hung wooden display cabinet with glass shelves, glazed doors and internal lighting.

In use It keeps good china and other breakables well out of children's reach. It measures about 60cm wide × 35cm deep × 120cm high.

Watchpoint Make sure it is well secured, preferably on cantilevered brackets.

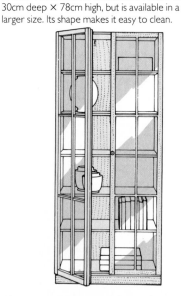
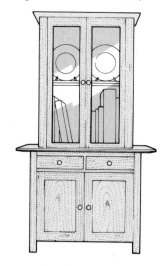

HIGH RISE

Style Modern, tall, glass-fronted cabinet with three fixed and two adjustable shelves. It is wood-veneered, available lacquered or stained.

In use As this piece is so tall (88cm wide × 44cm deep × 192cm high), it stands on a flat plinth rather than on legs, which gives it extra stability and wastes no space.

TWO-PIECE

Style Wood-veneered cabinet made up of a separate top and base unit like the traditional dresser. Top shelving unit is 90cm wide × 40cm deep × 110cm high. Base shelving unit is 114cm × 45cm × 84cm. Both available open or enclosed.

In use An attractive piece which doesn't display contents – but can hide a multitude of sins!

HIGH-TECH

Style This tubular metal shelving unit is supplied in a black, white or metallic grey painted finish for the latest high-tech look.

In use It stands 184cm high, 66cm wide and 38cm deep. The shelves are made from perforated sheets of metal. Look out for trolleys and chairs which match this style. Easy to clean.

AUDIO-VISUAL STORAGE UNITS

There is a wide choice of storage units available which are specifically made to house TVs, video recorders and hi-fi gear.

Many living room modular storage ranges offer a module for TV set, video recorder and hi-fi equipment, but there is also a huge number of stand-alone furniture pieces which are specifically designed to house these items.

High-tech, modern homes make a virtue out of their viewing and listening equipment and choose it to suit the style and decoration of the room.

However, in period settings and traditionally furnished homes, the overwhelming modern style of audio-visual systems tends to spoil the atmosphere. Consequently, some people try to hide the equipment away completely, while others prefer a compromise of convenience and looks.

Buying to fit TV sets are much smaller than they used to be, but it is impossible to generalize on size. Many people have a large set downstairs and a smaller one (often portable) for kitchen and bedroom viewing. The only way to tell if a unit is the right size for your TV is by measuring it.

As for the size of hi-fi equipment, there is even more variation; mini- and midi-stack systems, ones made up of independent components (amplifier, CD, tape deck and turntable) and music centres (one component and speakers).

If possible, choose an audio-visual housing system which is adaptable; this could be a unit with adjustable shelves or one big and versatile enough to accommodate combinations of equipment in the event of a change of equipment.

Style When it comes to a unit's appearance, there is plenty of choice. Reproduction, period and contemporary styles in wood finishes – natural and stained, and high-tech fashion units.

UNITS FOR TV AND VIDEO RECORDERS

The most important thing about a TV and video storage unit is that it should be sited where the screen can be seen easily. Experts say the ideal viewing height is a minimum 120cm.

Size When buying a unit, check it is the right size and height to house your TV and ensure it is suitable for your video recorder. Front-loading video recorders don't need to be moved for normal operation, but top-loading models need a slide-out shelf below the TV or a space above so there is access for loading.

Ventilation Most TV cabinets have ventilation slots in the back of them, others are even backless – if a unit is completely enclosed make sure it is at least 15cm deeper than the TV.

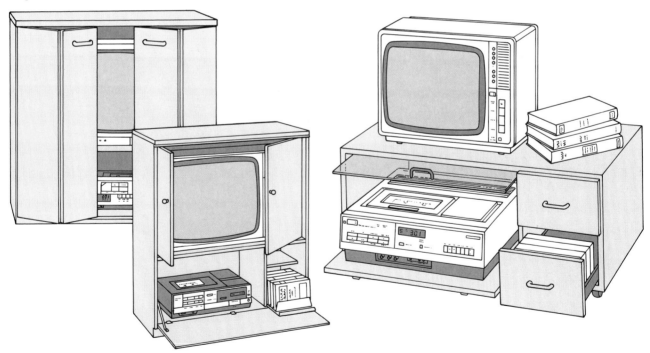

ENCLOSED TV AND VIDEO CABINETS

Style The TV is usually fitted into the unit and can be covered by a pair of doors, when not in use. And there is usually storage space (a shelf or slide-out tray) below for a video recorder. Occasionally, there is room for it above. Choose between the more classical piece of furniture which looks to all intents and purposes like a cocktail cabinet (above right), and the more modern wooden hide-away cupboard (above left) with concertina-style folding doors.

In use The doors may have special hinges to allow them to open flush with the sides of the cabinet or slide inside the cabinet itself.

OPEN TV, ENCLOSED VIDEO STORAGE

Style The TV sits on top of the unit while the video recorder is stored below, behind an up-and-over door or straightforward opening doors. The internal shelf may have a slide-out action (to give access to a top-loading video recorder). The area should allow for tape storage or there should be a separate drawer or compartment for tapes.

In use A glass or transparent up-and-over door keeps dust off the video recorder, but still allows you to see the digital read-out on the recorder telling you what it is recording, how it is programmed and it also enables you to see the digital time clock.

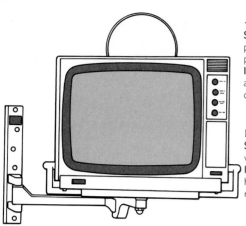

◁ **TV WALL BRACKET**
Style Steel support bracket swivels so you can position TV as desired. It has an adjustable base plate for it to hold different sized TV sets.
In use This can be screwed to the wall or ceiling and keeps the TV out of the way of inquisitive children and pets.

▷ **OPEN TROLLEY STORAGE**
Style A modern three-tiered tubular metal trolley with perforated metal shelves.
In use An ideal (and relatively cheap) way to house a portable or small TV set and video recorder.

HI-FI EQUIPMENT

Choosing storage units for audio equipment requires more care than for TV and video recorders, because there are more parts to consider. Measure each piece of equipment that has to go in the unit and then work out where they are to be positioned. It is disastrous if you buy a unit and then have to cram everything in to it when you get it home.

Everyday access Consider how you use the equipment and if there is adequate access to it – most hi-fi systems require access from the front and top. (Bear in mind that most turntable decks have opening lids, but tape decks and compact discs can be loaded from the front or top.) Operating height is important. They should be low so you can kneel or high so you can stand while loading tapes and so on. Avoid sizes in be-

tween. A few storage units include room for speakers. These look neat, but aren't necessarily the best position for speakers, so consult an audio dealer before buying if you are concerned about optimum sound quality.
Wiring Most hi-fi units have pre-drilled holes in their backs for wires. Electrical equipment should always have adequate ventilation – leave enclosed units open during operation.

ALL-ROUNDERS
Style This is a modular storage system made up of single units specifically for audio-visual equipment. It has various degrees of

enclosure and disguise for hi-fi, TV, videos and speakers.
In use Very versatile, as you can add more units to it as you acquire extra equipment, records and so on.

△ **ENCLOSED CABINET**
Style Usually with lifting lid and door-front opening, which may be disguised as a mock drawer-front. A fall-flap front is another alternative.
In use The ultimate disguise, and some say good for fooling prospective burglars. Keep open when in use.
Watchpoint It limits choice if you plan to change equipment.

STORAGE FOR ACCESSORIES

It is very handy when buying an audio-visual storage unit to have additional storage for LPs, tapes, video cassettes and compact discs. Look for drawers which are lined with slotted trays to hold tapes and discs (see above left). This enables you to keep them in order.

Record racks are standard with most hi-fi storage units. The

unit shown (above right) is a single piece of furniture solely for records. The neat, slide-in, slide-out cupboard (rather like the sort found in a fitted kitchen) allows you to find a record at the back without having to take out those in front first.

STACKING STORAGE
Style Space-saving, modern high-rise unit specifically designed for a stacking hi-fi system.
In use Most stacking types are fully enclosed with opening and lifting tinted glass doors. Shelves are adjustable to hold most hi-fi systems. Castors allow easy positioning of the unit in your home.

LIVING ROOMS: SOUND AND VISION

TV, video, hi-fi, and compact disc:
how to get the best from
your home entertainments system.

Loudspeakers should be positioned so that they give the best possible sound. Where you place the speakers – and, therefore, the quality of sound produced, depends, to a large extent, on the shape of the room and the type of loudspeaker cabinet – some are designed to sit on the floor, others on a bookshelf. Soft furnishings also affect sound quality.

Positioning speakers The loudness of the sound (particularly the bass sounds) coming out of a loudspeaker is influenced by where it is placed. The loudest position is on the floor (or on the ceiling) in the corner of a room.

Here, the sound output is being helped by the two walls of the corner and the surface of the floor (or ceiling). The next loudest position is on the floor (or ceiling) against one wall; here the sound is being helped by only one wall and the surface of the floor (or ceiling). The further away the speaker is from the ideal corner, the quieter it becomes.

In a small room, the loudspeakers are often so close to the seating that it is impossible to have background music without it interfering with conversation. In such a case, mounting the loudspeakers off the floor – on a shelf, or on one of a variety of floor or wall stands available – can help.

Some very expensive loudspeakers are supplied with detailed instructions as to where they should be placed for optimum listening. It's a good idea to follow these instructions faithfully as they are usually the result of exhaustive listening tests by the designers.

Soft furnishings, such as carpets and curtains, can affect the quality of sound from the loudspeakers dramatically.

A 'live' room has bare walls and floors which reflect the sound, making it much brighter, bigger and louder compared with a 'dead' room – one with fitted carpets and curtains. In an extreme case, a 'live' room can echo and confuse the sound, whereas a 'dead' room can make the sound seem small, dull and soft.

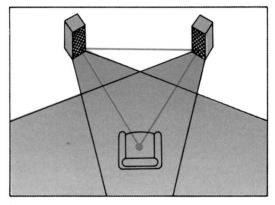

▷ *Serious listening*
If a line is drawn from the centre of the cone of sound coming from each speaker, the point where the two lines cross is the optimum position. For really serious listening, the distance between the two speakers must equal the distance between each speaker and the listener, forming a triangle of equal sides.

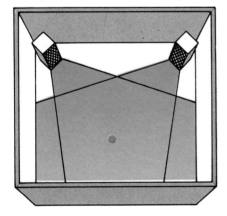

△ **Whole room sound**
Speakers facing diagonally into a squarish room from the corners of one wall give whole room sound.

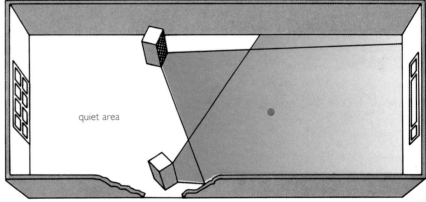

△ **Rectangular room with quiet area**
A long room can be more difficult to position speakers in successfully, but it is also more versatile. If you want a quiet

area in the room, for dining or study, for example, place one or both speakers partway down the wall, facing into the listening area.

POSITIONING THE TV

A television must be easy to view from the most comfortable seats but it shouldn't dominate the room. This seemingly conflicting set of conditions can be met by having the TV on a trolley, or keeping it in a cabinet or cupboard with closing doors.

Make sure the TV is positioned so that reflection off the screen from windows and lighting is avoided as far as possible. The recommended minimum height from the base of the set to the floor is about 120cm. This ensures that good seating posture is maintained. Unfortunately, most commercial stands are much lower than this, forcing the viewers to crane their necks down and forward or slump in the seat in order to see the screen.

It is a good idea to have some lighting near the TV when viewing. This is because looking away from the screen from time to time helps to reduce the eye fatigue caused by focusing on the small screen for a long time. This relief is most effective if you look at something of a similar brightness to the screen – otherwise your eyes have to re-adjust whenever the lighting conditions change.

CENTRAL CONTROL

The main hi-fi unit is the amplifier, if it is combined with a radio tuner it is known as a receiver. The amplifier receives low-level signals from the turntable, radio tuner, cassette deck, CD player, video and so on, and boosts them to a sufficient level to drive the loudspeakers.

Connecting your system Most of the connections made are between and among the amplifier and the above units, so it is a good idea to keep them all together to avoid trailing wires.

If your video recorder is stereo, it is worth connecting it to the amplifier along with all the main hi-fi units. This allows you to listen to video cassettes in stereo; you can also channel TV programmes through the speakers.

Most amplifiers have three or four sockets marked:
☐ phono, which is for the turntable only;
☐ tape for the cassette deck;
☐ tuner and/or aux which can be used for radio, CD, video or any additional unit you want to connect.

Power and connections If you do not have enough power points near the amplifier and other equipment, it's a good idea to plug everything into a fused adaptor strip socket. Sometimes the amplifier has built-in outlets providing power for additional units such as the turntable or CD player. This enables them all to be turned on and off with one switch and cuts down on the number of wall sockets you will need.

Once your equipment is arranged in position and set up, the only remaining connections to be made are:
☐ the loudspeaker cables;
☐ the cable from the video to the TV;
☐ and the cable(s) from the FM/TV aerial sockets or indoor aerials to the tuner and video unit.

If you need longer speaker cables than those provided by the manufacturer, use a thick stranded or automotive cable, as this will preserve sound quality over the longer distance. Long cables (sold as '75 ohm co-axial') suitable for the video unit/TV and tuner to aerial socket interconnections are readily obtainable from most video and hi-fi shops.

Block diagram of suitable wiring-up scheme

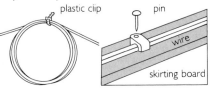

speaker — turntable — speaker — receiver — vhf aerial — CD player — fm aerial — cassette deck — VCR — TV

◁ *Connecting your system*
Most connections are made between the units inside the dotted line. If they are kept together, the wires and plugs can be neatly ordered and concealed. The speakers and TV can be positioned anywhere you like in the room.

plastic clip — pin — wire — skirting board

△ *Keeping wires neat*
Run cables close to skirting boards and architraves, pinned with plastic clips. Never twist or bend wires, wind unnecessary lengths in a loose circle and secure with a plastic grip.

CARE AND STORAGE

Always leave enough room around and above the turntable to allow the lid to be opened and records changed. Similarly, allow space above any other top-loading units, such as some videos, cassette decks, and CD players so that they may be loaded and unloaded.

To prevent units from overheating, it is important to leave enough space above and below them for air to circulate; for this reason, don't leave record covers or magazines on top of any electrical equipment that is switched on. If video or hi-fi units are mounted in a cupboard, make sure the doors are open when the units are operating.

The main enemy of records, cassettes, and compact discs is heat from the sun, a gas or electric fire, or even a video or hi-fi unit. Records buckle or warp in heat, and it causes magnetic tape, including audio and video cassettes, gradually to become erased. Moisture can also cause damage, so always ensure that your records and tapes are

video cassettes — compact discs — audio cassettes — task lighting — VCR — cassette deck — CD player — albums with vertical dividers — singles — receiver — turntable

stored in a cool, dry, clean place.

Stack records vertically with the spines facing outwards, and use dividers to break them up into groups of twenty or so. This allows easy access and, more importantly, means that they have no weight on them as they would in a horizontal pile. Audio and video cassettes and compact discs are also best stacked vertically for ease of access.

There are a number of units designed specially for record and tape storage, or you can simply treat them as you would books and build a series of shelves. Storage at eye-level is a good idea to avoid a frenzied search for a favourite record or tape. Avoid using the same shelf for the turntable and storage, otherwise the stylus will jump every time you touch an album.

FIREPLACE WALLS

A wall which contains a fireplace needs careful attention, whether or not you like to have open fires.

Traditionally, the hearth has always been regarded as the heart of the home. Particularly before the advent of radio and television, the family would gather round a glowing fire in the evenings to read, play games or talk.

For a while, though, it seemed as if the open fire was a threatened species as gas and electric fires, and later central heating, became increasingly common. Many fireplaces were blocked up, and elegant surrounds discarded in favour of undoubtedly more efficient forms of heating.

Recent years have seen a revival of interest in the open fire. Although no longer regarded as a practical or efficient way of heating an entire house, the contrast between the comforting glow of flickering flames and bleak winter weather cannot be denied. Many families now lay a fire only in the living room, where its inviting warmth can be best appreciated by family and friends. And it is, of course, possible to retain a distinctive fireplace for its decorative value, to provide a handsome focal point for seating, even if it is not used.

The choices If you have a fireplace, think carefully before deciding how to deal with it, both in practical and decorative terms. You could replace the surround, install a more modern heater or block it up and remove the surround. A fireplace which has been covered over by a previous owner of the house can be re-opened without great difficulty, providing the chimney hasn't been blocked up. If you have no chimney at all, don't despair. A new flue, made from ceramic lined metal sections, can be built up outside the house and clad in brick or built inside and concealed by a false chimney breast.

Decoratively, the fireplace itself must be viewed in relation to the chimney breast above and the side recesses. How these are treated affects the atmosphere of the entire room and plays an important role in highlighting or playing down the fireplace itself.

On the shelves
A modern room heater (an enclosed open fire) has been installed in this room. In winter, the seating can be rearranged to focus on the fireplace; in summer the coffee table acts as a focal point.

DECORATING IDEAS

It goes without saying that the way you decorate the fireplace wall must blend in with the decor of the room as a whole. But because a fireplace wall has a structure of its own – generally with a protruding chimney breast flanked by recessed alcoves – it does require special attention.

Start by asking yourself how often you light a fire during cold weather – every day, at the weekends or only on rare winter evenings? Your answer should influence the way you treat the fireplace wall. A frequently-used fireplace should take pride of place in the room since it forms a natural focal point for warmth and interest; one which is infrequently lit should be allowed to merge into the background.

The fireplace If the existing fireplace is not to your liking, it should be easy to find one which suits your taste and budget and matches the style of your home. Antique, modern and reproduction versions are widely available.

Scale is important – a tall, imposing fireplace tends to overwhelm a small, low-ceilinged room, while a plain, modern fireplace can become lost in an imposing Victorian or Edwardian room.

Also bear in mind the fact that modern technical improvements can greatly increase the efficiency of the fire. And if you want the pleasure of real flames, without the bother of a real fire, consider a room heater (basically an open fire behind glass doors), or a gas or electric fuel-effect fire. In most cases a back boiler for heating radiators and hot water is optional.

The chimney breast and alcoves are almost always arranged symmetrically, so it's important to reflect this in the decoration. It is, for example, best to stand a pair of lamps on the mantelpiece or a standard lamp in each alcove rather than have a single, unbalanced lamp.

Traditionally, a large painting or mirror is centred above the fireplace, and both alcoves are treated identically. The

△ *Blue and white*
This elegant fireplace is painted white to match the intricate coving and picture rail. Thus the architectural detail of this period room emphasizes the lines of the chimney breast and alcoves, against a background of gentle Wedgwood blue. A picture over the fireplace emphasizes the chimney breast and draws the eye away from the alcove.

alcoves should not fight for dominance with the chimney breast and fireplace. If the fire is often used, focus attention on the protruding chimney breast, perhaps by using a different colour or wallpaper to the one used in the alcoves.

If you light your fire less often, plenty of interest in the alcoves prevents the fireplace from dominating the room. Traditionally, built-in bookshelves or display shelves use the recess to best advantage, frequently with small cupboards at floor level. Another solution is to install modular storage or a small sofa in the space.

◁ **Old and new**
A period setting need not be furnished totally traditionally. In this alternative to the treatment below, an up-to-date tubular storage trolley in each alcove fits in well with both the fireplace and the coving.

▽ **Traditional elegance**
Symmetry is all important when decorating the fireplace wall. Here, a traditional approach has been taken – a large mirror tops the imposing fireplace and the alcoves have been arched over to frame glass display shelves. The arches and cupboards below are outlined in mouldings of a similar style to that of the cornice.

MAKING CHANGES

If the fireplace has been removed entirely or blocked up, or it simply is never used, the wall to which it belongs needs a special approach.

An unused fireplace How you decorate such a fireplace depends largely on whether or not the surround is attractive. If it is, decorate the entire fireplace wall as you would if the fireplace were in use. After all, no fireplace is used all the year round, however bad the weather may be!

There are many ways of preventing the empty grate from becoming an eyesore. Traditionally, a fire screen was used. Other alternatives include a pot plant, an arrangement of dried flowers, leaves or even logs and fir cones. Whatever you choose, ensure that it is harmonious with both the fire surround and the decoration above and next to it.

A blocked off fireplace It's always worth considering opening up such a fireplace – you never know what delights may have been hidden away behind a layer of boring hardboard. Opening up a fireplace should be done with care – it can be messy, and the condition of the firebricks, the chimney itself and the hearth must all be carefully checked if the fireplace is to be used again.

Treat a fireplace where the opening has been closed off (perhaps with a sheet of hardboard) but the surround has been left in place, in much the same way as you would a fireplace which is not being used. It's often a good idea, though, to plan on using a fairly substantial display in order to hide a possibly unattractive covering.

If the surround has been removed it's best to treat the entire wall – chimney breast and the alcoves – as a single

△ *Modern simplicity*
In this home, two rooms have been combined into one – and the fireplaces in both have been removed. In one, the opening has been completely plastered over – in the other a perfectly square hole has been left. The result is an elegant sequence of angular recesses.

entity in order to create a unified sense of space and to avoid the impression that something is missing. Try building cupboards or shelves out to the line of the chimney breast to hide all traces of the recessed alcoves.

Installing a fireplace in the absence of an existing chimney can be easier than you might think. Ready-made masonry chimneys, which can be installed either inside the house or on an outside wall, are now available, as are stainless steel prefabricated chimney systems.

Using the chimney breast Where a fireplace has been removed, the redundant chimney breast often provides an excellent location for a central heating radiator.

The radiator could be unattractive in so prominent a position, and so an open latticework 'box' has been built around it. The lattice, which allows heat to radiate freely, is painted cream to tone in with the rest of the wall. The front of such a cover should be removable to allow access for repairs.

▽ *Supplementary heat*
Although central heating is a more practical and time-saving way of providing warmth, a real fire undoubtedly adds an inviting glow.

Here, one fireplace has been removed while the other (in the sitting area of the room) has been left in place, to be used in conjunction with the main form of heating. A modern surround with simple lines blends well with the overall decor.

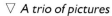
▷ *An unusual effect*
The installation of a floor-to-ceiling mirror on the back wall of one alcove creates a novel effect by reflecting an interesting statue. In practical terms, such a large mirror also makes a small room seem larger.

The single picture hung centrally over the fireplace directs attention to the chimney breast, and away from the alcoves. In effect, this can narrow a wide room.

▽ *A trio of pictures*
The normal width of a chimney breast usually means that there is room for only a single large picture – or possibly several small ones – above the fireplace. In this room, however, the alcoves have either been filled out so that they are in line with the chimney breast, or the chimney breast protrudes outwards from the house.

This has created a straight wall which allows a series of three pictures to be ranged above the fireplace, giving the room a feeling of added width.

FIREPLACES
The traditional fireplace is making a comeback and there's a shape and style to suit every home.

MATERIALS

The surround and interior (infill or slips) of the fireplace can be made from a variety of both natural and man-made materials.

Ceramic tiles were popular as decoration on the interior (slips) of the fireplace in Victorian and Edwardian times. The tiles used were ornate and often decorated with flowers, fruit or leaves. Heavily-embossed tiles in colours such as green, mulberry, brown and cream, or blue and white Delft designs, were also used. It was not until the 1920s that fireplaces were completely decorated with tiling which could be plain, embossed, incised, or made to imitate stone, slate or marble. Tiled fireplaces are still made today. Tiles are easy to clean, but chip and crack if anything heavy is dropped on them.

Stone and slate Both are popular for 'rustic' style fireplaces. Stone comes in a variety of colours, including off-white, honey, gold and grey. Quartzite, which has bands of colour running through the stone and a slight sparkle, is a popular choice. Stone can either be carved to the shape of the surround or pieced from regular or random-shaped blocks. The surface of these blocks can be textured (chip-like surface) or smooth. Slate ranges in colour from blue-green to dark grey and black. Like stone, it can be polished or textured.

Metal has always been a popular material for fireplaces. The Victorians made elaborate cast iron fireplaces. Today, copper, brass, wrought iron and stainless steel are used to make canopies, surrounds, fire opening edging and other accessories.

Briquettes are made from reconstituted brick. They vary in size from actual house brick dimensions to much slimmer versions, half the thickness, and are available in a variety of colours and effects. They are used to build fireplaces in all sorts of styles and are most common for DIY fireplace kits.

Marble has been a popular material for building fireplaces since the late 17th century. It comes in a range of colours, including white veined with grey or black, rose, green, brown and dark grey. Today reconstituted marble (lighter and cheaper than the real thing) is often used on the fireplace interior. Real marble is used to make expensive surrounds and is used in sheet form on the fireplace interior.

Fibrous plaster can be moulded to imitate classic designs formerly made from marble or carved stone, but is much lighter in weight and cheaper. It is usually accompanied by an interior of real or reconstituted marble. Plaster surrounds are available from specialist shops.

ANATOMY OF A FIREPLACE

Before buying a fireplace, it is useful to know the names of the various parts.

Surround This can also be called the mantle. It is the outermost framework around the fire, usually consisting of two vertical uprights and a horizontal plinth with a shelf on it – the shelf is known as the mantleshelf.

Fireplace opening This is the hole in the centre where the fuel is housed. It is often edged with brass or other metal edging.

Interior, infill or slips The area – often marble or reconstituted marble – separating the fireplace opening from the surround.

Firebox, basket or firegrate These hold the burning fuel.

Hearth Strictly speaking this is the concrete or stone base upon which the fireplace is built.

Decorative hearth This is the slab on the floor which extends (by a minimum 30cm) in front.

Fireback Traditionally decorative cast iron, but can be made of stone, fire clay or firebricks. This is the backplate against which the burning fuel is housed. It protects the back of the chimney from the heat of the fire.

Wood Pine, oak, walnut and a variety of hardwoods are used to make surrounds. When used for a classic style fireplace, the wood is combined with a marble, tiled, or cast iron and tiled interior. Modern and rustic styles usually have an interior of real stone or briquettes.

INGLENOOK
Style The traditional cottage fireplace – a big alcove which contains a fire, and sometimes seating. Modern inglenook designs are made from briquettes or stone.
In use The inglenook cannot be bought off-the-peg. It is either an original feature or can be custom-built. The fire itself is usually housed in a firebasket on a raised plinth and the smoke guided into the wide chimney via a brass canopy or hood. A freestanding or solid fuel appliance suits it well.

TUDOR
Style Large stone fireplace with a carved surround and big, arched opening. The fuel is housed in a firebasket. In the summer when not in use, the fireplace opening can be filled with a traditional tapestry firescreen.
In use Strictly for big rooms, preferably those furnished in dark oak and with period features. Originally Tudor fireplaces could stand around 2m high and 2m or more wide. Nowadays, reproductions are available in more modest dimensions; typically around 140cm high × 150cm wide.

CLASSIC

Style This has a carved surround made from pine, fibrous plaster, white-painted hardwood or marble. The interior is usually made of real or reconstituted marble slabs and the fireplace opening edged with brass or stainless steel. Alternatively it can be made without an interior so a firebasket can stand in the wide opening.
In use Not suitable for small rooms with low ceilings as this fireplace typically stands around 123cm high and 175cm wide.

DRAUGHT-ASSISTED FIREBOX

You can now buy draught-assisted fireboxes which enable you to adjust the rate at which solid fuel burns. Basically, dampers (manually-operated levers) or a small fan (electric or battery operated) control the flow of air from the room into the fireplace. This makes burning efficient and helps to stop heat from disappearing up the flue. It also means the fire can be kept on all night by reducing the rate of burning to a smoulder. It looks just like an ordinary grate, but has dampers at the side or bottom. The fan-operated type blows air into the room.

TILED

Style Tiled fireplaces were popular from the 1920s onwards with many post-war examples made in two-tone coloured tiles. More recently these have been updated with more stylish and streamlined 'designer' styles.
In use The tiles of baked clay are easy to clean and maintain, but do have a tendency to chip or crack if heavy objects – a poker for example – are dropped on them. Sizes vary; modern examples are typically around 80cm high × 122cm wide.

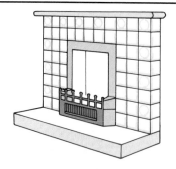

VICTORIAN

Style Can be either ornate cast iron with a wide arched or square opening and fire basket for the fuel or a carved wooden surround combined with ornate interior (infill) tiling and opening edged with cast iron, topped by a small canopy.
In use Sizes vary enormously from the large – around 150cm high × 140cm wide – to those much smaller, originally intended for bedrooms. Those with a pine surround are suitable for cottage-style interiors; bigger designs look best in large, period-style rooms.

RUSTIC

Style Various designs made in briquettes or stone, available in kit form or custom-built.
In use For small rooms, look at neat briquette fireplaces with arched openings, or the smaller stone fireplaces which usually have a wooden mantel and shelves on each side of the surround. If you have the space, choose from a range of larger fireplaces. These consist of a low plinth topped by wood or stone, built into the alcoves at either side of the chimney breast. The chimney breast can also be stone clad.

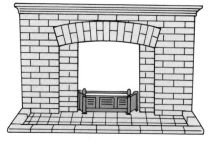

HOLE-IN-THE-WALL

Style As the name suggests, this is simply an opening in the wall or chimney breast, fitted with a basket to hold burning fuel. Many fireplace stockists sell brass edging to fit around an old fireplace opening and turn it into a hole-in-the-wall fireplace. More elaborate hole-in-the-wall designs have a stone, slate, or brick plinth below the fireplace opening (as shown).
In use The opening must be a minumum of 40cm wide. Especially suitable for a modern house.

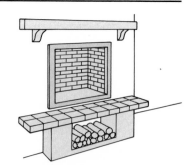

FIRE-IN-THE-MIDDLE

Style Modern, high-tech or rustic, depending on materials used. The fire, as the name implies, stands in the middle of the room. It comes in many styles; built into a chimney breast where the walls either side have been knocked through, as shown; alternatively, at a cost you can have a central chimney professionally built. Or the fire can be housed in a basket on a raised stone

platform in the centre of the room with a copper, wrought iron, or steel chimney, which starts as a wide canopy above the fire then narrows to a circular or square flue.
In use Often installed in large, open-plan rooms as a dividing line between one area and another. The room must be large for this sort of fireplace to look effective.

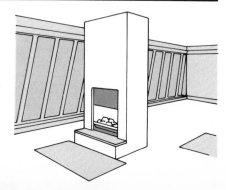

TABLE AND FLOOR LAMPS AND SHADES

Floor and table lamps can create atmosphere, provide background light or direct light on activities.

Good lighting is essential so it is important to choose the right fittings.

This chapter covers freestanding light fittings (table lamps, desk lights and floor lights). These are plug-in fittings run off a wall or floor socket so they are easy to install and portable. This makes them an ideal choice if you require flexible fittings or if you are not prepared to rewire to use fixed fittings.

Freestanding lights are, however, best avoided in young children's rooms where they might easily get knocked over. The next two chapters cover ceiling-mounted and wall-mounted fixtures (including spotlights, fluorescent strips, downlighters and uplighters) so that you know what is available when planning the lighting scheme for any room.

The style of a light fitting should be compatible with the style of a room, but most important of all you should work out what you want any individual light to do and where it will be positioned in relation to other lights. There are three main types of lighting:

Background lighting provides a general view of visibility. It is indirect and restful, and is a direct replacement for natural light.

Task lighting is strong localized lighting which provides illumination for specific activities and includes work lights and guiding lights (on a stairwell for example).

Decorative lighting is used to accent or highlight attractive objects in a room and to create atmosphere/effects.

Most rooms require a combination of the first two types, and in general living areas you may also want to add some decorative lighting to spotlight a picture or ornaments.

CHECKLIST

Here is a checklist of points to consider when deciding what kind of light fittings you want. Appearance and cost will, of course, also play a part.

☐ What is the style of the room – traditional or modern?
☐ What atmosphere or mood are you aiming to create?
☐ What is the room primarily used for – relaxed conversation and reading, sleeping, studying, craftwork, household tasks?
☐ Do activities move around and require flexible lighting?
☐ Is there space for free-standing lights?
☐ Do you want to highlight plants, paintings or ornaments?

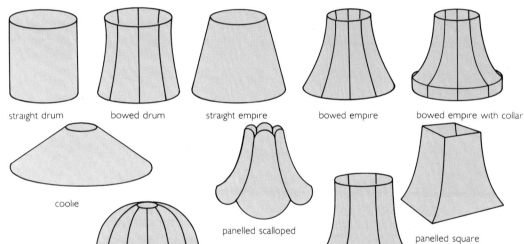

straight drum   bowed drum   straight empire   bowed empire   bowed empire with collar

coolie

panelled scalloped

panelled square

tiffany

bowed oval

TABLE LAMPS

A table lamp provides a warm, intimate glow and is primarily used for low-level background lighting. It is a useful supplement to other lights in living rooms, bedrooms and hallways and is often a decorative object in itself.

Depending on the amount of light thrown downwards by the shade, a table lamp can also be used for task lighting (for armchair reading or as a conventional bedside lamp) or for display lighting (to illuminate a table display of favourite objects for example).

Shades with open tops can also bounce light off the ceiling.

The bases and shades can be bought separately or together.

TRADITIONAL TABLE LAMPS

Style Bases and shades come in a variety of styles suitable for both traditional and modern furnished rooms. Simple pottery bases look good in both settings and so do candlestick, greek urn and some chinese styles.

As a general rule, the simpler the shade the more suitable it will be for a modern decor.

In use Choose a fine 2-ply electric wire rather than a bulky 3-ply wire when wiring up a lamp.
Watchpoint A shade contributes to the colour of the light produced when lit so it is best to see it illuminated before buying. The shade must be in the right proportion to the base and deep enough to shield the light bulb.

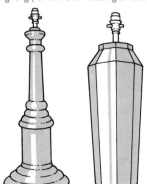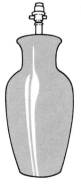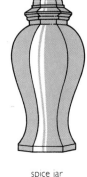

candlestick   column   ginger jar   urn   chinese vase   spice jar   small globe

DECORATIVE TABLE LIGHTS

tiffany

modern

oil

art deco

ART NOUVEAU TIFFANY LAMP

Style A coloured, stained glass shade on an ornate metal base. There are several variations on the basic petal shade. This old-style opulence adds a decorative touch best suited to traditional settings.

ART DECO TABLE LAMP

Style This design must be used with care, but can look equally at home in a modern home as well as a 30s style room. The base often consists of a draped female figure holding a globe-shaped shade.

In use The lamp provides general lighting and, at the same time, is a very distinctive object.

OIL LAMP

Style A brass lamp with a frosted, etched or clear glass shade which is best suited to cottage and country settings.
In use New oil lamps are available converted to electricity – old ones can easily be adapted.

MODERN TABLE LAMP

Style A range of styles usually with a streamlined look.

FLOOR LAMPS

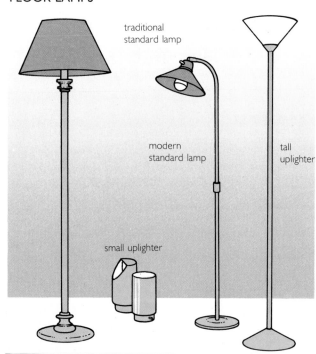

traditional standard lamp

modern standard lamp

tall uplighter

small uplighter

These give general background lighting, and some can also be used for task lighting.

Use mainly in living rooms and dining rooms (and possibly hallways) and position near a wall or next to furniture and away from circulation routes.

CONVENTIONAL STANDARD

Style This traditional light looks pretty in cottagey rooms or more formal in a traditional setting, depending on the type of shade. Use larger versions of those on previous page.
In use Provides a pool of light for reading when set beside or some way behind a chair.
Watchpoint Look for a sturdy base and keep flex well away from circulation routes.

MODERN STANDARD

Style Simple, stark lines suit most furnishing styles and particularly those with a contemporary look.
In use More versatile than the

standard lamp, they can often be angled, raised or lowered.
Watchpoint Ask to see the lamp lit before buying so that you can check whether glare is a problem when you are seated.

TALL UPLIGHTER

Style The streamlined, vertical lines of uplighters are mainly suitable for modern settings.
In use Most of the beam is bounced off the ceiling to achieve a soft background glow. Best reflected off white or pale-coloured surfaces.
Watchpoint Should be tall enough to shield bulb and avoid glare at sitting and standing level. Needs a stable base.

SMALL UPLIGHTER

Style Unobtrusive modern shape is suitable for any setting.
In use Position behind a sofa, low table or plants to flood the walls with light.
Watchpoint Do not place too close to plants.

TASK LIGHTS

traditional desk lamp

modern desk lamp

angled work light

flexible neck spotlight

Designed to give localized areas of bright light for detailed work, they can also be used for background lighting if redirected to bounce light off walls or ceiling. For maximum flexibility choose adjustable lamps so that you can direct light exactly where you want it.

DESK LIGHT

Style Available in both traditional and modern designs.
In use Gives an efficient, even spread of light for desk work. Some shades can be angled to alter the area lit. Some modern fittings take a miniature fluorescent bulb which is cooler to work under.
Watchpoint The shade should be at eye level to avoid glare.

ANGLED WORK LAMP

Style The strong, angular lines are appropriate for workrooms and some modern styles but may not suit a traditional setting.
In use Versatile spring-loaded arms and swivel head are easily adjustable. Clipped or clamped to a suitable surface, it takes up little space so is ideal for cluttered areas. Also available with a heavy, stable base.

FLEXIBLE NECK SPOTLIGHT

Style A small neat lamp which is equally at home in the workshop, on a desk or as a bedside lamp.
In use The flexible stem can be adjusted to almost any angle and the lamp is small and light enough to move around easily. (A clip-on version is available.)
Watchpoint The area of illumination is limited by the small size of the lamp.

CEILING LIGHTS
A central pendant is not the only choice – look, too, at downlighters, strips, spots and tracks.

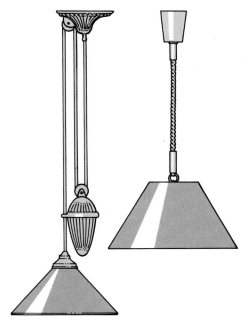

Most rooms have some sort of ceiling light, usually a single, central pendant fitting, but the choice also includes fluorescent strip lights, downlights, spotlights and track systems. The light they give can be background, task or decorative, but unlike floor and table lamps, most ceiling lighting is fixed, with the wiring hidden in the walls or above the ceiling, so any change in position will involve some re-wiring. It is important, therefore, to choose the right position first time as it may be difficult to change without making a mess of your decorations or having the wiring exposed and visible.

PENDANT LIGHTS
The most common type hangs on a flex from the ceiling and gives background lighting or a more directional light, depending on the style of shade and the length of flex. If the fitting or shade is heavy, it will need additional support, usually a chain fixed into a joist.

A central pendant light can give a flat look to a room and cast ugly shadows. If you are redoing your lighting, consider installing a dimmer switch for the pendant to use with other lamps in the room or consider positioning it off centre, low over a coffee table for example. Alternatively, an extended flex can be looped and fixed at another point on the ceiling.

Rise-and-fall fittings
When fitted to pendant lights they make them much more flexible. Positioned over tables or work surfaces, they can be pulled down or pushed up at will. There are two types of mechanism available: one works on a pulley and balance, the other on a spring.

When rise-and-fall lights are lowered they can be uncomfortably bright, so choose shades carefully or use dimmer switches to control the intensity of the light. If this is not possible, use a low wattage bulb.

SHADES
Many of the shades shown for table and floor lamps are suitable for pendant lights, so you can match the shades in a room. A wide base opening distributes the light, while a narrow base opening concentrates the light downwards. Light from an open top shade reflects off the ceiling, adding to the general background lighting. The material the shade is made of makes a difference – opaque materials direct the light, while transparent materials diffuse it more evenly.

Decorative pendant shades
In addition to the fabric shades, there are pendant shades made from cane, paper, glass (plain, etched, stained and frosted), china, metal and PVC. Some metal frames have an inner reflective surface – to avoid glare use a crown silvered bulb.

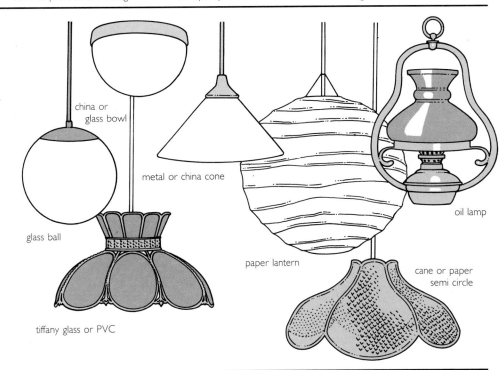

china or glass bowl

metal or china cone

glass ball

tiffany glass or PVC

paper lantern

cane or paper semi circle

oil lamp

CHANDELIERS AND LANTERNS
Style These range from the traditional crystal to the simpler branched metal or wood. Most are designed to take candle fittings and bulbs and/or small shades. Reproduction Georgian lanterns have round or hexagonal sides.
In use Chandeliers suit rooms with high ceilings such as classically furnished halls, living and dining rooms best. Lanterns should only be used in porches and halls.

Watchpoint The more elaborate the fitting, the more difficult it will be to clean. These heavy fittings must have strong support. Suspend them from joists above the ceiling·

DOWNLIGHTERS

There are three types of downlights – recessed, eyeball and surface mounted – and each can have minor variations. Downlighters direct light away from the ceiling and make pools of light on horizontal surfaces and walls. Light is not reflected off the ceiling, so they are ideal for rooms with high or dark ceilings.

As the light is directional rather than diffuse, several downlights may need to be used. If they are wired to two different circuits, and dimmer switches are used a more flexible scheme is produced. To avoid glare the inner surface of the cylinder may be grooved to help direct the beam and reduce brightness when you look directly at the light.

RECESSED DOWNLIGHTERS

Style Fitted flush to the ceiling with just the rim showing. Although modern in feel, these unobtrusive fittings work in traditional rooms too.

recessed downlighter

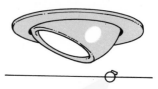

eyeball downlighter

surface mounted downlighter

In use Most have fixed position bulbs which direct a broad beam of light downwards but some angled bulbs are available to spotlight a particular area. Wallwashers, which have up to half the opening covered, direct the beam over a wall where it is reflected back into the room.
Watchpoints A hole must be cut into the ceiling to fit the downlighter so once installed they are not easily moved. Check the depth between the ceiling and the floor above.

EYEBALL DOWNLIGHTERS

Style This semi-recessed spherical light is available in a white, silver or brass finish.
In use Can be swivelled to any position to highlight objects or reflect off the walls.
Watchpoint Slightly more obtrusive than the recessed downlighter. Can look out of place in traditional rooms.

SURFACE MOUNTED DOWNLIGHTERS

Style The circular or square mounting is fixed to the ceiling, eliminating the need to cut a hole in the plaster.
In use Suitable for high ceilings or those without sufficient space between ceiling and floorboards above for recessed downlighters.
Watchpoint More obtrusive than the recessed downlighter. There are fewer styles to choose from.

SPOTLIGHTS

Style Spotlights can be circular (eyeball), have a drum or cone shaped shade or a parabolic (controlled beam) reflector. They can be ceiling mounted singly, in pairs or threes on a base; track mounted; or with a clip-on attachment.
In use They produce accent lighting to illuminate a work area, show off a decorative object or reflect light off a

wall or ceiling. Framing spots can be adjusted to light a specific area such as a picture.
Watchpoint They were particularly fashionable in the 70s and some models can look dated, so use with care.

TRACKS

Style Tracks for spots are usually ceiling mounted but they can be recessed, wall-

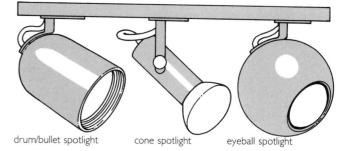

drum/bullet spotlight   cone spotlight   eyeball spotlight

mounted or suspended from the ceiling. Lengths can be cut or clipped together for longer runs. Rigid L or T junctions or flexible connectors are available.

Mini tracks with small spots are much less obtrusive than the standard size track. Single tracks work off one switch, multitracks work off two or more. Recently introduced tracks can take both tungsten and fluorescent bulbs so you can mix spots and strip lights.
In use The whole track carries the power so you can position spots anywhere. The number of

spots on any one track is limited by the wattage on the electrical circuit. Check with the shop when you buy. Position tracks parallel to walls or behind pelmets.
Watchpoints Tracks carrying spotlights add up to a very deep fitting, unsuitable for low ceilinged rooms. As the track is live do not use in bathrooms. Track systems are not usually interchangeable between manufacturers so you cannot choose a track from one manufacturer and lights from another.

triple spot fitting

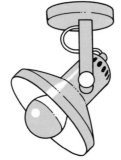

parabolic spotlight

STRIP LIGHTS

Style The bare strip light has been superseded by a range of attractively designed lights using warm fluorescent or tungsten bulbs which give an even spread of light. The most basic fitment is the batten attachment which is fixed to the ceiling or the underside of a wall cupboard; the bulb is slipped between the ends.

Boxed fitments with a grooved or etched glass shade gently diffuse the light and some come with a shaver point for use in bathrooms. Box shades with

louvres set at right angles to the bulb, minimize glare when looking directly at the tube.
In use Ideal for concealed lighting under a run of kitchen wall cupboards, inside display cupboards, behind pelmets and bookshelves. A control box can be fitted to direct the beam.
Watchpoint Clip in batten fitments can be unattractive so try to position them with the tube out of sight.

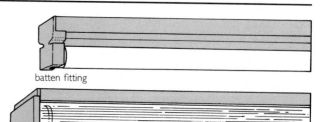

batten fitting

boxed fitting

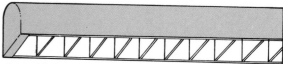

louvred fitting

WALL LIGHTS AND BULBS

Use wall lights for versatile background lighting, and choose the right bulb for every light fitting.

Wall lights are mainly used for general background lighting although some can also be used as task lights. Their position on the wall means they don't take up space but once they are fixed, with the wiring chased into the wall, they are impossible to move without disturbing the decorations. It is important, therefore, that you are really sure where you want the lights so that they do the job required. Those for general background illumination will need to be high enough to bounce light off the ceiling; for reading, they should be lower.

The styles range from the traditional to the ultra-modern. Try to see them lit before buying, as the shades are usually positioned at eye-level making them particularly noticeable.

Wall lights are best wired to a separate circuit with dimmer switches giving a range of light intensity to suit every occasion. Some have an on/off switch on the fitting itself, others are controlled from a wall switch.

There are four basic styles – bracket, bowl, bulkhead and strip – in both modern and traditional designs.

Bulbs (or lamps as they are called in the trade) are described overleaf to help you make the right choice of bulb for every fitting.

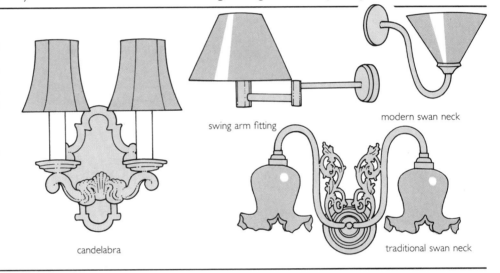

swing arm fitting

modern swan neck

candelabra

traditional swan neck

BRACKET WALL LIGHTS
Style Both single or double brackets are available. Traditional styles include the swan neck fixed with the shade facing up or down, single or double candelabra made in metal or wood, and more modern styles such as the swing-arm fitting.
In use Choose fittings and shades that are in keeping with the decorative style of the room. Many shades are available which match those used on pendant lights and lamps (see Options page 11).
Watchpoint If there is glare from the bulb when the shade faces down, try a crown silvered bulb.

BOWL

Style Made from plaster, ceramic, glass or metal, and fixed flush to the wall. Designs range from half hemisphere, cone or fan to more decorative shapes. Choose plaster or ceramic for traditional rooms; chrome or glass for a modern setting.
In use Glass shades diffuse a soft warm light, while plaster and metal shades reflect light upwards. Some metal shades have an acrylic inset at the base, which reflects light downwards and against the shade. Plaster shades can be painted to match the wall.
Watchpoint For general lighting they must be positioned high on the wall so that light can be reflected off the ceiling.

 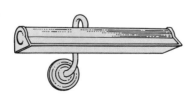 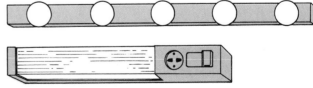

BULKHEAD
Style These functional lights have a high-tech utilitarian look.
In use Mainly used as task lights, so position them to cast light on the activity. As the bulb is totally enclosed they are particularly suitable for bathrooms.

PICTURE LIGHTS
Style Usually made in brass with a swan neck arm and swivel joint to angle the shade.
In use Can be fixed to the wall or to the back of the picture. Use a double ended tungsten strip bulb for best effect.

STRIP
Style Wall mounted strip lights are usually found in bathrooms above mirrors. A modern variation is the row of small bulbs, mounted on a natural wood or metal strip, Hollywood dressing room style.
In use The boxed shade fitment diffuses the light gently and may incorporate a shaver point.
Watchpoint Buy one with a cord pull switch for safety in a bathroom.

THE DINING AREA

To do justice to a carefully prepared meal, whether it is served to the family or to invited guests, you need room to savour it in style and comfort. This chapter tells you all you need to know about making dining at home a pleasure, whether you have a kitchen/diner, eat in a corner of the living room, or enjoy the luxury of a separate dining room.

Assessing your needs is the key to successful planning, so all the options are clearly presented to help you avoid what could prove to be costly mistakes. Foremost considerations are comfort and convenience, so advice is given on choosing the best location for your dining area, selecting the furniture you need, and how to get the lighting right. Diagrams and floor plans illustrate precisely how much space you need and how to make the best use of it.

The way you decorate a dining area plays a large part in creating the right atmosphere for both family meals and dinner parties. This chapter is lavishly illustrated with dining areas of every possible size, style and shape. There are dining rooms both traditional and modern, alongside others designed to double up as family rooms. Combined living rooms and kitchen/diners are also covered in detail and you will find plenty of bright ideas for simple dividers and space-saving furniture to help ease the squeeze.

Rounded off with an illustrated guide to choosing tables, chairs, glassware, china and ovenware, this chapter is a treasure trove of ideas to help you make the best of any dining area.

ROOM TO DINE

A dining room can be separate, in the kitchen or tucked in a corner, but it must be inviting and comfortable.

In today's smaller homes and with the busy lifestyle of most families, it is tempting to neglect the dining area and make do with a table in the kitchen or living room. Even if the whole family eats together only once a week and you entertain rarely, it is worth making your dining area comfortable.

Eating should be an enjoyable experience, a time for families to gather at least once a day. Balancing a tray on your lap in front of the television, or making do with a breakfast bar is no way to enjoy food – it also destroys the social aspect of family meals.

There's no need to go overboard for a formal separate dining room – unless, of course, your lifestyle includes regular entertaining. Most family dining rooms can double for other uses, such as study, letter writing or homework, or with the addition of a sofa bed, become an extra guest room. Alternatively, you can establish a dining area in the kitchen, in a conservatory or at one end of the living room.

ASSESS YOUR NEEDS
Before planning a dining area, think how it is likely to be used.

☐ How many people will regularly use the room?

☐ What is the maximum number of people likely to use the room? (Do you entertain regularly? If you often give large parties buy a table which extends.)

☐ Are there other facilities for eating in the kitchen? (A breakfast bar or wall-hinged table can be used for snacks.)

☐ How often is the dining room likely to be used? (Most families eat dinner in the dining room on weekdays and three meals at weekends. Think about other uses for the space.)

SITING THE DINING ROOM
For maximum convenience, the dining room should be close to the kitchen, preferably connected by a serving hatch so that crockery and hot dishes need not be carried any distance.

Existing dining room Is it in the right place and do you really use it? If the room is inconvenient and under-used, think about making better use of the space, as a study perhaps, or as a family room. Eating can be moved to a kitchen diner, or into a conservatory.

Kitchen/diner For many families, a kitchen/diner is the best solution to the space problem. Try to screen the area from the main part of the kitchen. You can do this by installing a counter with storage beneath between the cooking and eating areas (it can double as a breakfast bar), or, if there isn't enough space for a counter, a low wall. A ceiling-mounted venetian or roller blind can be pulled down to wall level so that diners can't see into the kitchen – few cooks enjoy being watched at work.

Living room/diner Modern through rooms where a central dividing wall has been removed often have a dining area at the end nearest the kitchen. If possible, make a hatchway through to the kitchen to make serving and clearing easier.

Ventilation Try to site the dining area near a window which can be opened to disperse smoke and food smells. In the kitchen, an extractor fan positioned above the cooker helps.

△ **Custom-built dining**
This cleverly designed dining area is divided from the kitchen by open shelving which doubles as a serving hatch.

BRIGHT IDEA

Make a fold-down table A simple fold-down table top (which can be used with folding chairs) is a space-saving way to add a dining area to the kitchen.

To make the top, fix wooden battens to the wall, as shown right. Hinge a length of laminate-covered or wood kitchen worktop to the battens, then attach folding hinges to the underside. Folding hinges which come in a variety of sizes are available from good DIY and hardware stores.

ROOM TO MOVE

People need elbow and leg room and enough space to get in and out.

Elbow room Each person needs about 60cm (2ft) of space when sitting at a table on a chair without arms. If the chair has arms, add 5cm (2in) each side.

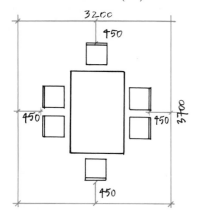

△ *Rectangular setting for six*

Leg room There should be enough leg room for the average adult to get his or her legs under the table with ease. As a general rule, the chair seat should be 25cm (10in) from the top of the table.

Getting in and out It is annoying and uncomfortable if people have to climb over one another to get to or leave the table. Ideally, there should be 45-60cm

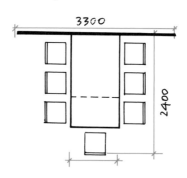

△ *Wall-mounted table for seven*

(1ft 6in-2ft) of space behind the chair so that it can be pushed away from the table and allow enough space for the person using it to stand up.

If lack of space means you must have fixed bench dining seating which cannot be moved, make sure you choose a table which isn't too heavy to be pushed out of the way.

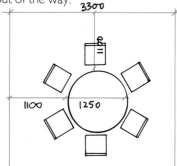

△ *Round setting for six*

BUYING DINING FURNITURE

First make a plan of the room, marking doors, windows, radiators and furniture you want to keep. List the following and take the list with you.

Table size What is the biggest size table the room can accommodate comfortably? Buying a table which extends to a large size makes no sense if the room is too small for it to be used to full capacity. When buying a table with an extension, ask to see the table with the extension in place. On some tables, the legs stay in the same place when the extension is inserted – usually right where they will restrict leg movement.

Table shape Dining tables come in round, oval, square and rectangular shapes. In a small room, a round or oval table is less visually restricting than a rectangular table – and you won't bump your hips on the corners. To work out the number of people the table can seat, measure sides and ends or the circumference of the table then divide the measurement by 60cm (2ft) which is the average amount of space needed per person.

Number of chairs Work out how many chairs are needed for daily use and how many for guests. Folding chairs, which can be stored flat or hung in a

cupboard, are useful for the times when extra seating is needed but should not be used for small children who can easily slip between the seat and the back. If the folding chairs are too low for your dining table, add cushions.

Storage space Remember that you are likely to need a place either in the dining room or close by to store glasses, cutlery and china. This can be a traditional sideboard (which can also be used for carving and serving food) or modern unit furniture. If there is not enough space in the dining room for storage, look for a suitable area close by and use a trolley.

△ *The right position*
This table extends with the legs at the ends where they don't impede diners.

△ *The wrong position*
The position of the legs makes this table uncomfortable when extended.

△ *The gate-leg table*
Gate-leg tables are always uncomfortable for dining.

SPACE-SAVING DINING

Build a bench Corner bench seating is a good way to create a dining area in limited space. Benches and tables are available from DIY stores. If the dining area is in the kitchen, a low

wall behind the bench makes a good divider.

Custom-built dining Another way to solve the problem of separating the dining area from the kitchen is to ask a fitted kitchen manufacturer to

design a scheme which incorporates a table and an open shelf room divider. Look through some catalogues and interior design magazines for ideas which might suit your room.

LIGHTING THE DINING ROOM

Lighting plays an important role in creating the right atmosphere for family meals or dinner parties.

The aim of dining room lighting is to create an atmosphere which is comfortable to dine in. The contrast of light and shade in a dining room should be planned as carefully as any other aspect of the room, whether it's the position and style of furniture, or the overall colour scheme.

Your choice of lighting scheme is obviously influenced by the way you use your dining room. Some are used almost exclusively for formal dinner parties, others are family dining rooms first and foremost, which are occasionally used for entertaining guests. Some must double up as work rooms or study areas.

The lighting must be sufficiently subtle and adaptable to accommodate all these uses and moods. You need to be able to see what you are eating as well as your neighbours at the table. Yet the light must not be so bright that it kills the atmosphere you are trying to create.

Before making decisions, take a tip from the professionals and try to study the lighting in other people's homes as well as in restaurants and cafés, where the lighting has almost certainly been professionally designed.

A light fitting over the dining table itself is a definite advantage. In addition, you will need to light the serving table or sideboard – and it's a good idea to create some focal points in addition to the table. Finally, of course, there must be sufficient overall lighting.

So long as these criteria are met, you are free to choose fittings that match the style of the room – ranging from elaborate and formal chandeliers to modern, streamlined lights.

Simple and effective
On bright, sunny days this dining table needs no artificial lighting. In overcast weather (and, of course, at night) a simple pendant over the table adds to the glow of the candles, and a converted oil lamp lights the dresser.

LIGHTING THE TABLE

A light fitting directly above a table enables you to see what you are eating and defines the dining area, especially in a multi-functional room.

A pendant lamp is the most common choice, partly because the fitting itself helps to define the table. Pendant lamps need to be carefully positioned above the table (see Bright Idea). Other alternatives include surface-mounted or recessed downlighters. The latter can also discreetly boost the light from a pendant fitting.

◁ *A graceful curve*
The long, flexible arm of this standard lamp reaches over the dining table and can therefore replace an ordinary pendant fitting.

▽ *Modern lights*
The tungsten halogen uplighter in the corner of this dining room bounces light off the ceiling on to the table. Candles alone therefore are sufficient to light the table itself.

△ **Twice as bright**
A long dining table is best lit by two or three pendant lamps. If the table is extendable, hang one pendant above the centre and others at each end.

◁ **Classically simple shapes**
A black lampshade to match the chairs sets the style in this dining room.

BRIGHT IDEA

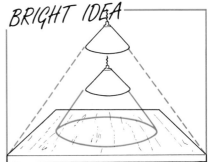

Hang a pendant lamp high above a table to shed a large but relatively diffuse pool of light. For more intimate meals, a lamp nearer the table will cast a more concentrated pool of light.

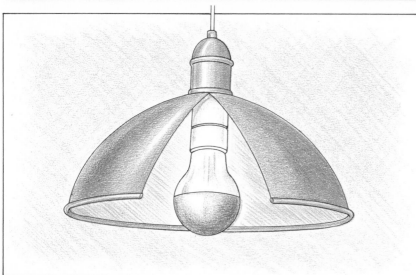

△ **A variety of light sources**
The lighting of this dining room has
been planned so that several sources of
light are available, as the occasion
demands. The wall unit, which has an
integral light source to illuminate the
display of china, is flanked by modern
uplighters. A table lamp on the
sideboard makes serving easy.

◁ **A crown-silvered bulb**
If the light bulb projects below the
shade of a pendant lamp, fit a crown-
silvered bulb which is decorative in itself
and reduces glare by masking the
filament. Used in a reflective shade, a
crown-silvered bulb also produces a
sharper beam of light.

LIGHTING THE WHOLE ROOM

As well as adequate general lighting, a dining room benefits from good task lighting and one or more focal points in addition to the table itself.

Overall lighting is particularly important if a dining room is not used solely for evening entertaining. Wall lights, often hung on either side of a fireplace, are a traditional solution and are available in modern as well as classic styles, perhaps to match an elaborate chandelier over the table. Recessed or surface-mounted downlighters or a tungsten halogen uplighter are other suitable solutions.

Focal points and task lighting While the table is a natural focal point in a dining room, it's a good idea to create additional points of visual interest in the room. That way, you can highlight the table without having to dine in a single pool of light surrounded by semi-darkness.

A table or sideboard that's used for serving needs clear lighting while it's in use. If you fit a dimmer switch for this light, the lighting can be turned down when you have finished working there, or when the meal is nearing its end, to hide dirty plates and empty serving dishes.

Other focal points could include a painting, a flower arrangement, or a large and attractive ornament on a bookcase or occasional table – even architectural details such as an attractive fireplace. Use picture lights, wallwashers and spotlights to create glowing pools of light. A standard lamp adds visual interest as well as creating a focal point.

If the dining room boasts an attractive bay or bow window, consider installing strip lighting behind the pelmet to draw attention to the window and the curtains or blinds. Strip lighting hidden above a pelmet or coving will bounce light off a pale ceiling to produce a gentle glow round the room's perimeter that's ideal as background.

△ *Side lights*

A serving table or sideboard in a dining room should be as well-lit as other work areas in the home. Downlighters positioned above the sideboard can therefore serve a dual function: they provide working light as well as highlighting the sideboard, creating a focal point in the room other than the dining table.

A row of recessed or surface-mounted downlighters can be positioned to cast separate or overlapping pools of light.

CANDLELIGHT

Although candles throw a romantic glow, just one or two candles on a dining table rarely cast enough light to eat by. To boost the light without sacrificing the intimate mood, either group a number of candles together or direct the beam of a downlighter on to the candles. A rise-and-fall lamp can be raised so high that you feel you are dining solely by candlelight.

△ *Dining by candlelight*
By scattering subdued lighting at various points in this dining room, sufficient light is provided without disturbing the gentle atmosphere.

▽ *A gentle glow*
For a very intimate atmosphere, the light of a single candle is boosted by a pair of wall-hung candle brackets and a lamp on the sideboard.

BRIGHT IDEA

Mirror image For a really unusual and attractive focal point on a festive occasion, mass a collection of candles in front of a mirror. The reflected flames are magnified, throwing a sparkling light.

DINING IN STYLE

Furnishings for the room you eat in deserve special attention.

The basic requirements for a dining room are a table for eating at and chairs to sit on. Although style is largely a personal matter, you'll almost certainly want something in keeping with the rest of the house. This doesn't necessarily mean being chained to a particular period: Victorian style furniture in a turn-of-the-century house, for example. Modern furniture can look good in an older setting providing there's empathy between furniture and surroundings.

Think, too, of your normal eating needs. If there are children about, you don't want to be forever anxious about delicate surfaces, so compromise with a scheme for relaxed everyday gatherings that can be smartened for guests.

Make sure the room is really comfortable and easy to manage – spend time sorting out details like easy-care surfaces and handy storage. The most elegant furniture won't hold much appeal if the lighting is gloomy or harsh:

use dimmers as part of an adjustable scheme, perhaps with rise-and-fall pendants above the table and wallwashers, picture lights or downlighters for subtle focal points elsewhere.

A fine meal is far less appetising in a room that's distinctly chilly, so good heating is important. Though there's nothing quite like a blazing coal fire, be honest: will it be lit for quick family meals or only grander occasions? Coal-effect gas may be more practical as a cheerful focal point and to provide a source of extra heat, particularly on chilly nights.

Modern lines
An unusual solid beech underframe and curved chairs give distinction to this suite. It's a classic style that isn't likely to date, and would sit nicely in a modern or traditional setting. In this room the soft creamy backdrop is kept deliberately sparse.

TRADITIONAL STYLE

Few of us are in a position to collect together a Regency table and six or eight matching chairs. It is, though, possible to give a traditional feel to a room without spending a fortune.

Borrow library books on traditional interiors to catch the essence of an era: adapt ideas as faithfully or freely as you please. Edwardian copies of antique furniture are less pricey and can have a fine patina. Alternatively, some modern reproduction furniture is very good indeed: the best isn't cheap but usually has the advantage of being easier to care for than the real thing.

If you're working to a budget but are determined to have authentic pieces, scour junk shops and auction rooms for interesting old chairs that are superficially dilapidated but structurally sound; if they have a similar feel they don't need to match exactly. Improvise by draping a big cloth over a round chipboard table, with a lace overcloth for enter-taining. For everyday use some firms will coat a favourite fabric in plastic for wipe-clean convenience.

For a country air genuine old pine is expensive and hard to find. However, modern well-seasoned pine with a distressed finish looks convincingly aged. distressed finish looks convincingly aged.

Let wallcoverings follow the style – anything from a Regency stripe to whitewashed simplicity. Paint effects like marbling or ragging could work well. And catch the appropriate mood at the windows: fringes and frills, flouncing drapes with cord tiebacks, pretty lace or café half-curtains.

Often it's little details that give the flavour of a period. Search around for extras to give a cumulative effect: an antique or modern butler's tray, wall sconces, a good mirror over the mantel, candles, old brass fixtures, polished glass decanters, even a luxuriant aspidistra in the corner to produce a distinctly Victorian spirit.

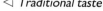

◁ *Traditional taste*
A gradual accumulation of just the right accessories gives a definite identity to a room. Handsome old furniture in this room is enhanced by a fine service and well-chosen accessories: touches of brass and polished glass about the room combine for a warm gleam. Most of the ornaments are placed fairly low to be appreciated by diners. Some accessories can be rotated from time to time so they don't grow stale!

A dado-level border is cleverly diverted to frame the window, and the translucent blind is a good idea as it shields a glaring sun and gives privacy while still admitting natural light into the room.

▷ *Dining comfort*
Fully upholstered chairs are ideal for lingering over a meal: for a practical finish treat fabric with stain-resistant spray. Curved arms allow the carvers to be drawn up comfortably to the table. An appropriate backdrop is provided by painted dado and cornice teamed with traditional wallpaper.

◁ **New into old**
A kitchen connection need not prevent you having a traditional dining room, if that's what you want. This interior has been given a period feel, and the dining room reflects that old-fashioned charm though the oak gate-leg table and chairs in 18th-century style are in fact modern, and built to withstand the rigours of everyday use.

From the contemporary wooden blinds to the mirror with candle sconces – a genuine old piece – this room is an admirable mix of old and new. For example, you can see how the lighting combines traditional grace with modern practicality. Once the company is assembled the functional kitchen lights can be switched off and recessed downlighters dimmed so that the meal is enjoyed in candlelight.

MODERN MOOD

Though there's adventurous new dining furniture about, a modern suite doesn't necessarily involve a break with tradition. If you don't want to play conventionally safe, investigate the latest Italian designs – very cool, very chic – but take care that you don't end up with a style you'll tire of or something that soon dates.

For sleek city living, look for stained black tables and leather and chrome chairs. Modern classics, such as the cantilevered Bauhaus chair, fit in well with this sophisticated elegance. If black is too sombre, build up the style with sleek light-wood furniture.

The coolly modern city look is nowhere near as spare as would satisfy a minimalist. For this, nothing must distract from the simplicity of pure line. Root out anything that's even a touch sentimental or romantic. Store everything but the barest of essentials well out of sight. Unless you're an out-and-out purist you may find an empty void too stark. A little skilful compromise is quite in order – perhaps a big pot with dried seedheads, or a well-lit wallhanging. Once you get a feel for a style you'll soon gain enough confidence to be able to discriminate between appropriate and jarring elements.

Have a neutral ground for your modern dining room, with clear accent colours used sparingly and plain roman or venetian blinds at the window. Hang large abstract prints on the wall, look for concealed lighting or leggy Italian lights. Choose plants or flowers with a strong architectural quality rather than softening foliage.

◁ **Material mix**
A combination of marble table with leather and chrome cantilevered chairs makes a dramatic dining centrepiece: on this sort of scale, and with such splendid materials, little else is needed in the room. A plain rug helps define the dining area, and is sensibly big so that chairs can be drawn in and out without difficulty.

If you like a spare, disciplined approach look for basics in first-rate materials with simple but satisfying lines. Limit accessories to a well-considered minimum. Proper organization of storage is essential so all that precious emptiness doesn't attract clutter.

LIGHT STYLE

For a modern chandelier effect, hang several lights above a dining table. Mix the colours to suit your room scheme and experiment with lights suspended at slightly different heights. A separate dimmer switch for each light would allow a great variety of mood.

If you want to use curly cable – and it does look attractive – let thin wire take the weight of the lights so the cable stays curled.

▽ **Dining space**
Chrome on table and chairs adds a gleam to the starkness of black in a grouping that has an almost Japanese purity. Venetian blinds give a muted light to augment the general calm. It's all offset by an elegant beech floor.

Once the basics are established, attend to those details that give an uplift. Here, the severity is softened by coral table dressings, including fan-fold napkins that introduce just the right degree of shape and light relief to the table.

△ **Contemporary classic**
Good modern furniture fits in well with a variety of settings. Here, hand-built pieces look comfortably at home in an old country rectory though they could equally well grace a modern scheme. There's no absence of sunlight in this dining corner, but light wood is a particularly good choice in a room that's inclined to be dark.

All the pieces in this range – display cabinet, table and seating – are in solid ash with distinctive rounded detailing. Different types of seats – side and carver chairs and a cane-backed banquette – provide interesting variation in shape.

Some of the finest new furniture around today is inspired by the best traditions of the past but nevertheless retains a distinctly modern quality. First-rate materials are combined with strong, pleasing lines to produce good-natured furniture that will stand the test of time.

◁ **Dining den**
Not everyone has a separate – or even a large – dining area. Here, the awkwardly narrow shape has been turned to advantage. Red gloss is a bold choice for a small space, but it gives friendly warmth to this area, and the built-in sofa, upholstered to match the chairs, is nicely plump and inviting.

This sort of fine old table seems to demand the special magic of candles, which can be boosted with other lighting that's versatile enough to meet different needs. The whole area looks just the place for guests to linger over coffee at the end of a meal.

▷ **Table arrangements**
In many flats and conversions space is at a premium, and ingenuity and an open-minded approach to planning are called for. A dining table doesn't have to be placed right in the middle of the room; in fact an alternative arrangement, perhaps ranged along or butting up to a wall, is often more intimate for dining and won't obtrude at other times.

If the room is used for other purposes, the table can be a display area for collections like these ducks and a grand old pot. The very modern strip light is a good surprise element in a featureless corner.

DINING ROOMS FOR ENTERTAINING

A separate dining room should be decorated and planned to suit the way you do your entertaining.

A dining room used for the sole purpose of entertaining is one of those rare rooms where you have extensive freedom of choice in both design and planning. Used for only a few hours at a time, and mostly during the evening, this is one area where you can exercise the creative rather than the down-to-earth side of your decorating skills.

Wall- and floorcoverings, furniture, furnishings and lighting can all be chosen largely on aesthetic grounds, for their ability to create mood and atmosphere rather than to withstand the rough-and-tumble of family life.

Of course, you cannot totally ignore the practical aspects of a room in which food is served, but you can afford to experiment with some more dramatic schemes which maybe you would not contemplate trying out in regularly-used family rooms.

Siting the room Ideally, the dining room should be close to the kitchen, with an interconnecting door or serving hatch. In practice, though, your choice is likely to be influenced by the position and functions of other rooms.

An outside view is unimportant for evening entertaining, but for day-time use, a dining room that leads on to the garden is particularly pleasant. An adjoining patio or balcony is the perfect spot for aperitifs or coffee in summer.

The dimensions are also important, as a minimum of 12-16 square metres is usually required to accommodate six people comfortably around a table with enough room for them to get in and out. But even a dining room which is too small to house storage units or a sideboard as well as the dining table and chairs is an improvement over the living/dining room or kitchen/diner arrangement as all the preparation and clearing away can be done out of sight of the guests.

Patterned co-ordination
Strongly patterned wallpaper and curtain fabric – which might seem overdone elsewhere in the home – form the basis of the decor of this dining room. The off-white, pinky-red and green are echoed in furniture, crockery, tablecloth and cushions.

GETTING THE STYLE RIGHT

Within reason, there's no need to curb your imagination when decorating the dining room. The colours and patterns can be bold and dramatic – chosen to enhance the sense of occasion rather than to relax.

The style depends on the type of entertaining you prefer. A room used mainly for having supper with close friends may well be entirely different from one in which formal dinner parties or business suppers are to be held. The two need not be mutually exclusive, though. With creative planning, it is possible to incorporate both styles in the same room – it is surprising what a switch of tableware and linen and different lighting can achieve.

Lighting Good lights enhance a well-laid table, highlight and complement the food and help create an atmosphere that makes people feel at ease.

For the best effect, a combination of

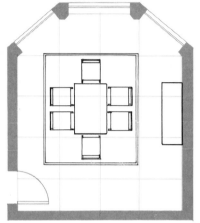

Scale: 1 square = 1 metre square

◁ *Up to date*
Traditional bay windows and wooden flooring blend well with smart, modern furniture and furnishings.

▽ *Formal elegance*
Rich shades of gold, luxurious velvet fabrics and a polished parquet floor make this dining room perfect for formal dinner parties.

light fittings is the answer. It's unwise to rely on a single ceiling fitting which tends to restrict your flexibility. Similarly, wall-lights, or floor lamps standing in the corner of the room, should not be used as the sole source of light as they cast a shadow over both the guests and their meal.

So you'll need some sort of lighting immediately above the table. The table light must enable diners to see what they are eating without subjecting them to a harsh glare. A rise-and-fall fitting above the table is an excellent choice – but do not place it so low down that it obstructs the guests' view of each other.

A dimmer switch allows you to adjust lighting levels to create the right mood for the occasion.

Away from the table, the illumination of the serving area should be slightly stronger and can be provided by a standard or table lamp, or spotlights mounted on the wall above.

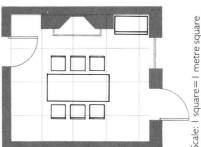

Scale: I square = I metre square

△ **A friendly atmosphere**
Informality is the keynote to this farmhouse-style dining room, ideal for family get-togethers. The pine table in the centre of the room allows easy access all round and a glass-fronted dresser combines storage and display.

◁ **Country classic**
A change of wall treatment, lighting and floorcovering, and the addition of co-ordinating curtains and a set of matching chairs, give the room above a more sophisticated yet still casual feel.

CHOOSING DINING FURNITURE

Although a dining suite placed centrally in a room may seem to have a generous amount of space around it when not in use, it's important to think about the comfort and safety of both diners and host when the room is actually in use. In terms of space, you should allow about 60cm for each diner and chair, and a minimum of another 45cm for the diner to push the chair back, or for the host to pass behind with a serving dish. A dado rail at chair-back height helps to protect precious wallpaper from being damaged by careless guests.

The dining table When buying a new or secondhand table, bear in mind that a full place setting is between 60 and 70cm long, so a minimum size for six diners is about 150cm long for a rectangular table and 120cm in diameter for a round one.

In a small room, a round table accommodates more people comfortably than a rectangular one and, with no one at the 'head', tends to suit informal occasions. If space is tight, an extendable table might be a better choice, to seat four in comfort and stretch out to six or eight by means of a drop-in or pull-out leaf. In a generously-proportioned rectangular dining room, a large rectangular or oval table is the obvious choice.

Dining chairs need not match each other, or indeed the table, but they must be comfortable, especially if you like guests to linger over coffee after a meal. Good back support and cushioned seats are desirable, and arms add additional comfort but take up more space. Allow at least 25cm of knee-room between the table and chair.

Serving tables Whether you prefer to serve guests, or let them help themselves, you need a small table on which to put serving dishes, carve meat, set out coffee cups and so on. A narrow table with a drawer for place mats,

△ *Glowing red*
A dramatic colour scheme, with spotlights focusing attention on the painting, overcomes the uninteresting shape of this box-like room. The large expanse of strong colour combined with the bold painting might seem overpowering in, for example, a living room, but here they help to create an exciting atmosphere for dinner parties.

A fairly small round table which has an additional drop-in leaf can be extended for larger parties.

napkins and so on is ideal. A stable trolley or a shelf at a comfortable height for working on positioned in an alcove or beneath a serving hatch also does the job just as well.

For dining room storage, a traditional sideboard or a modern wall unit is a practical choice and can also sometimes double up as a serving table, providing its height suits the host.

Lighting trick Dining just by candlelight is rarely a good idea unless you are having an intimate dinner for two. It is difficult to carry on a conversation, or see what one is eating, in such dim light. But candles do throw an inviting glow, and it is a good idea to supplement the light by directing the beam of a downlighter on to the candles.

▷ *Simplicity*
Dining room furniture need not necessarily be bought as a matching set. Here a heavy pine table is quite at home with lightweight bentwood chairs.

▽ *The modern touch*
High-tech furniture complements the painted brick walls of this dining room. The doors on to the patio make this an ideal spot for summer-time gatherings.

▷ **A traditional feel**

The architectural detail of this dining room – the shutters, cornice and fireplace – is complemented by carefully chosen fabrics, furniture and tableware.

For less formal occasions, the lace tablecloth, fine china dinner service and crystal glassware can be replaced by a simple printed cloth and, perhaps, the everyday crockery. The choice of wallpaper lends itself to both formal and informal gatherings, and the blue carpet helps to disguise stains.

▽ **Practical and pretty**

Natural materials combine with an abundance of greenery to create a fresh, inviting atmosphere in this dining room. The table could easily be dressed up with a floor-length tablecloth and tableware to match, or 'dressed down' with simple place mats instead of the tablecloth.

By locating the dining room next to the kitchen, the cook can serve piping hot food with a minimum of delay. If necessary, the pine dresser can double as a serving table.

DINING AREAS IN LIVING ROOMS

One comfortable room that combines both a living and a dining area can be an ideal arrangement.

The most used room in the house – the living/dining room – should be designed for comfort and convenience. This is where you spend time sitting, relaxing or watching TV, and where you eat evening meals and entertain.

Depending on the shape of the room and how it is decorated and furnished, it can be treated as a single room where the living and dining areas are integrated, or planned so that the two areas are separate.

Dividing the two areas The room may be divided physically by a change in shape, floor level or by an archway. Lighting can be used to change the emphasis in the two areas, or you can create the same effect with decoration, using different paint, wallpaper and floor coverings to make a definite boundary.

Another way to divide the room is with furniture, perhaps with a series of low-level cupboards that open out into the dining area or with a sofa facing towards the living room area.

Unifying the room The alternative approach is to treat the room as a single entity. Use the same decorative finishes throughout, linking the two sections with details such as a wallpaper border, or using the same fabric for the main curtains and the tablecloth. The dining area will also look less separate if you choose dining chairs that can be used for extra seating in the living room area.

LIVING/DINING ROOM LAYOUT

Where you locate each area depends largely on the shape of the room. There may be an alcove, a narrow end, or the short leg of an L-shape that is ideal for a table and chairs. Otherwise the obvious place is close to the kitchen. Modern houses are often designed with the eating area as an integral part of the living room. In older houses, the wall between the living and dining rooms may be opened up to give more space with the dining area at one end.

Versatile living
This good-looking practical space serves as a living/dining room and incorporates a study area too. The sofa, facing into the living area, creates a natural division and is backed by a console table conveniently placed for serving. Notice how the black and white floor changes level, emphasizing the difference between living and dining areas.

STORAGE SENSE

Any dining area needs to have enough storage space to house your china, glass, table linen and cutlery.

Old-fashioned sideboards are very useful in living/dining rooms, being slightly higher than their modern equivalents, which has a dual advantage: they are the perfect height for carving and serving food from as well as providing more storage space.

Low-level cupboards can be used for storage and as room dividers, while tall cupboards, possibly glass-fronted, make the best use of floor space.

LIGHTING

A lot of activities other than sitting and eating take place in a living/dining room, so it needs flexible lighting.

It is important to work out exactly what you use the room for and how much time you spend doing what. Identify what you do where as well as what sort of moods you want to create.

Task lighting for reading and to illuminate areas such as the stereo and

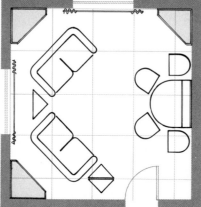

the TV are a good idea, and so is a dimmer switch. You need good lighting over the table so you can see what you're eating but at the same time, the light should be subtle and flattering to faces and food. Avoid non-adjustable overhead fittings which may be in the wrong place if you decide to move the furniture around. Table or floor lamps close by give a softer glow and can also serve as task lights when the table is used for other activities.

△ **Corner wise**

The three corner cabinets have a surprising amount of storage space.

During meals, the sofas can be moved back and the table opened out into the room, (see plan, below). When not in use, the drop-leaf table is pushed against the wall and the dining chairs are turned round, (see plan, left).

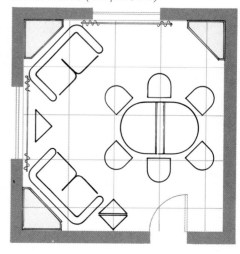

scale: 1 square = 1 metre

A flexible lighting scheme should include an adjustable light for the dining table, such as a rise-and-fall pendant or wall lights controlled by a dimmer switch, and some general light with plenty of power points for task lighting and table lamps in the living area.

wall light

rise-and-fall

uplighter

table lamp

▽ *Folding solution*
Here, instead of the drop-leaf, a long modern table which folds in half lengthways has been chosen.

As shown in the diagram right, it opens out into a full-size dining table and when folded, it makes a handsome console table, pushed back against the wall. An elegant dining chair fits neatly at either end and additional seats can be carried in from other rooms when needed.

SOFAS AND CHAIRS

As the living/dining room is used for more than one purpose, versatility should be a priority. Space may be tight, so choose chairs and sofas that aren't too bulky. If the living room furniture has to be pushed back to make room for the dining table when it is extended, make sure everything is fitted with castors or is light enough to be carried.

TABLES

Rectangular or oval tables that can be made longer or smaller are perfect for dual-purpose rooms, provided there is somewhere to store a detachable leaf when it is not required. If you don't have the room, choose a drop-leaf table, or one where the leaves are attached at either end and can be pushed into the body of the table to reduce its size.

The dining table is likely to become a social centre for a wide range of activities – conversation, homework, games and hobbies as well as mealtime get-togethers – so the table has to survive everyday wear and tear and still look its best when you are entertaining.

A table top that is durable is the most practical choice. Laminated plastic immediately comes to mind – it is tough and easy to keep clean, and although somewhat utilitarian in appearance, can be dressed up for formal occasions. Natural wood, such as oak, beech or pine, looks good and can be treated with a polyurethane seal to give a

hardwearing, natural-looking finish.

A glass topped or polished wooden table needs to be safeguarded from heat, spills and scratches with a thick tablecloth. If the tabletop is particularly good, use a felt undercloth for extra protection.

Entertaining As soon as your guests arrive and see the dining table laid for a meal it becomes the centre of attention, so it is worth dressing it up for special occasions. Even the shabbiest old table – a junk shop find, a garden or pasting table, or an old flush door supported by a pair of decorators' trestles – can be transformed with a smart linen tablecloth and a pair of candlesticks.

CHAIRS

Dining chairs don't have to match as long as there are some common visual elements such as colour, shape, upholstery and so on. Conventional chairs, tucked in position around a dining table which is not being used, can look very formal. Instead, choose chairs that can do double duty – as extra seating in the living area, kitchen or bedrooms. Chairs that stack or fold flat, canvas director's chairs and even stools are also ideal.

Comfort and practicality are as important as appearance when choosing chairs. With a permanent dining area, fixed banquette seating either side of the table makes good use of space but it can be a rather uncomfortable arrangement. Compromise with a bench on one side, and chairs opposite.

▷ *Simple colour scheme*
Storage plays a large part in the success of this living/dining room. The storage unit has cupboards and drawers for china, cutlery and tablecloths, with open shelves and illuminated glazed cupboard sections for displaying treasured possessions.

Sleek, matching chrome furniture, upholstered in pale grey against a background of peach carpets and walls, gives a feeling of space.

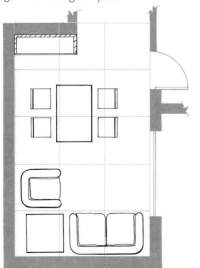

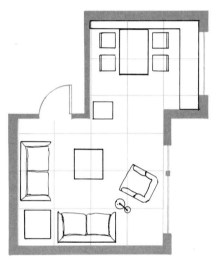

◁ **Through room**
This airy living room was designed with a dining alcove off the main seating area. The two zones are clearly defined by the change in shape but are held together, visually, by the use of the same curtain treatment and carpet.

During meals, the desk under the window becomes an extra surface for serving food and the rise-and-fall light can be lowered over the dining table.

BRIGHT IDEA

A folding screen forms a light and adjustable divider between the seating and dining area in a small living room. This makes the dining area cosier while you are eating and hides a messy table when you are relaxing after the meal.

This openwork screen divides the room without cutting out the light. Its pale colour goes well with the stripped and sealed wooden floor and simple beech dining table and bentwood chairs.

Painted antique screens can often be found in secondhand shops, or you could make your own: construct two or three rectangular wooden frames, hinge them together and drape with fabric to match your curtains or upholstery.

△ **Old and new**
The ground floor of this house has been knocked through to make one large living space.

The pretty round dining table is covered with a PVC cloth to protect it from scratches and spills during meals. Modern director's chairs can be used round the table or moved through into the living area for extra seating. The cheerful matching rugs provide warmth and decorative interest.

▷ **Serving hatch**
Easy access to the kitchen is necessary for serving food and clearing away dishes.

This extra wide serving hatch is open and provides a permanent link between the kitchen and dining area, allowing the cook to be included in conversation. The bright red pans and kitchen accessories match the lampshade, emphasizing the connection between the two areas.

ENTERTAINING IN THE LIVING ROOM

Transform your living room into a congenial backdrop for social occasions.

The living room needs to be one of the most flexible areas of a home. It must be comfortable enough for the family to sit down together and relax in at the end of the day. But it's also the room that's used when you have guests, so it should look specially good when occasion demands.

At the planning stage, consider having two layouts, one for everyday and one for entertaining. When initially furnishing the room, you can take into account the main type of entertaining you are likely to do. Social events can usually be divided into four situations:

Family gatherings, such as at Christmas and for anniversaries. These may include making provision for small children, like putting precious ornaments beyond reach. Perhaps it would be thoughtful to supply a comfortable chair for an elderly relative to get into and out of easily.

Informal gatherings of friends for an evening. The traditional layout around the fire is unlikely to accommodate more than six guests, so consider providing two or three focal points around which seating can be grouped.

Larger parties may require space cleared for standing room, but highlight ornaments in wall units or pictures so the room doesn't look bleak. Extra surfaces for drinks could be provided by clearing bookshelves.

Formal occasions such as dinner parties may involve living room use for drinks before or after the meal. Fold-up or director's chairs could be brought in from other areas. A side table for pouring drinks would be useful.

Glowing welcome

There's nothing so welcoming as a live fire: together with warm, rich colours, it makes an inviting picture. There's a good-sized table for food and drink just a stretch away from the seating. A practical point is that the patterned carpet and soft furnishings won't show every crumb that falls. When guests are due, lamps and candles can be lit and extra chairs drawn up.

SITTING COMFORTABLY

A little forethought and some readjustment of your normal seating arrangement can make a great deal of difference to a congenial atmosphere. An evening is unlikely to go with a swing if your guests are jammed into a meanly-proportioned settee, or if chair positioning subtly excludes some of the company from full participation.

Seating combination should be decided from the outset, to serve first family requirements and be flexible enough for entertaining. Guests need to be close enough to make pleasant social contact without being squashed: seating that's too close, or too distant, will impose a strain on congeniality.

Positioning is important. Guests need not face each other directly. Settees and chairs placed at right angles may be more convivial than a face-to-face encounter over the canapes. Whatever your arrangement, try to leave a passage clear so a social group isn't disturbed by people coming and going.

Large gatherings need special provision: possibly you could arrange seating in the living room, but have ready another room for serving drinks and food, or use a dining table if you have a combined living/dining room. If you are bringing in chairs from other quarters, try to find seats of similar height. Make sure no one is left perched high and dry on the edge of the party.

◁ ▷ Gathering point
Space to spread is a great benefit when the company is large, but take care to arrange seating and lights to allow guests to collect together into pleasant conversation groups. The plan on the right shows possible positioning of extra chairs (coloured pink) and a rearrangement of tables (beige) and lighting (yellow).

▽ ▷ Coolly inviting
A modern room that would lend itself well to a social gathering. Tables are handily placed for setting down drinks, and have wipe-clean surfaces which won't be damaged by spillage. On the right the plan suggests a layout for a larger group. Additional seating is shown in pink, tables are beige and lighting is coloured yellow.

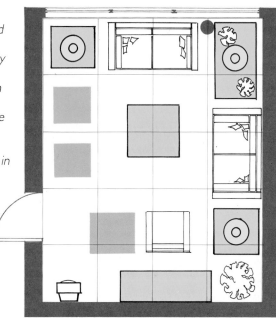

Scale: 1 square = 1 metre square

◁ On the move
If you don't have a convenient table or other surface for drinks and glasses, a trolley may be a useful investment. It can also be used to transport party fare to and from the kitchen. One with adjustable shelving will prove the most versatile; if you don't want to use it at other times, look for a version that folds flat for storing. There are both traditional and modern styles of trolley on the market.

△ ▷ Party manoeuvres

The arrangement above would be fine for a gathering of six people, but some adjustment is needed for a larger group. As the alternative in the picture and plan shows, additional seating by the window can be included in the social circle, with a table added or shelf cleared for drinks.

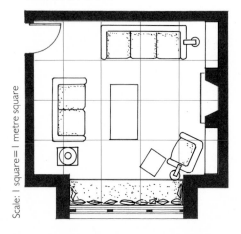

Scale: 1 square = 1 metre square

Sparkling fresh These candles not only cast an attractive glow over a corner of the room, but they provide a tactful solution to a possible nuisance. There's nothing worse than a room full of stale smoke. The candle wax has been specially treated to give off a scent that will help disguise the smell of tobacco smoke. The atmosphere in a crowded room can easily become thick. A slightly-open window will allow air to circulate, but make sure no-one is in a draught.

IN THE MOOD

Lighting needs to be as versatile as possible and is an essential aspect of setting an inviting scene. The effect will of course vary according to the nature of the gathering. On a fine summer's evening you will have the benefit of natural light; guests may even want to spill out on to the patio.

Generally, lighting for entertainment should be cosily intimate – a dimmer switch is ideal, with a flexible system of freestanding table and standard lamps. You may want to cast more light on your store of drinks or music centre. Make sure that no light glares in a guest's eyes, and avoid the danger of trailing flex in a crowded room. The unused edges of a room shouldn't be left unlit; you could gently highlight special features, like a painting.

A fire will add a lovely glow to the room, and softly-flickering candles can brighten a dark corner. Sweet-smelling candles are available, and those that freshen smoke-thick air. Take care when there are many guests about – fit a guard to keep party frocks well away from a fire, and site candles safely.

Music speakers should be positioned away from a seating group, preferably at high level. If you want to put them directly on a hard surface such as wood, use an insulating mat or small carpet sample to deaden reverberation. The deck will need to be sited for easy operation, but keep it well away from a surface used for drinks to avoid accidental damage.

△ *Dancing light*
Candles have their own special magic which can transform even an ordinary room into a marvellous setting for a social occasion. Group different heights together for added sparkle.

◁ *Conversation piece*
A pleasant setting for six, which can easily be enlarged to contain a sizeable gathering. A nest of tables could provide versatile surfaces for drinks.

SET-DOWN POINTS

Guests don't want to sit with a glass (and perhaps a plate) in hand all evening. Having no convenient surface to offload on to except the floor is awkward and risky, particularly in a crowded room. If the seating is to be arranged around a central occasional table, can everyone reach?

Tables for setting down drinks can be brought from other areas, and placed at strategic points. A nest of tables would lend itself to flexible arrangement. For a large makeshift surface for drinks, you could place a long piece of chipboard between two small square tables, and cover it all with a nice cloth. You could also clear a temporary space on a bookshelf or wall unit that's within arm's reach.

Remember to protect any polished surfaces with mats, coasters, or a sheet of attractive PVC.

Trays and trolleys are a great asset when you are entertaining. Large trays placed on occasional tables will protect a delicate surface from spills, and they can be carried straight out to the kitchen at the end of the evening. A trolley can be used as a set-down point for food and drink. It can also transport party fare from the kitchen and remove all the used glasses and general debris when guests depart at the end of the evening.

◁ *Swinging spirits*
It's good to have your stock of drinks readily available for entertaining, but you may not want them displayed at other times. This concealed drinks cabinet swings away when the party is over. Whether you keep your drinks in an open or closed unit, if you have an extensive range try to provide storage space that allows room for the pouring and mixing of drinks.

▽ *Entertaining style*
An elegant room that has everything on hand for a special occasion. Drinks and glasses are housed in the wall unit, and a nest of tables can be drawn out and placed conveniently close to the seating arrangement.

DINING TABLES

Whether you want a table for formal dining, family meals or a kitchen/ diner there's a shape or style to fit.

When choosing a dining table, whether new or second-hand, there are four things to bear in mind: the style of the table, what it is made of, shape and size. **Style** should be influenced by the room setting and the chairs you plan to use with it. There is a wide range to choose from, whether you are looking for a practical table to fit into a kitchen/diner or finer furniture for a more formal dining room.

Finish The high cost of solid timber means that most dining tables – whether reproduction or modern in style – are blockboard veneered with a thin layer of wood. Very cheap furniture is sometimes veneered in paper printed to look like wood and with a waterproof seal-

ant. Always check what the veneer is made of and look out for poor finish and chipped edges on wood veneers.

If the table is to be used by children or for other purposes, such as dressmaking or typing, choose a sturdy design and a hard-wearing finish. Melamine is a tough all-purpose surface available in a range of colours. Any wood with a polyurethane varnish is easily wiped clean and is relatively heat resistant. An advantage of solid wood tables is they can be stripped, sanded and refinished if the surface gets badly damaged.

Size and shape The height of a dining table should be between 70-75cm and must be related to the height of the

chairs. Allow 65cm space for each armless chair and 70cm for carvers. A rectangular or oval table must be at least 75cm wide to allow table settings on both sides (see page 86).

Round tables can seat more people more comfortably than square or rectangular tables but when you take into consideration the room the chairs need, they take up more space in a room. A central pedestal leg is less obtrusive than four separate ones. A 900mm diameter table seats 4; 1.2m-1.4m diameter seats 6; 1.5-1.7m seats 8.

Square tables usually seat 4 comfortably, 8 at a push. The legs at the corners can be a problem when seating more than 4.

Rectangular tables seat more people than square tables of the same area. Extension flap(s) or draw leaves present fewer problems with legs than leaves which are inserted centrally. Check the position of the legs in relation to place settings with and without extensions.

Oval tables are a good compromise between round and rectangular tables. They give the most flexible seating, particularly if on a pedestal base, and take up less space than a round table.

FARMHOUSE
A sturdy design usually made from solid pine or oak. Seats 6-8 people depending on size. The thick turned legs support a firm working surface, ideal for kitchen/diners. When choosing chairs to fit note the frame (which often incorporates a drawer) under the table top. Suits the farmhouse or country cottage-look kitchen or dining room – the weight may mark a soft floor covering.

REFECTORY
A 16th century table design with solid panel end supports through which the stetcher bar passes and is pegged. The end panel can be carved or have decorative cut outs and the stretcher bar can be at floor level or midway up. Check to see if people can be seated comfortably at the ends. The table's weight is spread across the wide panel feet so it is less likely to mark a soft floor.

TRESTLE
One of the simplest designs, particularly popular if space is limited as the top and folding legs can be stacked away separately when not in use. The top is usually made from veneered wood, melamine or glass and the legs from chrome or brightly enamelled metal or wood. Check the weight of the top if you intend to stack the table regularly.

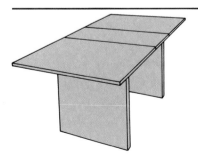

MODERN SOLID END
A simple streamlined design which has solid panelled supports linked by a stretcher bar instead of legs. The simple rectangular design means it is usually made from veneered particle board and the clean lines suit a contemporary setting.

ROUND PEDESTAL
A simple circular table with traditional curved tripod legs, or a more streamlined modern design made from glass with chrome legs or veneered wood. Some of the traditional styles have a hinged mechanism which allows the top to tilt vertically so that the table can be pushed against the wall when space is limited.

TWIN PEDESTAL
A long oval table based on Regency designs often has two pedestal legs, with or without a stretcher bar between for extra stability. Some designs incorporate a flip out central panel (see Flip leaf overleaf).

DRUM

A simple circular table supported by four legs. Styles vary from the traditional, with turned legs, to the modern, with chrome or sleek panelled legs. Tops can be made from wood, glass, melamine or marble. Check for leg room if there is a frame under the top.

GATE LEG

Originally an early 17th century Jacobean design, there are both reproduction and modern versions. A lightweight table which is easily moved, the narrow centre panel is traditionally supported on four turned legs, with or without stretcher bars. Modern designs are variations on this style. The deep semi-circular or square flaps are each supported by a leg which swings out from the central section. This versatile table takes up little space when folded and can be used with one or both flaps up. Check the space for knees at the central panel. Made from solid wood or, for modern designs, a wood or melamine veneer.

CENTRE LEAF

These square, circular, oval or rectangular tables can be extended by pulling the table apart and inserting a separate central leaf. Some designs have a second and even a third leaf. The leaves must be stacked carefully to avoid being scratched when not in use and unless they are inserted frequently, there is the problem of the part which is in regular use changing colour with exposure to light and more frequent cleaning.

DROP LEAF

The central panel is considerably larger than that of the gate leg and is either square or rectangular in shape. There is a square or semi-circular flap at one or both ends which is supported by a fold out bracket or slide when raised. The lack of leg support makes the flap unsuitable for a heavy weight, such as a sewing machine or typewriter, but more comfortable for dining as there is no leg to get in the way of knees. Available in both traditional and modern styles.

A Pembroke table is a light elegant drop leaf table with square or shaped drop leaves which are supported, when raised, with hinged fold out brackets. There can be a central pedestal or four legs at the corners of the central panel, under which a drawer is often found.

DRAW LEAF

This traditional rectangular design has extension leaves which fit under the top at each end. When the extensions are pulled out the central panel lowers to fit flush. With age, use and exposure to light the main table top tends to change colour while the leaves remain the same as when new, if they are not extended regularly. The legs may be panelled as here or turned.

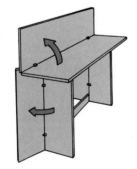

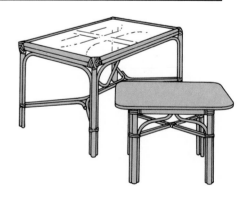

FLIP LEAF

The two halves of the table top pull apart to reveal a central fold out panel which is hinged across the middle and swings out. Some styles have a second panel for greater extension. In this way, a round table turns into an oval and a square into a rectangle.

FOLDING CONSOLE

The central join runs the length of this table so that when it is folded in half it fits neatly against the wall like a console or side table, ideal for a living/dining room. When pulled out and the top opened out the leg divides to support the second half. The decorative brass or silver metal hinges are more obvious in a dark wood.

RATTAN/BAMBOO LOOK

Much bamboo furniture is, in fact, made from steamed and bent beech which has been given a bamboo look. The table top is often made of toughened glass, set into a frame or resting on adhesive pads, which adds to the light open look of the furniture. Wood veneer tops are also available.

MODERN DINING CHAIRS

Contemporary dining chairs are made in an exciting range of materials, upholstery and styles.

Many modern dining chair styles are based on traditional designs but with a cleaner, more streamlined look. Others are completely original in their own right.

The same principles of size, construction, upholstery, etc, outlined on page 85 apply equally to these designs. Bear in mind that many modern tables and chairs are slightly lower than period ones so if you are going to mix your styles check heights carefully.

A universal characteristic of modern styles is lightness, both in weight and visually. This does not mean strength has been sacrificed in most cases, but check the construction carefully if you plan to put the chairs to strenuous use.
Materials As wood has increased in price, designers have experimented with cane, bamboo, metal (especially chrome) and plastics, and these materials have allowed for new designs.
Upholstery Most manufacturers offer a choice of fabrics and, if you ask, many will cover the chairs in your own fabric.

The same design often has a choice of seat style. Fabric, cane, rush and leather are used when appropriate.
Finish As well as natural wood finishes, many modern styles are stained in various colours, lacquered or painted.

WOODEN CHAIRS

SQUARE AND ROUNDED UPHOLSTERED
The seat and back panel are fully upholstered and the high back is curved to fit the shape of the body. The curved back has a particularly elegant line. Square legs and stretcher bars make a sturdy chair; slimmer legs without bars give a lighter feel. Also made with a cane back panel and seat and the wood can be natural, stained or lacquered.

PANELLED UPHOLSTERED
Just the central panel of the high chair back is upholstered, giving it a lighter look. A carver is usually available for most square backed styles.

MODERN LADDERBACK
A streamlined version of the traditional design. Note the higher stretcher bars between the legs which add strength unobtrusively.

Similar in concept is the square or rounded back with a series of narrow or two or three wide vertical bars. The seat is upholstered or rush/cane and the wood is natural, stained or lacquered.

SOLID PANEL BACK
This chair has a mid-height, rounded or squared back with a solid central panel. The seat is cane, rush or upholstered.

LOW BACK UPHOLSTERED
This very basic chair design is relatively inexpensive. The low curved back panel gives limited support. The seat can be cane, rush or upholstered.

TUB
The low back curves round to form the arms and sometimes there is a similar curved bar at the base into which the legs are fitted. It is also available with conventional legs.

The seat is cane or upholstered and the back panel can be filled with vertical or horizontal bars, or a cane or upholstered central panel.

METAL CHAIRS

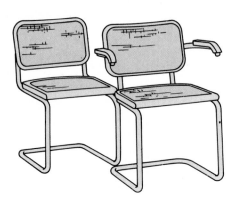

SPAGHETTI
The tubular metal frame comes in a range of bright enamel colours and the seat and back are made from lengths of clear or coloured plastic tubing wound round the frame. The chairs are designed to be stacked one on top of another.

BAUHAUS
A modern classic. The original was leather and chrome but modern versions are made from cane, chrome and wood, which is left natural or stained black. The S shape can be sharply angled or have fluid curves. There is a carver and armless version.

CANVAS AND METAL
Tubular metal framework supports an all-in-one padded canvas seat and back. The covers come in a range of colours and are washable. Simpler versions have a canvas seat and back panel stretched across the frame.

FOLDING CHAIRS

Folding chairs are useful for back up seating although they can, of course, be used as permanent dining furniture. Take care with young children as the chairs may tip and little fingers can get pinched.

WOODEN FOLDING
Available in natural wood finish or stained in various colours. The seat is solid, slatted or cane. Quite bulky when folded.

METAL FOLDING
The tubular metal framework in a range of bright colours has a solid, perforated or mesh seat and back rail. The classic Plia chair is in chrome with a clear acrylic plastic back and seat instead of metal. The legs are joined at the base with a rail front and back or are separate and finished with rubber caps. Folds into a neat narrow shape.

CANVAS AND WOOD
The 'director's' chair frame comes in natural wood or painted in various colours. The canvas seat and back can be replaced when old or stained. They are bulky when folded.

RATTAN/BAMBOO LOOK

Bamboo furniture is no longer exclusively used in the conservatory. It gives a light airy look to a dining room but is relatively fragile and will not stand up to very rough treatment. Much of the furniture sold today is, in fact, made from beech which has been stained and given the bamboo look. Both materials can be steam bent into fluid curves and the intersections are bound with split cane. Painted chairs, usually in pastel colours, are also available. Loose cushions used for the seat and/or back add comfort.

Spoon back An elegant lightweight chair.

Tub The low back rail curves round to form the arms. The space between the rail and seat or just the back panel is completely filled with cane.

Pagoda back A high backed chair with an oriental feel.

Square back A neat low-backed style with cross stretchers to strengthen the legs.

DINING CHAIRS IN PERIOD STYLES

Reproduction or antique dining chairs are usually classified by period or by cabinet maker.

Dining chairs and tables are often chosen at the same time, as a matching set, particularly if they are to go into a separate dining room. But do not feel you have to stick rigidly to this – an elegant modern set of chairs can look good with a traditionally designed table. Don't be afraid to mix periods and styles if you think they look right.

When choosing dining chairs bear in mind that they are often put to other uses; for example, at a desk, a sewing table or to provide additional seating in the living room. If your chairs have to serve different purposes make sure they are light enough to move easily and look right in the different settings.

Style Most period designs come in two versions, a carver with arms and an armless chair. Carvers are usually more expensive and take up a lot of space but some people find them more comfortable. A combination, with two carvers at the ends of the table is popular.

Size To work out how many chairs will fit round a table allow about 65cm for armless chairs and 70cm for carvers. The space between the seat and the under side of the table or rim is important. Allow 30-35cm between them and bear in mind that modern tables are usually lower than period styles if you plan to mix them.

Comfort The only way to find out

whether a chair is comfortable is to sit on it long enough for any discomfort to make itself felt! Your feet should rest flat on the floor and the seat should be wide and deep enough and should not slope back. The back should be angled to give support when sitting up to a table – some people find a space between the seat and the back support more comfy than a solid back.

The arms of carvers should be shorter than the seat so you can pull the chair right up to the table and preferably they should be lower than the table top so that the chair can be tucked away when not in use. Check that the chair arms are low enough to allow easy movement when eating and that your arms are in a relaxed position when resting.

Upholstery Dining chairs may have the food spilled on them, particularly if there are young children in the family. Drop in seats are easier to replace than fixed upholstery and removable cushion covers are the most practical.

Construction Chairs take a lot of hard wear – being pushed back and forward, tilted and even used to stand on – so look for firm, strong joints. Stretcher bars across the legs also add support and strength.

ELIZABETHAN
A carved panelled back – solid or with a break just above the upholstered seat – and stretcher bars between the legs make these particularly sturdy chairs.

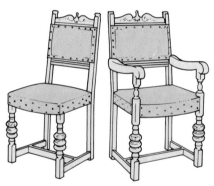

CROMWELLIAN
Strong chairs with leather covered back panel and seat fixed with brass studs. Leather is easily scratched or stained and is expensive to replace.

QUEEN ANNE
An elegant chair with elegant cabriole legs without stretcher bars. The high rounded back has a solid central splat and the seat is upholstered.

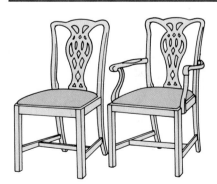

RIBBON BACK CHIPPENDALE
A high square back with a lattice carved central splat gives the chair a lighter look. A drop-in upholstered seat is more easily re-covered than a fixed one.

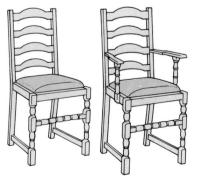

LADDERBACK
The back rungs can be plain or carved; the seat is usually upholstered and dropped in – modern versions can have rush seats. Made in a range of woods.

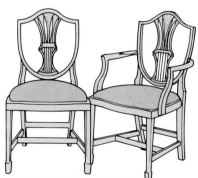

SHIELD BACK HEPPLEWHITE
A light, elegant chair with a drop-in seat. The front of the seat often is curved in a serpentine shape. The shield back can be carved or upholstered.

ROUND BACK HEPPLEWHITE
Slim elegant legs without stretcher bars make these unsuitable for rough wear. Hepplewhite chairs also look good in living rooms and bedrooms.

SQUARE ARM ADAM
This square shaped chair has a low back with a carved panel, tapering legs and upholstered seat. Adam furniture is also called neo-classical.

UPHOLSTERED ADAM
The back panel and seat are upholstered and there are sometimes upholstered pads on the carver arms. This style can also make an elegant bedroom or living room chair.

SCROLL ARM REGENCY
The back panel can be elaborately carved or with a simpler design. The seats are upholstered and the curved legs reasonably sturdy without stretcher bars.

VICTORIAN BUCKLE BACK
The back is curved to fit the body with a rail which can be decorated with carving. The seat is upholstered. Looks good in both formal and informal settings.

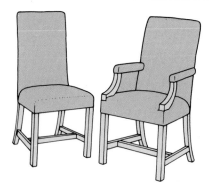

UPHOLSTERED PANEL BACK
Derived from 17th century styles, the fully upholstered back and seat give a solid appearance and shows off boldly-patterned upholstery fabric effectively.

BUTTONED LEATHER PANEL BACK
Similar in appearance to the upholstered panel back but the buttoning allows for a more sculptured back. Solid carver arms give a heavy appearance.

SPINDLE BACK
A country chair with many variations in style. The back is made up of either a single or a double row of spindles and the seat can be wood, rush woven or upholstered.

COMB BACK FARMHOUSE
Developed from the 18th century spindle back chair, the back rail curves to fit the sitter and the seat is moulded. Add squab cushions for extra comfort.

WINDSOR
Styles range from the sturdy to the more finely turned. The back is often supported with two struts for extra strength and the carver arms can continue round the back.

WHEELBACK WINDSOR
A development of the Windsor chair, with the central spindles replaced by a carved splat, often incorporating a wheel. Windsor chairs are made in a range of woods.

BENTWOOD
Simple curved lines made by steaming and bending the wood into shape, with various styles for the back. Usually made from stained beech with a solid or cane seat.

VERSATILE DINING

Even if you have a separate dining room, tables that expand are far more useful than ones that are fixed.

Few people have the space nowadays to devote an entirely separate room in their home to dining, and nothing else. In most homes, whether flats or houses, space is at a premium and the chances are that you will have no choice but to make the dining room double as something else as well.

The kitchen/dining room is – not surprisingly, given the close association between cooking and eating – the most popular partnership. But there are several other possibilities. These include the dining/living room, the dining/guest room, the dining/work room, and even the dining room/hall – often a good solution in converted flats where halls can be positively spacious in relation to some of the other rooms. At the drop of a table leaf and the unfolding of a few chairs, you can accommodate all the family and friends you want.

The most common arrangement of all is the dining area which is no more than a corner of another room. More often than not, this is the kitchen or the living room.

Round in circles
A circular dining table is one of the most sociable arrangements for eating, but takes up a lot of space. This one has two drop leaves, either one or both of which can be used, which makes it a very versatile solution to the problem of seating family and friends for dinner without taking up too much space permanently in the kitchen.

*▽ ▷ **Dropping in***
A simple drop-leaf table such as this makes for maximum versatility. An oval table with two leaves which fold away easily, it will readily seat up to six people, or you can put up just one leaf and use it as extra work space or for supper for two.

GETTING EQUIPPED

The secret of a successful versatile approach to dining is to make the most of the space you have available and to use it sensibly. And that means both maintaining a flexible attitude and, possibly even more important, finding the right sort of furniture which lends itself to this treatment.

Perhaps, for example, you want a dinng table that doesn't look like one most of the time. This means being able to use it easily for something else – as a console table in the hall or for stacking books, say, though this does mean you need somewhere convenient to move them to when you use the table for eating. It helps too if you don't have to surround it with chairs all the time, which is where folding or stacking chairs, which are great space savers, come in useful.

Even if you do have a completely separate dining area, you may not always want to cater for the same number of people. Four people can feel uncomfortably out of place sitting round a huge table that would happily accommodate ten, and – conversely – eight people bumping elbows crammed around too small a table are unlikely to feel at ease.

Do, if you have the space, look for a dining table whose size can be altered by adding an extension or extra leaves.

*▷ **Flexible seating arrangements***
Both these tables lend themselves to versatile seating arrangements, depending on how you set them up.

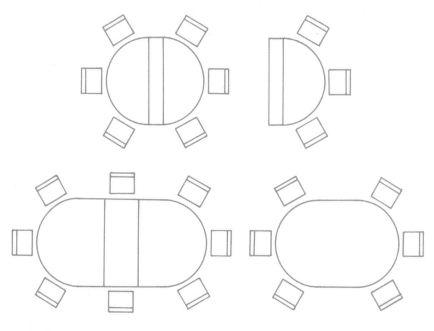

◁ **Practical styling**
Combining easy practicality with elegant styling, this dining table is 1624mm long and extends to 2328mm with an extension leaf, when it will seat eight people. A traditional-style mahogany table, this is suitable for a dining area as well as an entirely separate dining room.

▷ **Doubling up**
This simple drop-leaf kitchen table seats two or three people when positioned against the wall. It can also be extended to provide an extra storage surface or to seat up to six people for an informal supper.

BRIGHT IDEA

AN OPEN AND SHUT CASE

Here are two good ideas where space is limited. A butler's table (right) is a folding table-cum-tray on legs, which can be used for a cosy supper or a quick snack. A trestle table (above) can be stored away beside a cupboard or even under a bed and brought out when you want to entertain.

▽ **On the shelf**
This sliding shelf in a tiny, well thought-out, custom-built kitchen can be pulled out to provide an extra surface, whether for working, for storage, or on which to grab a quick breakfast or a hurried snack on the run.

△ Swivel top
A large Victorian dining table on a central pedestal can be stored with its top swivelled flat against a wall, where it takes little space.

▽ The story unfolds...
This simple pine dining table can be folded up into a special wall recess. The ceiling light is on a pulley system and can also be raised out of the way.

IMPROMPTU DINING

It is nice to be able to set up table and eat virtually anywhere in the home when the fancy takes you. The kitchen is the most obvious choice, but what about a cosy supper in front of the television; a romantic breakfast *à deux* in the bedroom; or even an informal dinner with friends in the conservatory (with a view to moving outside, perhaps, if the weather holds)?

A great aid to impromptu dining is to bring out folding varieties of both table and chairs for the occasion, which deals effectively with the problem of where to store all that extra furniture. After use they can be put away in a hall cupboard or even hung out of the way on a wall.

The clear perspex or plexiglass type of folding chair is a particularly good idea, because you can see right through them and they take up very little 'visual' space. The brightly coloured wooden sort is another attractive alternative, particularly if they go well with your decor.

Another solution is to cover all your chairs in a neutral fabric that will go with virtually any colour scheme. Then they can be moved round the house and brought together for dining when needed.

Any part-time dining area will benefit greatly from a trolley or serving cart, which forges the link between eating and cooking. They are also useful as an extra surface for serving and storage.

◁ **Breakfast blues**
An old marble-topped washstand has been converted to form the base of a dresser by fixing a hand-crafted and painted dresser top to the wall above it. This makes a convenient place for a family of three to enjoy a simple breakfast in the corner of an old-fashioned country-style kitchen.

▷ **Kitchen ease**
This modern, multi-functional tiled island unit makes the maximum possible use of space in a small open-plan flat. It forms an ingenious and convenient room divider between the kitchen and living area, as well as doubling as work surface, storage unit and dining area that comfortably seats four or six.

CHOOSING GLASSWARE

There are many different types of glasses available and it can help to know their correct uses.

Glass is a man-made substance which is the result of a long process of turning different chemicals into a transparent solid at very high temperatures.

There are three groups of glass which are generally used for domestic glassware. Crystal glass contains oxide of lead and has good optical qualities. Lower-priced soda-lime glass – which is based on sand, soda ash and limestone – is a good all-purpose glass, while 'borosilicates' (a mixture of glass and ground stone) are used for cooking utensils and for heavy duty glassware.

Lead glass is sturdy and elegant; the highest quality is known as full lead crystal. This and crystal glass are light materials and are most often used for luxury drinking glasses.

Soda lime glass can be produced by hand or by automatic machine processes; it can be plain or opal coloured. Cut crystal (which is crystal with decorative carvings) is frowned on by wine-lovers, because, they claim, it disguises the wine's colour. And many people believe that the most expensive type is not necessarily the best.

Glassware is made in many different shapes and patterns. If you want a complete set of glassware, simply choose the pattern you like and then buy pieces as you can afford them. But be sure it isn't a fashionable design that will go out of production.

It is always a good idea to shop around first and then choose a design that best complements your china and cutlery – so if both of these are modern, a similar glassware set is best.

CARING FOR GLASS

☐ Wash glasses separately to avoid chipping. Use a plastic bowl or rubber mat in the sink and stand them properly to dry.
☐ Wash glasses in warm soapy water, and avoid abrasive powders; rinse with warm water.
☐ Polish with a soft cloth and store upright: the rim is the most delicate part of the glass.
☐ Clean engraved patterns with a soft brush.
☐ If glasses stick together, pour cold water on the inner glass and hold the outer glass in warm water.
☐ Use a little cooking oil to move sticking decanter stoppers.
☐ Remove lime deposits with tea leaves soaked in vinegar. Other obstinate marks can be shifted by soaking glassware for 24 hours in a strong solution of household detergent and water.
☐ Allow decanters to dry properly before corking – trapped water can smell unpleasant.
☐ Glassware should not usually be cleaned in dishwashers. Valuable crystal, in particular, should always be washed by hand.

STYLES OF GLASSWARE

RED WINE
HOCK
WHITE WINE
CHAMPAGNE FLUTE
CHAMPAGNE SAUCER
WHISKY
BRANDY
SHERRY
LIQUEUR

RED WINE
Style Glasses for red wine usually hold about 6fl.oz.
In use These glasses are generally used for Burgundy and similar wines, which need space so that they can release their aroma.

WHITE WINE
Style Round-bodied wine glass on a stem for holding 6fl.oz of white wine.
In use Ideal white wine glasses are on a stem; chilled wines can be made tepid if the hand is clamped around the bowl of the glass, and a stemmed glass makes it easier to swirl the liquid about to release its smell.

HOCK
Style Hock glasses traditionally have a long stem. Larger in size than ordinary white wine glasses, but also designed to hold 6fl.oz.
In use Hock glasses are normally used for wines from the Rhine, the Mosel and Alsace.

CHAMPAGNE FLUTE
Style Traditional style, tall champagne glass. Many styles of champagne flutes come in cut or lead crystal: plain glass is unusual as the drink is usually served in something rather elegant. Champagne can also be served in goblet-shaped glasses.
In use These usually hold 5.5fl.oz.

CHAMPAGNE SAUCER
Style Plain saucer-type glass with a wide, shallow bowl that became fashionable in the 1920s. Champagne saucers are not approved of by connoisseurs.
In use Holds 4.5fl.oz.
Watchpoint Storing these glasses needs particular care: ensure plenty of space to avoid chipping.

WHISKY
Style Short tumbler made of uncut, full lead crystal.
In use Whisky glasses are fat, heavy glasses with a thick base. Modern styles are often plain, but many are elaborately cut.

BRANDY
Style Round-bodied, balloon-shaped glass on a short stem. Holds 14fl.oz.
In use The balloon glass allows the warmth of the hand to release the spirit's aroma.
Watchpoint These glasses are not meant to be filled to the brim!

SHERRY
Style A slender glass on a tall stem.
In use Sherry and port glasses should contain no more than about 3fl.oz of wine. True sherry glasses are narrower and taller than port glasses but nowadays many combine the functions of both.

LIQUEUR
Style Long-bodied, tapering glass on a very short stem.
In use Liqueur glasses come in many different sizes but the smallest, designed to hold 2fl.oz, is the most common.

GOBLET
Style Large, round glass on a thick stem. Goblets are thicker and heavier than wine glasses.
In use Goblets can be used to hold many different drinks and make an excellent all-purpose glass.

LONG GLASS
Style Plain, tall glass.
In use These tall glasses are called by the American name Hi-ball.

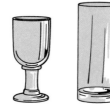

COCKTAIL GLASS
Style Cocktail glass available in plain or patterned glass. Most types of a similar style hold 5fl.oz, while tall cocktail glasses have an 11fl.oz capacity.
In use Cocktail glasses are designed to make mixed drinks with a spirit base. These glasses can nowadays be bought at relatively low prices.

IRISH COFFEE GLASSES
Style Looks rather like a glass mug on a short stem.
In use Used to serve black coffee, with Irish whiskey and double cream.
Watchpoint Glass is generally a poor conductor of heat. When a glass is filled with boiling water the inside heats up and expands, but the outside expands more slowly and the result is a crack. To avoid this, put a spoon in the liquid to draw away the heat.

BEER GLASS
Style Popular shapes are the Straight beer glass. (Pilsener) or the glass tankard. They come in measured ½-pint or pint sizes.

NOVELTY GLASSWARE
Style Novelty, fashion glassware decorated with coloured designs.
In use Suitable for any type of juice or soft drink: a good idea for older children as they tend to be more careful if they have their own favourite glass to use.

WINE DECANTER
Style Wine decanter in full lead crystal – traditional ones are in uncut crystal while the more modern ones are simply plain.
In use Most wine decanters hold 38fl.oz of wine.

SPIRIT DECANTER
Style Square spirit decanter usually

available in cut crystal.
In use This style holds 26fl.oz but there are larger sizes available in the same design.

SHIP'S DECANTER
Style Heavy-bottomed ship's decanter originally designed for use at sea.
In use Holds 35fl.oz.

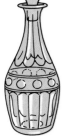

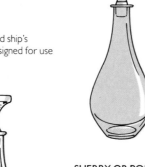

SHERRY OR PORT DECANTERS
Style Decanter in plain (uncut) lead crystal. These decanters can be used for either drink. The first (left) is rather modern; the second is more traditional and comes in full lead crystal. Holds 28fl.oz.

MAGNUM DECANTER
Style Top of the range, Magnum decanter. As its name implies this holds twice as much as the average sized decanter – 60fl.oz.

ICE BUCKET
Style Uncut, lead crystal ice bucket that comes complete with a pair of stainless steel tongs.
In use Ice buckets can be bought to complement or co-ordinate with a glassware set.

BISCUIT BARREL
Style Full lead crystal biscuit barrel in diamond cut pattern.

In use A glass biscuit barrel is an attractive display container but there are no special benefits to be gained by using glass.

SUGAR AND CREAM SET
Style Set made in lead crystal. This set has interwoven colourways.
In use These sets can be bought to complement your existing glassware.

FRUIT AND SALAD BOWL
Style Fruit and salad bowl with matching dishes in crystal.
In use A set of decorative tableware designed for everyday use at an everyday price.

LOW VASE
Style Low vase in ornamental full lead crystal.
In use A piece such as this – at the very top end of the market – is designed for its beauty and ornamental value rather than for heavy use; but sturdiness is part of its high quality.

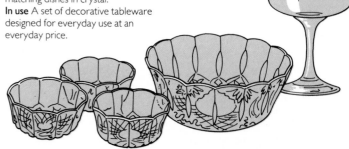

CHOOSING CHINA AND OVENWARE

From Sunday best dinner service to everyday ovenware, crockery can be practical as well as pretty.

Buying a set of china can be quite a bewildering experience as there are many different shapes and patterns available to choose from.

And in addition to these different shapes and patterns, crockery is available in different materials too. Porcelain and china are two names for the same thing: clay fired at a very high temperature to produce delicate but strong crockery with a glossy non-porous core.

It's called china, because Chinese potters were working on it as early as the 9th century. It was introduced to Europe by Italian travellers, who described it as 'porcellana', their word for the translucent, smooth, white cowrie shell.

Bone china is a purely British phenomenon, invented in the 18th century by Thomas Frye of Bow, in London's East End. He discovered that adding bone ash to the porcelain clay makes it extra white. It's a technique that's still used today.

Two types of clay are used in today's crockery. Porcelain is made from kaolin or china clay, which is a primary clay. That means it is dug from the ground where it is formed, untainted by other minerals. Secondary clays, like those used in earthenware, have been moved from their source, often by rivers for example, and tend to be tainted with other substances. This can make them more elastic (but less durable). Since

impurities reduce strength, bone china is not as strong as porcelain.

Designs, including plate shapes and patterns, vary from manufacturer to manufacturer and range from traditional through to classic and modern styles. No one can really tell you which is the right design for you – that comes down to personal taste. But the most important thing to remember is that the service you choose to collect – few can afford to buy a whole set in one go – will be a lifetime's investment.

Classic shapes and patterns wear better than modern sets. For example, something in cream and purple is not likely to last as long as a plain white plate with a gold border, and there's less risk of manufacturers discontinuing classic styles as fashion changes. If you are unlucky and the manufacturer does stop making your set, they usually give two years' notice. If you're not aware that your service has been discontinued, look in reject china shops for any extra pieces.

Buying a full dinner service is quite an investment, especially if you plump for more expensive china. Generally speaking, you get what you pay for, so the higher the quality of the porcelain or the more bone ash present in bone china, the more expensive the outlay.

Price is also governed by pattern. The cost of hand-painted china – which tends to be most intricate – reflects the time and energies employed by the

skilled craftspeople in making it.

Nowadays it is more common for patterns to be applied by screen printing, in which enamelled colours are built up to make a pattern.

Upmarket designs are often 'lifted' by the addition of gold or platinum. Burnished gold is the best quality and is made from an amalgam of brown gold and mercury. It is fired so that the mercury can evaporate and leave a layer of pure gold.

So-called 'bright' gold has a brassier quality and tends to be less durable, so it may be worthwhile paying more in the first place. However, bear in mind that as gold or gilded decoration is fired at a lower temperature than enamelled colours, it does wear away quite quickly, making the service unsuitable for everyday use.

If this huge variety of options is a bit daunting, it may help to know that gourmets often prefer to eat off the plainest and purest white porcelain. They say it's the best setting for any food.

SIZES

Full dinner services often include a confusing amount of similar but variously sized pieces. Plates can come in five sizes, typically 15, 18, 21, 23 and 26cm sizes. The 26cm is the usual dinner plate, 21cm is a dessert plate, and 15cm a side plate. If you prefer a larger side plate the 18cm can be used while the 23cm makes a handy salad plate. Some manufacturers also include a 31cm service plate for use beneath smaller plates.

The shapes and sizes of cups depend on the beverage they contain and meal they're intended for. Generally speaking, a breakfast cup holds 9fl.oz, a tea cup 7fl.oz and a coffee cup 4fl.oz.

Be careful when buying what is described as a 'tea service' as it doesn't include a tea pot, milk jug or sugar bowl. Normally, you get six tea cups and saucers and six side plates.

CHINA STYLES

PLATE SHAPES
Plates come in several different styles but their shapes tend to be fairly uniform and you can expect to find dining plates which are either round, oval, octagonal or with fluted edges. Which plate shape is included in a full china set is the decision of the manufacturer but many offer a choice. Modern, unorthodox china sets are more likely to include some rather unusual shapes. The dining plates shown here all belong to dinnerware sets and, as can be seen, the plate design will also influence the plate shape.

CHINA PATTERNS
Your choice should largely be governed by your personal tastes, your decor, the type of food you are likely to serve and even your personality. Patterns tend to fall into three main categories: traditional, classic and modern. Traditional styles (shown left) tend to be well known and much loved designs – they work equally well as wall plates and often antique styles in the same pattern can be found. Classic patterns (centre) are likely to be the longest lasting as their simplicity means that they won't date easily or clash with food or decor. These styles work well for daily use or as a special dinner service. Modern styles (right) are designed to incorporate the latest fashion trends and for that reason are best for daily or frequent use as the pattern may not be so appealing a few years later.

TEA AND COFFEE SETS
According to your tastes and your needs, you can have a tea or coffee set that matches the rest of your dinnerware, you can have one that is completely different, or you can combine both options and keep one set for special occasions. And as you're likely to use a teaset more often than you use your full dinner set, a different design is sensible for everyday use. The set here has a bold, attractive design and its size make it ideal for breakfast. These sets do vary in size and shape (see those shown in the china and ovenware photographs too). Classic styles (flatter and more oval than the one shown) are available as well, so try to see as many as possible before you choose.

OVENWARE
This china can go straight from the oven to the table so you don't have to worry about putting the food in special serving dishes. If you want dishes that can go on direct heat, look out for sets that are flameproof too. Expect to find casserole, soufflé, flan and gratin dishes, ramekins, platters, soup bowls and plates all available in these services. Materials are usually earthenware and stoneware – either glazed or unglazed. Stoneware is fired at a higher temperature than earthenware, making it harder and a bit more expensive but it is versatile and can go straight from freezer to microwave. Earthenware retains heat and is ideal for slow cooking.

CHINA SETS
Some sets consist of just plates, cups and saucers and sometimes a tea or coffee pot. Such sets are usually low priced and designed to be bought in one go. But a full dinner service should consist of dinner plates, side plates, saucers, casseroles, meat platters, a cake or bread and butter plate, a gravy boat and stand, a soup tureen and soup dishes, an open jug and more often than not, a full tea service too. However, there is no need to collect every single piece from a china set: just what you need. Often manufacturers will include two or three different styles of the same piece as a choice. Modern sets can even have matching cutlery and glassware to give a totally co-ordinated look. However, this option does tend to be at the lower end of the market and is thus more suitable as a set for daily or frequent use.

It is usual to have enough for six people (ie, six plates, bowls, saucers, cups, and so on) but buy more, or less, to suit your needs.

A GUIDE TO KITCHEN KNIVES

Knives for the kitchen can last for many years – some even a lifetime. So take your time and choose carefully.

Preparing a meal becomes a much simpler task if you have a selection of knives suitable for cooking. Although there are many different types of kitchen knives available, most people manage with just three or four specialist knives. Look at what's available to see which ones best suit your needs.

Most kitchen knives have stainless steel or carbon steel blades, with a variety of handles, usually black plastic or wood, securely riveted to the blade. Stainless steel is much easier to keep clean, but carbon steel takes a better edge. And as the metal discolours and rusts easily, carbon steel knives should never be left wet. If they are stored and not used for a while, wipe them with olive oil when you are going to use them again.

So long as they are kept well sharpened, plain-edged blades give the smoothest cut; serrated or fluted-edged blades need little or no sharpening, and are also cheaper.

Price is usually an indication of quality. The best kitchen knives are craftsman-made from forged steel, and cannot be cheap. Several excellent ranges come from France and West Germany, as well as Sheffield. Look for a guarantee (this may be for 15, 25 or 50 years), and buy from a specialist cutler or kitchen equipment shop (one which is used by the catering trade).

Blunt knives are not only inefficient but are also potentially dangerous, as applying too much pressure can cause your hand to slip. The traditional tool for use on plain blades is a fine carborundum stone or a sharpening steel. The latter are easier to handle but eventually create a crinkled edge.

In either case it pays to have good knives professionally re-shaped and sharpened from time to time. Knives with fluted or serrated edges may not need any sharpening – or they may require special techniques. Check when buying. Store knives in a knife block or on a magnetic rack to preserve the edges and prevent accidents.

Many different types of kitchen knife are made, and it's important to use the right one. The sizes given below are for the blade, not the whole knife.

PREPARATION KNIVES

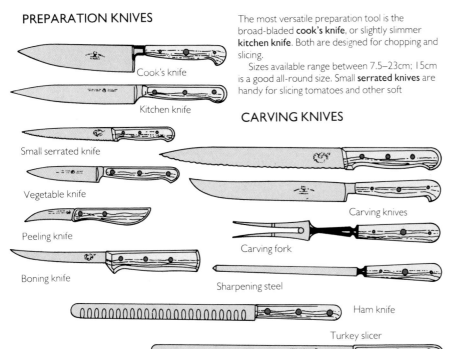

Cook's knife

Kitchen knife

Small serrated knife

Vegetable knife

Peeling knife

Boning knife

Carving knives

Carving fork

Sharpening steel

Ham knife

Turkey slicer

The most versatile preparation tool is the broad-bladed **cook's knife**, or slightly slimmer **kitchen knife**. Both are designed for chopping and slicing.

Sizes available range between 7.5–23cm; 15cm is a good all-round size. Small **serrated knives** are handy for slicing tomatoes and other soft vegetables thinly, and if they are kept sharp they can double as steak knives.

Do not confuse small cook's knives with **vegetable or paring knives**. The latter are lower quality, and so cheaper, as they are only meant for scraping and peeling. However, if you prefer to buy knives designed for a particular purpose, special **peeling knives** are available too. Blades for these knives can be straight or curved, serrated or plain. Sizes available range from 6–9cm.

Boning knives have narrow blades about 12cm long, designed to slip easily between flesh and bone. Filleting is best done with a special flexible-bladed knife.

CARVING KNIVES

A traditional carving set consists of a **carving knife**, a **twin-pronged carving fork** and a **sharpening steel**. Smaller carving knives are more versatile (particularly useful for filleting) but you really do need a long carving knife if you are going to be able to deal with a large joint neatly and efficiently.

Special carvers with long, round-ended and straight blades are made for slicing ham, salmon and turkey. Small carvers with upward-curving blades are handy for carving and jointing poultry. These knives tend to range from about 18–28 cm in size.

SPECIALIST KNIVES

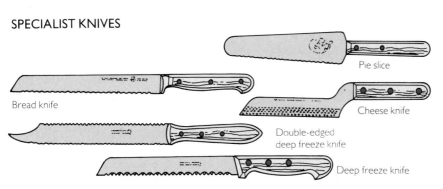

Bread knife

Double-edged deep freeze knife

Pie slice

Cheese knife

Deep freeze knife

A **deep freeze knife** has a strong, coarsely serrated blade for dealing with frozen meat. If you need to carve large quantities of frozen meat, it's sensible to use the right knife – although a carver might seem suitable it could easily be ruined. A **bread knife** is long enough to slice a large loaf, but does not have to be razor sharp; serrated blades are traditional. A combined **pie slice** and spatula is convenient for cutting and serving pastry, but don't use it on non-stick bakeware. For cutting large quantities of cheese use a special **cheese knife** which has an etched blade which prevents the cheese you are cutting from clinging messily to the knife.

THE KITCHEN

Creating a kitchen that looks good and works well takes more than money. You need a basic knowledge of kitchen planning, information about what equipment is on the market, plus inspiration and effective, practical ideas.

There is no one 'ideal' kitchen. What is perfect for you depends on your personal lifestyle. The first stage is planning the layout: the vital key to making your kitchen easy to work in. After setting out the ground rules for positioning kitchen units and appliances, there are separate sections on typical kitchen layouts: the L-shape, the U-shape, the single-line and the island kitchen. The very small kitchen is also given special attention, with space-saving and storage ideas a top priority.

As with all rooms, the use of lighting is fundamental, and in the kitchen there are certain areas where it must be bright for safety reasons – where the cooking and preparation of food takes place, for instance. So valuable advice about lighting is included; also on the use of colour to create the atmosphere you want; on the range of materials available for worktops and splashbacks; even on how to make use of any gaps between units.

CLASSIC KITCHEN LAYOUTS

A kitchen, above all else, is a place of work. Plan to make that work easy and efficient and it will be enjoyable too.

Surprising as it may seem, the efficient use of a kitchen depends more on how it is laid out than how big it is. Although many people long for something larger, small kitchens have plenty of potential, given the right layout.

The work sequence When you are planning the kitchen you should always aim to make the food storage, the preparation, the cooking and the serving areas as practical and energy-saving as possible.

A great deal of research has been carried out into the most efficient way to arrange a kitchen. Cooking a meal follows a predictable pattern. The three main areas of activity are food storage – fridge and food cupboards; preparation – worktops and sink; and cooking – oven and/or hob.

Although you often have to double back on yourself, expert planners have established that the most sensible layout should follow this pattern: fridge/worktop/sink/worktop/cooker and hob/worktop. If it is possible this should be arranged from left to right in an unbroken sequence.

THE WORK TRIANGLE

The sequence of storage, preparation and cooking is known as the work triangle. Obviously, the dimensions of the triangle vary, depending on the size and shape of the kitchen but the basic concept should be applied to the design of every kitchen.

Ideally, the total length of the three sides of the triangle should be between 4 and 7 metres. Distances any greater will only create needless kitchen mileage; any less will leave you feeling cramped.

The classic layouts A kitchen can be almost any shape or size, depending on the architecture of the building. But there are just six basic layouts that, working within the guidelines of the work triangle, will give you a practical kitchen that is a pleasure to work in.

◁ *The single line*
Suitable for one or two people, this kitchen can be fitted into a very narrow space. The units and appliances are all lined up along one wall. Place the sink in the middle and choose

built-under appliances so you don't lose any of the limited worktop space.

The room should be at least 2m wide to allow enough space for two people to pass each other. The single line kitchen is often a corridor and through traffic can be a problem.

Eating will have to take place elsewhere, unless a pull-out or flap-down unit can be incorporated.

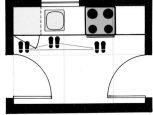

scale: 1 square = 1 metre

▷ *The double galley*
Similar to the single line, the double galley has units lined along facing walls.

Most layouts will be dictated by the position of existing doors and windows but, ideally, the sink and cooker/hob should be on one side, with the fridge and storage opposite.

The double galley is a compact and easy layout for one or two people to work in, but make sure there is at least 1.2m between facing units, otherwise bending down to get something from a low-level cupboard

becomes a contortionist's act. Traffic can be a problem if there is a door at either end of the room.

scale: 1 square = 1 metre

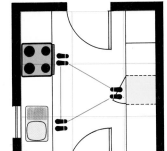

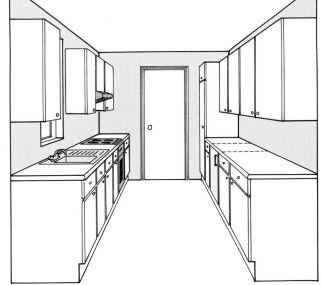

▷ The L-shape

This is a very versatile layout. The units and appliances are arranged on two adjacent walls, creating an efficient work triangle protected from through traffic.

Make sure that the corner is used to best effect – a carousel fitting inside the corner cupboard is a good solution. Separate the sink, cooker/hob and fridge with stretches of worktop to avoid the areas of activity becoming too congested.

The sides of the L can be adapted to suit an awkwardly shaped room and should be able to accommodate two cooks without them constantly getting in each other's way.

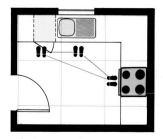

scale: 1 square = 1 metre

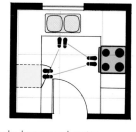

◁ The U-shape

The best kitchen layout of all, the U-shape has three walls for units and appliances, uninterrupted by through traffic – an efficient and safe arrangement in a compact area.

Scale is important: you need enough space between facing units to allow two people to work without banging into each other, while too large a space leads to unnecessary walking about. The flexible shape can often accommodate a dining area with ease.

scale: 1 square = 1 metre

▷ The peninsula

In a larger room, or kitchen/dining room, the peninsula is a flexible layout. The short arm jutting out into the room divides the cooking and eating areas; it can be used to house a sink or hob with an efficient extractor hood above, or it can be a breakfast bar or serving area.

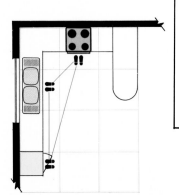

scale: 1 square = 1 metre

▽ The island

Essentially, the island layout is a larger version of the L- or U-shape with an additional work area in the middle. It can look stunning but is only practical in a spacious room. Careful planning is needed to avoid wasteful journeys around the island.

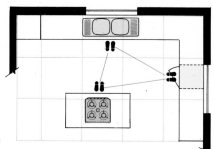

scale: 1 square = 1 metre

KITCHEN CHECKPOINTS

Spend time carefully assessing your needs when designing a new kitchen.

Installing a new kitchen is a major outlay and a long-term investment. Don't approach the venture in too much of a hurry as any mistakes at the planning stage will prove costly as well as a nuisance to the user.

The plan below gives you an at-a-glance guide to the main considerations in good kitchen design and over the page is a questionnaire to help organize your thoughts in detail before you start.

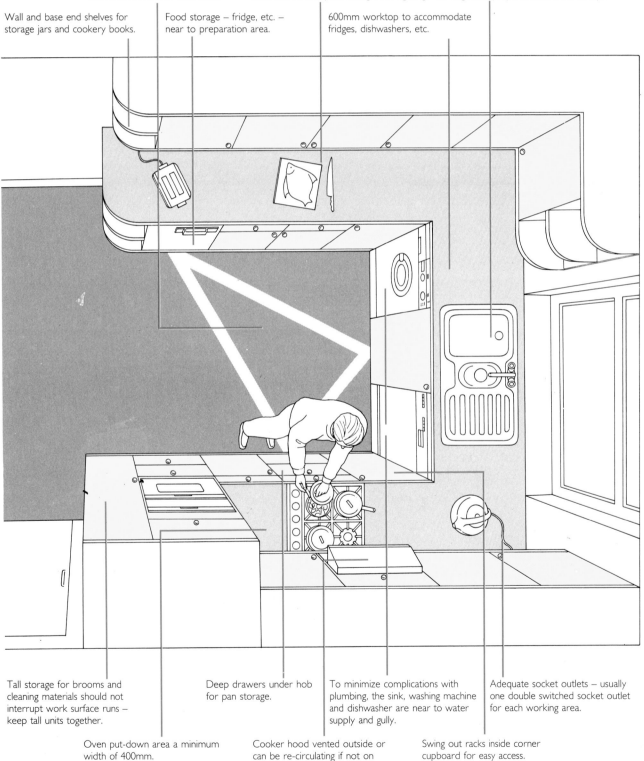

Keep work triangle down to minimum, usually not more than 6.6m and no shorter than 3.6m.

Task lighting provided by strip lights under wall units – there must also be adequate background lighting.

Double bowl sink – one bowl taking waste disposal. This allows for washing up and still leaves room for vegetable preparation and use of taps.

Wall and base end shelves for storage jars and cookery books.

Food storage – fridge, etc. – near to preparation area.

600mm worktop to accommodate fridges, dishwashers, etc.

Tall storage for brooms and cleaning materials should not interrupt work surface runs – keep tall units together.

Deep drawers under hob for pan storage.

To minimize complications with plumbing, the sink, washing machine and dishwasher are near to water supply and gully.

Adequate socket outlets – usually one double switched socket outlet for each working area.

Oven put-down area a minimum width of 400mm.

Cooker hood vented outside or can be re-circulating if not on outside wall.

Swing out racks inside corner cupboard for easy access.

KITCHEN CHECKLIST

A kitchen that works and looks just the way you want it to is not easy to achieve. It requires a detailed analysis of your needs, a careful assessment of the potential of the space and a thorough investigation of the merchandise available to implement your ideas. You must also always bear in mind the basic principles of kitchen planning.

Designing a kitchen is a complicated and intricate procedure, which with our guidance you should be able to do for yourself. Professional help is now available from many retail outlets free of charge but no professional kitchen planner can help you unless you first work a bit at helping yourself. This is essential as the professional design solutions provided by planners can only be as good as your briefing.

The questionnaire below is designed to help you clarify your thoughts and to get your ideas into a workable form.

FAMILY/LIFESTYLE

☐ What do you and your family like about your present kitchen?
☐ What don't you like about the kitchen you have now?
☐ What is your idea of a dream kitchen?
☐ Who uses the kitchen and how old are they?
☐ How many people tend to use the kitchen at the same time?
  You'll need more space if two or three people often combine to help with cooking and washing up, or if toddlers or young children are to play in the kitchen.
☐ Does anyone using the kitchen have special needs? For example, is the cook left-handed?
☐ Is anyone in the family elderly or disabled?
☐ Do you have pets that eat or sleep in the kitchen regularly?

EATING

How often and what kind of meals are taken in the kitchen and for how many people?
☐ Breakfast only.
☐ Snacks.
☐ All meals.
What kind of eating facilities are needed/ preferred?
☐ A table for sit-down meals.
☐ A fold-down table.
☐ A bar with stools.
☐ A serving hatch through to the dining room.

ACTIVITIES IN THE KITCHEN

What takes place in the kitchen, apart from storing, preparing and cooking food and washing up?
☐ Eating.
☐ Laundry.
☐ Leisure activities such as watching TV, listening to music, reading, or hobbies which might involve using the sink or cooker.
☐ Homework.
☐ Entertaining.

BUDGET

☐ How much money is available to spend on your new/improved kitchen?
☐ How is finance to be provided?
  A new kitchen is a major home improvement/ investment. It should last for many years. It may be worthwhile raising extra finance (for example, by extending your mortgage or applying for a grant) to give yourself the kitchen you really want.
☐ Are you thinking of moving within the next few years?
  If so, avoid the temptation to overspend. A new kitchen puts a certain amount of value on to a house, but usually not as much as the kitchen itself costs. The next occupants may well have very different ideas of what a kitchen should be like.

STYLE

☐ What style are you aiming to create?
☐ What colour schemes appeal?
  Choice of colours will be influenced by the type of light your room receives as well as personal preference. Kitchens with a cold aspect tend to feel friendlier when decorated in warm colours; while those with a warmer aspect can take cooler ones. Some people find cooler colours more calming and relaxing to work with; others respond more positively to the lively nature of warm colours like red.
☐ What type of flooring do you prefer?
☐ What wall covering?

SPACE/STRUCTURE

☐ Can you work within the space available?
☐ Can you find ways of providing more space?
☐ Can you take in space from an adjacent area such as a walk-in larder, a large hall or a little-used dining room?
☐ Would removal of the wall between kitchen and living area provide an open plan arrangement to give more space for kitchen activities?
☐ Can you remove a chimney breast?
☐ Can you expand your kitchen area with an extension to your house?
☐ Could you re-site your kitchen in a larger room?
  Always obtain professional advice before carrying out any structural alterations.
☐ Is there a boiler in the kitchen? Could it be moved, possibly to another room?
☐ How much work surface will you need, and what type do you like?
  Consider the work surface height. This is usually dictated by the dimensions of appliances but if you are very tall or small you can adjust the height by using plinths.

APPLIANCES

☐ What kind of fuel do you plan to use?
☐ Gas.
☐ Electric.
☐ Solid fuel.
☐ A combination.
☐ What type of cooking appliances will you have?
☐ How many small electrical appliances will you have, or plan to have in the future? You will need sufficient electric sockets and storage space.
☐ What combination of fridge and freezer will you have?
☐ Do you use a lot of·frozen food?
  If you do, obviously you need a large freezer. Perhaps it would be better kept out of the kitchen, in an outhouse or garage.

SINKS

☐ What arrangement.of sink(s) is best suited to your needs/space/budget?
☐ A single sink.
☐ A double sink.

☐ An extra half sink.
☐ Where do you want the draining boards?
  Consider whether you prefer to wash up from left to right or right to left; or if you want drainers on both sides.
☐ Is the kitchen a long way from the dustbin, or do you not have room for a very large bin in the kitchen?
  Consider installing a waste disposal.
☐ Where could you site a draining rack? If possible, attach this to the wall to save worktop space.
☐ Do you want a dishwasher, now or in the future?
  Make sure you plan adequate space and plumbing to save additional work later.
☐ Is there enough storage space near the sink for cleaning materials, mops and buckets, tea towels, etc?

STORAGE

☐ How much food/equipment must your kitchen contain?
  Think about all the kinds of food you have to keep in the kitchen. This will guide you towards the size of fridge/freezer needed and amount and size of cupboards/shelves required. Think about a larder.
☐ How about utensils and pots and pans?
☐ Where are you going to keep your crockery, cutlery, glasses?
  All these considerations will determine what sort of cupboards you need. Look through manufacturers' catalogues and visit a few showrooms to see the vast choice available. Consider carousel cupboards and deep, wire drawers as well as traditional shelves and cupboards.

LIGHTING AND VENTILATION

What kind of lighting do you prefer?
☐ General overhead light.
☐ Fluorescent strips behind diffusers.
☐ Clusters or strips of spotlights.
☐ Electrified tracks.
☐ Recessed downlighters.
☐ Special under-cupboard lighting.

Is there adequate ventilation in the kitchen?
☐ Should you consider a cooker hood or an extractor fan over the cooker or hob?

LAUNDRY

☐ What kind of washing machine will there be?
☐ Will there be a tumble drier? Will it be stacked or adjacent to the machine, or a combined system to save space?
☐ Is there enough space for soap powders, pegs, laundry basket, drying rack?
☐ What facilities will you need for ironing? Where will you keep the ironing board and iron?
☐ Could the laundry be sited in the bathroom or a separate utility room?

PLANNING A FITTED KITCHEN

An accurate plan with everything worked out will save tears when it comes to fitting a kitchen.

Before you decide on what appliances and units to have in your kitchen, and what style you like, you need to work out exactly how everything is going to fit in, in the right place.

The first stage is to get an accurate, scaled floor plan of the room on graph paper.

Measuring for a fitted kitchen calls for more accuracy than any other room. Watch out for uneven flooring and corners that appear to be square but in fact are not 90°; care will have to be taken, especially when fitting corner cupboards or appliances.

Make a list of all the appliances you plan to have and their dimensions, not forgetting allowances for pipes, wires and ventilation at the back. Make scaled cut-outs for each appliance, and move them around on your plan, following the work triangle principles set out on pages 137–8, until you find the best possible set-up for your kitchen.

Make cut-outs of the units too, and add them to your plan. There are different sizes available; the choice varies according to the manufacturer but, usually, the more expensive the range, the more choice you will have.

Once you have finalized your plan, it's a good idea to stick masking tape down on the floor where all the cupboards and appliances are to go to check that the layout works.

If new plumbing, drainage or wiring is involved, check that your plans conform to regulations.

CUPBOARD UNITS

Wall and floor units usually come in standard widths starting at 200mm, and increasing in 100mm steps to 600mm for single cupboards and 1200mm for double units.

Wall cupboards are almost always 300mm deep and floor units are either 500mm or 600mm deep. Most appliances are 600mm deep so choose the same sized cupboard if you plan to build in the appliances. Alternatively, you could set all the floor units slightly in from the wall, using a deeper work surface to cover the gap at the back, this is ideal if you are likely to end up with lots of pipework that would be best concealed behind the units.

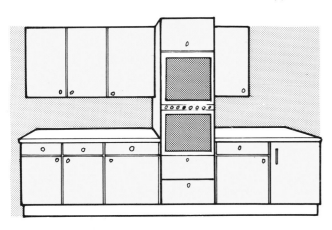

◁ *Tall units should never be placed in the middle of a run of units as they will interrupt the work surface.*

The wall space in between base units and wall cupboards can be lined with narrow shelving, about 100mm deep, or with hooks or pegs for utensils, or with a metal grid storage system.

△ *Wall units should be positioned about 450mm above the work surface. Any lower and you won't be able to see the back of the work surface without bending down. Any higher, and the top shelves will be difficult to reach.*

▷ *Corners are the trickiest areas to deal with. It is very important that doors don't open into each other.*

If you are housing an appliance near a corner you must be able to open the door to its fullest extent without banging into the wall. Here, extra tray and tea towel storage space solves the problems.

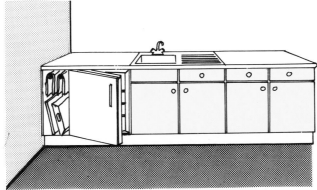

WORK SURFACES

The standard height for a work surface is 900mm. If you are tall, this may be too low, particularly for the sink, where you work with your hands below the work surface level.

It is worth experimenting to find the height that suits you, but bear in mind that units come in a standard height which will have to be built up to match unless you can alter the height by adjusting the bottom plinth. Other possibilities include setting special surfaces in the work surface at different heights, such as a butcher's block for chopping or a slab of marble for rolling out pastry.

Work surfaces are generally 600mm deep, but most manufacturers make a deeper one for peninsula units, eating areas or to cover extra-deep appliances.

APPLIANCES

Sinks, dishwashers and washing machines are usually best sited on an outside wall to allow for straightforward plumbing. Other appliances, such as ovens, hobs and fridges, should be positioned in relation to the sink, following the

Ovens Should be placed at least 300mm away from a corner to allow doors to open easily. Never position an oven within the radius of an inward-opening door. Position an eye-level oven at the end of a run of units, with plenty of work surface to one side for setting down dishes. Watch out for side-hinged doors – the handle should be on the side nearest the work surface.

Dishwashers Best placed as close to the sink as possible for rinsing plates and for convenient water and waste connections. Under the draining board is often a good place for built under models. Avoid positioning a dishwasher near a corner as you will need plenty of room to open the door to its full extent for loading and unloading.

principles of the work triangle.

For every major appliance, allow for an electric socket below work surface level. This will avoid the need to run cables through the work surface and will free the high level sockets for smaller appliances.

Hobs Should have at least 300mm of work surface to either side and should never be placed near windows with flapping curtains. Gas hobs should be positioned out of any draughts in case the burners blow out. Do not place a hob under wall units unless you install an extractor hood.

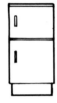

Fridges and freezers These are usually hinged on the right but some models can be hinged on either side. Allow at least 100mm between the hinge side and an adjoining wall or run of units so that you can open the door wide enough to remove shelves. For tall fridge freezers, an adjacent put-down area of around 300mm is useful.

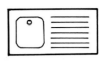

Sinks A minimum length of 1000mm for sink and draining surface is recommended. The size of sink you need will depend on how big your household is and whether or not you have a dishwasher, but the bowl should be big enough to cope with bulky items such as chopping blocks and pastry boards. Round sinks, although they can be very attractive, are usually impractical in this respect.

If there is enough space, a one-and-a-half or double bowl sink is useful, especially if one of the bowls is fitted with a waste disposal unit. Allow at least 300mm of work surface or drainer either side of the bowl for stacking dishes and pans.

Washing machines and tumble driers If there is no space for a separate utility room, and the washing machine/drier must be fitted in the kitchen it is more hygienic to keep them separate from the food storage and preparation zones. Position the washing machine on the same wall as the sink and/or dishwasher for ease of plumbing.

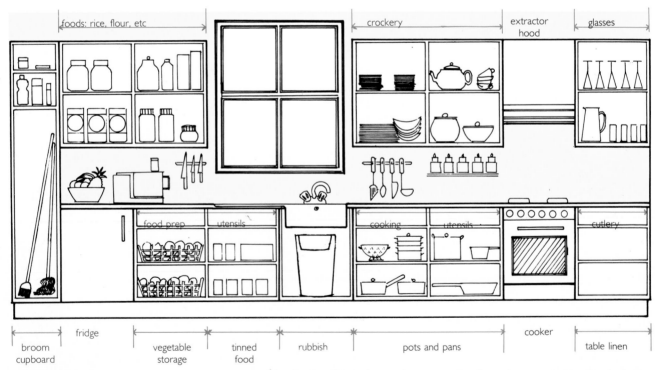

STORAGE

For greatest efficiency, organize storage around the three zones of the work triangle (see Home Planner page 11-12).
Food storage centres around the fridge, well out of the way of heat and steam. Use wall cupboards for dry goods such as flour, sugar, biscuits, etc – and store tins and jars of food in floor cupboards. Keep cleaning materials in a separate

cupboard – foodstuffs tend to pick up powerful tastes and smells.
The preparation area is near the sink. Keep kitchen knives, strainers, graters, peelers and so on in drawers or hung from racks on the wall, and china and crockery handy for the washing-up and serving areas. This is also the place to keep a rubbish bin, ideally under or beside the sink.

Small appliances can be kept along the back of the work surface or in drawers or pull-out units underneath. Don't keep heavy items in wall units as they are awkward to lift down.
In the cooking area you need deep drawers or double floor cupboards for pots and pans, baking dishes and so on, and wall racks and shallow drawers for cooking utensils.

THE L-SHAPED KITCHEN

This layout is one of the most functional, giving you a traffic-free zone in which to work.

The L-shape is one of the most versatile kitchen layouts, with its units and appliances ranged along two adjacent sides. It is also one of the most functional because the work triangle isn't interrupted by through traffic.

The L layout is suitable for almost all types of room, except narrow ones or those with lots of doors, and is often used to create a kitchen in a corner of an open-plan living room or in an awkwardly shaped corner.

The L is particularly suited to kitchens that incorporate eating areas. It almost always allows space for eating – even if only a breakfast bar – and in most a table can be fitted in comfortably. Not only is it a neat, space-saving arrangement, but it is an extremely sociable set-up, allowing the cook to join in the life of the room – ideal for relaxed informal entertaining and family meals.

COOKING
The long continuous run of work surface is marvellous for cooking and, when the sides of the L are not too long, this is a very efficient and energy saving arrangement for the cook.

If one, or both, sides of the L is over-long, keep the work triangle compact and use the extra space at the long end for storage of cleaning equipment and materials and for less frequently used cooking utensils and appliances.

Once you have decided on the position of the essentials such as fridge, hob, oven and sink with its attendant plumbing, there are still plenty of ways you can vary, improve and extend the use of the L. And, of course, there are dozens of looks to choose from.

Space to work
A double sink, built-in hob unit, and fridge on the far left behind a matching door panel still leave a good stretch of continuous worktop for food preparation. There is plenty of space for two people to work at the same time in this medium-sized room and the arrangement allows space for a table for informal meals.

BRIGHT IDEA

Utensil rack A towel rail fitted under a wall cupboard and hung with S-shaped hooks provides an attractive and handy place to keep small pots and pans and kitchen tools.

CHOICES

As well as being extremely practical, the L-shape is a very adaptable arrangement. These three kitchens, for example, are the same size with basically the same layout, but they work in different ways according to the needs and means of their owners.

There are a number of factors that will affect how you organize your kitchen once you've decided on the basic layout and where the appliances should go. You need to consider how much storage you need and where; whether to include an eating area; how many people use the room; what kind of look you want, and so on.

If you are a very keen cook and prefer buying fresh food as you need it, you won't want a lot of storage space for food, or even a very large fridge –

Cook's choice
The three L-shaped kitchens shown here illustrate the variety of uses to which the same basic layout can be put as well as the different looks that can be achieved.

The practical laminate kitchen below is designed for a keen cook who prefers

but you may want extra space for cooking equipment and utensils. On the other hand, you may not have the time or inclination for daily shopping, or perhaps you live in an isolated spot and tend to buy in bulk – in which case you probably want plenty of food cupboards and a large fridge and freezer.

BUDGET

Obviously, too, the amount of money available will affect your decisions. But there's no reason why you can't proceed gradually.

Once you've established the work triangle and where to put the sink, cooker and fridge, you can start with a modest set-up of cupboards set under a work surface, replacing old appliances with new, and adding extra floor and wall cupboards as you can afford them.

to have the maximum amount of work surface rather than an excess of cupboards. A wipeable table provides even more space for food preparation.

Floor cupboards are kept down in number with a space left under the worktop by the window for an eating or work area.

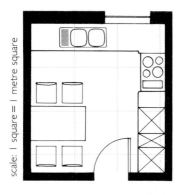

scale: I square = I metre square

Floor to ceiling

These two kitchens are designed for owners prepared to sacrifice a certain amount of worktop to gain storage space. Both rooms feature cupboards up to the ceiling but that is where the similarity ends.

▷ Open shelving and a glass-fronted cupboard contribute to the light, open look of this kitchen.

▽ A streamlined kitchen with similar features has been achieved with a totally built-in look.

SPOTLIGHT ON CORNERS

Every L-shaped kitchen turns a corner – in the best designed ones, every inch of this space is used to positive advantage.

Deep corners formed by adjacent units can be a problem but there are now dozens of well-designed corner cupboards available, and almost every manufacturer features at least one kind of carousel or lazy Susan device which fits into a floor corner unit using circular trays or shelves. And you can fit wall and floor units with bi-folding doors so it's easy to reach inside.

A simpler solution is to use open shelving around the corner, at wall or floor level, allowing everything to be seen at a glance.

The corner of the worktop is often a problem area too. It's too deep and awkward to use for work space, but it is an ideal place to keep small appliances when not in use. Another idea is to cut across the corner at an angle and build in a sink or hob, or install a built-under oven. This very smart solution allows you additional space at work surface level behind the appliance.

With all these options, there's no reason why the corner of an L-shaped kitchen should be under used.

▷ *Simple corner*
The corner worktop area is a useful place to keep wooden spoons, spices and the like next to the hob. The cupboard underneath houses a swing-out shelf unit. The angled open unit on the wall takes decorative dishes and breaks the line of solid cupboard doors.

▽ *Clever corners*
From left to right:
☐ *A bi-folding door opening out on itself for an unobscured view right to the back.*
☐ *A revolving carousel unit ensures nothing gets lost at the back.*
☐ *A single door with two circular lazy Susan trays that swing out for easy access to small jars and spices.*
☐ *A single cupboard next to a compartment for trays and wine.*

 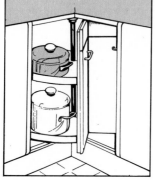  

◁ **Sink solution**
A sink unit placed at an
angle across the corner.
Although this is a fairly
small kitchen, it makes
sense to sacrifice a
little cupboard space for
such a good-looking,
streamlined effect.

A wall grid between the
wall cupboard and worktop
and a hanging rail over
the sink provide
additional, attractive
storage for small
utensils.

Often a large cupboard
under the sink unit is
merely a rather scruffy area
for cleaning materials, so
the smaller cupboard space
under the sink is no
disadvantage.

The roll-up door on the
corner wall unit is
another good idea and one
less door to bang your
head on.

▷ **Slide-in option**
Cutting off the angle and
tiling the walls between top
and bottom cupboards
is the corner solution in
this cheerful kitchen.

There is a space
between the units for a
slide-in cooker (the tiles
making a sensible
splashback). This is a less
expensive alternative to a
built-in hob and built-under
oven and incidentally allows
you a double rather than a
single oven.

The space above the
cooker hood is filled with a
small wall cupboard which
aligns with the rest of the
units.

▷ **Using every spare centimetre**
This tiny room uses the L arrangement to maximum effect and usefulness. All the essentials are neatly incorporated and every bit of space is made to work for its living, with storage cupboards and shelves taken to ceiling height and a sensible amount of cupboard and drawer area. And there is just enough room for a small table – both this and the chairs fold up when not in use to give the cook more room to work.

◁ **A family kitchen**
A working kitchen which is also a pleasant place for meals with family and friends. Here the 'business' area is confined to the window recess and along one wall. Elements such as the inlaid linoleum floor and a long cloth on the round table help to define the eating areas and give it a relaxed mood.

▽ **Room to entertain**
A dining area ideal for informal entertaining is created in the opposite corner of this pastel coloured, L-shaped kitchen.

THE U-SHAPED KITCHEN

This is probably the safest and most efficient of all kitchen layouts, offering maximum storage and workspace.

This arrangement, where units and appliances are ranged along three sides of a square or rectangle, is both functional and flexible. There is scope for choice in the positioning of work-tops and appliances as well as room for plenty of storage, often on at least two complete sides of the U-shape.

Size is less of an obstacle in creating a U-shaped kitchen than awkwardly-positioned doorways. In a true U-shaped kitchen no doors break up the line of work surfaces so that the cook is not disturbed by through traffic.

FIRST CONSIDERATIONS
The U-shape lends itself to the creation of an efficient work triangle whose sides should add up to between 4 and 7 metres. Too small a work triangle could feel claustrophobic; an over-long triangle involves extra walking.

A small kitchen can accommodate a successful U-shape although it is important to allow space for two people to use the kitchen at the same time – so you need a minimum of about 1½-2 metres of space between the legs of the U-Shape.

Larger kitchens More people seem to make mistakes with large rooms than with small ones. A spacious U-shape may give plenty of work surfaces but can give rise to an elongated work triangle; it's best to confine the triangle to the base of the U-shape.

Through view
A U-shaped kitchen, with a full complement of appliances, can be fitted into the smallest of rooms, Space-saving sliding doors and an open serving hatch separate this kitchen from the interconnecting living area.

△ Room for manoeuvre

This kitchen is wide enough to allow two cooks to work together and open a drawer, cupboard, oven or fridge and stand or bend down in front of them without banging into each other.

A lot of time in the kitchen is spent at the sink – even if you do have a dishwasher. By placing the sink underneath the window, the cook has a pleasant view while working – and a sunny yellow roller blind cuts out glare on hot summer days. Teamed with matching accessories, it also brightens up dark woodwork.

USING THE SPACE

Careful siting of appliances is important for an efficient and enjoyable layout – and the three-sided U-shape gives ample room for choice.

Follow the guidelines set out in Home Planner (pages 11-18) to find the ideal position for your sink, hob and oven, fridge and freezer, and other appliances. Apart from considering the work triangle, remember to think about plumbing requirements, access to power, and the need to allow space for doors to open comfortably.

The continuous run of the U-shape means that there is often room for a tall larder and broom cupboard. The usual rule applies, however; position them at the end of a run to avoid interrupting the work surface.

It is usually possible to fit in an eating area, even if it is only a bar with stools tucked under it along one leg of the U-shape. If this is separated from the work area by a tall unit, the bar could be at a lower level to suit children or elderly people.

BRIGHT IDEA

Smooth rollers A pair of special rollers under a slot-in appliance makes cleaning and repairs less of a chore by allowing you to roll the machine forward. The appliance must, of course, have sufficiently long and flexible water and power connections and there needs to be about 40-50mm above it for the added height.

◁ **A narrow U-shape**
In a relatively long and narrow room such as this, it's best to confine the work area to the base of the U-shape to avoid time-wasting journeys between the sink, hob and food preparation areas.

A work surface should not normally be broken up by tall cupboards or stacked appliances. In this kitchen, the fridge/freezer and a double oven are positioned at one end of the room, near the door.

▷ **A different arrangement**
This kitchen has been rearranged so that a separate fridge and freezer have been tucked under the worktop, replacing the breakfast bar. In addition, the double oven has been replaced by a single oven slotted in directly under the hob. This has freed space for two full-height cupboards, which could act as a broom store and a larder.

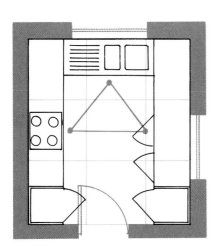

Scale: I square = I metre square

DIVIDING SPACE

A U-shaped kitchen is not necessarily self-contained. Often, the fourth wall which would close off the U-shape is absent, and instead the kitchen interconnects with another room.

Alternatively, a U-shaped kitchen can be linked to another room along one of its arms. Units can run along two walls, with the third arm making a room divider. The floor units which make up the room divider are best fitted with doors which open into both areas, with the worktop providing a convenient serving surface.

The area above the divider units can be left completely open, or open shelving or wall units can partly screen the cooking zone from a dining area. This also allows the cook to keep in touch with what is going on at the table.

∇ ▷ *Double use*
During the morning, this kitchen opens on to a breakfast area (below). Later in the day (right), the dishes are cleared away and the furniture moved aside to make room for a playpen. This practical arrangement allows a parent to prepare a meal while keeping a watchful eye on a child.

△ Breakfast bar
An extra wide worktop along one arm of the U-shape provides knee room for a breakfast bar.

◁ Extra storage
The installation of ceiling-hung units in the kitchen illustrated above greatly increases its storage capacity.

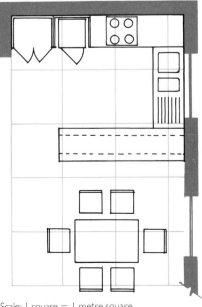

Scale: 1 square = 1 metre square

COPING WITH CORNERS

Making the best use of corners can be difficult in any kitchen and with a U-shaped layout you have two to deal with. When planning the basic layout, it is important to ensure that doors do not open into one another and that appliances are positioned at least 30 centimetres from a corner so that doors can be opened fully without banging into the wall.

Most manufacturers include corner units in their ranges – whether carousels for wall or base units or units with bi-fold doors.

▷ *A corner sink*
An unusual way of making full use of an awkward corner is to install a special sink that cuts across the corner. It's a good idea to install a strip light under the units above the sink.

▽ *Soft angles*
Corners can be used to advantage, as in this semi-circular kitchen. By angling the units and a cooker across the corners, the flow of the work surface is not interrupted. The interesting shape of the angular table adds to the visual interest and provides a useful working or breakfast table.

SINGLE LINE KITCHENS

Compact and easy to run, but often tight on space, single line kitchens need to be planned with ingenuity.

If your kitchen space is limited, a single line layout, where units and appliances are arranged along one wall, is often the most efficient arrangement. This layout is equally useful in a multi-purpose kitchen/dining/living room, as units and appliances can be neatly contained in one area, leaving the majority of the floor space free for dining and relaxing.

Cleverly planned, a single line kitchen can be as neat and work as well as a minute ship's galley. The road to success lies in allowing as much worktop space as possible, choosing the right units and appliances and having a flexible approach to storage.

PLANNING THE LAYOUT

The width of the room is a crucial factor in planning. You need floor space of about 1400mm so that you can move around comfortably and open doors.

Start your plan with the sink, which is best positioned in the centre of the single line, with the cooker and fridge at either end.

Ideally, there should be worktop space between the sink and appliances. If limited space means that this is impossible, place the draining side of

Perfectly plain
A single line layout is a good choice if you want to use the rest of the room for dining. Half-width doors on the wall cupboards save space when open and a laminated table such as the one shown here can double as an extra work surface if there is more than one cook.

the sink next to the cooker, so that you have somewhere to put down pans, and choose a fridge that slides under the worktop. A slide-in cooker with a pull-down glass top provides useful extra work space. Both the cooker and the fridge doors should open away from the sink for easy access. Most fridges and ovens are now sold with interchangeable hinges.

If you have a washing machine or dishwasher, tuck it underneath the draining side of the sink. This minimizes plumbing costs and means that it is quick and easy to transfer things from the sink to the machine.

Use the remaining space for base units. If possible, incorporate a larder unit with pull-out wire shelves or a carousel for storing small items. Fit an extractor in the space above the cooker between wall cupboards. If you have bought units with integral doors (special clip-ons which cover appliances), the extractor can blend into the run of cupboards. If not, look for a slimline pull-out extractor which can be positioned below a wall unit, or a standard extractor above which you can put open shelves or a cut-down cupboard.

A re-circulating charcoal filter extractor occupies less space than the ducted type where piping must be run through cupboards to the open air. If you can't afford an extractor, leave the space above the oven free, or add a couple of open shelves, starting halfway up the side of adjacent wall cupboards.

If a window interrupts the run, you could incorporate it in the overall design plan by hanging wall cupboards on either side, level with the top of the frame, then join them with a narrow overhead storage shelf. Make sure that wall cupboards allow good clearance of the work surface and check that all doors can be opened without them banging into each other.

THE CLASSIC SINGLE LINE KITCHEN

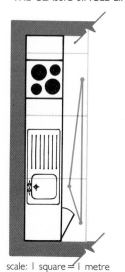

scale: 1 square = 1 metre

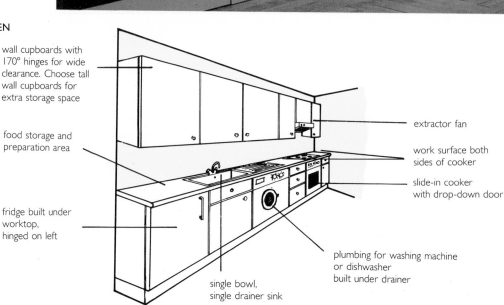

wall cupboards with 170° hinges for wide clearance. Choose tall wall cupboards for extra storage space

food storage and preparation area

fridge built under worktop, hinged on left

extractor fan

work surface both sides of cooker

slide-in cooker with drop-down door

plumbing for washing machine or dishwasher built under drainer

single bowl, single drainer sink

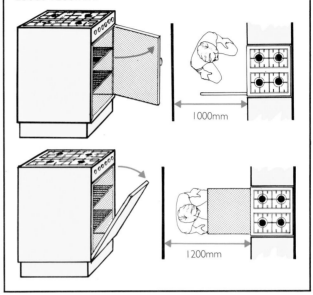

▽ *Oven door clearance*
Because you can stand at the side of a side-hinged oven door (below) you only need clearance of about 1000mm. You have to stand directly in front of a flap-down door (bottom), so allow slightly more room – about 1200mm.

1000mm

1200mm

◁ *Fully integrated*
This single line kitchen is part of a larger room; it has been planned to look good as well as work efficiently. The tall unit on the left houses the fridge, with two deep drawers underneath and a small cupboard above. The oven is built under the worktop with an inset hob above and an integrated pull-out extractor in the wall cupboard.

▽ *Built-under bonus*
Planned for maximum worktop space, there are no tall housing units in this alternative version of the same kitchen. The fridge, hinged on the left, fits under the worktop and the slide-in cooker has a toughened glass lid. A small cupboard with a work surface on top fits into the space between the cooker and end wall and is useful for putting down pans.

USING WALL SPACE

The wall facing the main run of units can also be put to good use. Narrow shelves, fitted from floor to ceiling, add invaluable extra storage space. For breakfast or light snacks, fix a hinged shelf to the wall which can be flapped up at mealtimes and folded back down against the wall to keep it out of the way when not in use. Folding chairs can lean or hang beneath the shelf when they are not needed.

CHOOSING APPLIANCES

In most single line kitchens there is not much space for appliances, so shop around for those which will work well in a limited area. Starting with the kitchen sink, there are dozens of shapes and sizes and some of the latest ranges of accessories are designed to make the most of space. Look for chopping boards and drainer baskets that fit over the sink. For a neat, streamlined look, go for an inset model in which the drainer is an integral part of the unit and choose a colour which matches the surrounding worktop.

If you have a dishwasher, you may be able to do without a draining board. Instead, fit a single inset sink with a draining rack or, if there is room, a pair of inset bowls, one with a waste disposal unit.

The new slide-in cookers are neater than the old-fashioned raised back models and are designed to match units at plinth and worktop level. A slide-in model is cheaper and takes up less space than a split-level separate oven and hob. Multi-fuel slide-ins, with a gas hob and electric oven, and models with halogen or ceramic hobs are available.

Some microwaves can be mounted between wall units and worktops – a great space saver in a single line kitchen. A microwave is a useful addition to any kitchen but it should not be seen as a replacement for a conventional oven unless it offers radiant and convected heat as well as microwaves.

▷ *Space at a premium*
As well as the usual kitchen appliances, a washing machine had to be fitted into this tiny kitchen. Tall wall cupboards stretch right up to the ceiling, making use of every inch of available space. The only practical place for the cooker was to the immediate right of the fridge (out of picture), so a slide-in model with extra insulation was chosen.

△ *Folding steps*
Maximizing storage space in a narrow kitchen often means that some shelves and cupboards are out of reach. Instead of balancing on a chair or ledge, keep some folding steps handy. These can be hung from a hook on the wall or slipped into a gap between units when folded down after use.

◁ **Pull-out larder**
Maximize the potential of cupboards with slide-out shelves. Here a pull-out larder unit is incorporated into a run of units under the worktop. Accessible from both sides, there is room for large bottles at the bottom, while smaller items can be kept in a shallow wire tray at the top.

With minimal cupboard space, storage must be organized efficiently. A small kitchen is no place for clutter, so store little used items in cupboards, keeping only what's absolutely essential close at hand.

▽ **Breakfast bar**
There is not enough room to fit any cupboards along the right hand side of this sunny yellow kitchen which has been brightened up with splashes of green.

Instead, a breakfast bar made from a narrow length of work surface to match the kitchen is attached to the wall by a hinge. This runs along the entire length so that it can be folded down against the wall when not in use.

▷ **Wall-mounted boiler**
Central heating boilers are no longer as large and cumbersome as they used to be. Neat, balanced flue boilers now come in a range of colours and styles, designed to fit between or be concealed inside wall cupboards.

▽ **Vegetable store**
The gap at the end of a run of floor units can be left open to accommodate a plastic-coated wire vegetable rack. If it is fitted with castors it can be easily pulled in and out.

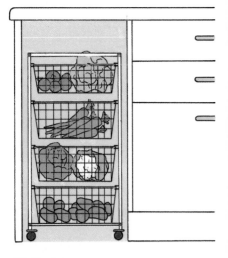

▽ **Useful space**
A small space between wall cupboards can be fitted with shelves, and a space between base units provides a tidy spot for trays. White walls and units with accessories picked out in a stronger colour make a kitchen feel spacious.

BRIGHT IDEA

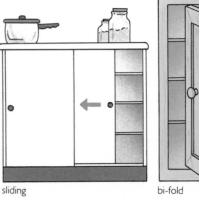

sliding   bi-fold

SPACE SAVING DOORS
When it comes to kitchen doors, side-hinged are not the only choice.
Bi-fold doors, hinged in the middle, fold back on themselves to allow access to the whole cupboard.
Sliding doors take up even less room. Fixed on a pair of parallel runners, one slides alongside the other, giving access to half the cupboard at a time.
   Other solutions include roller doors which slide up and over the top of the cupboard or use roller blinds to cover base units.

ISLAND KITCHENS

Best suited to larger rooms, a central island can become the functional heart of the kitchen.

An island kitchen is a U or L-shaped kitchen with an additional 'bit in the middle'. Purists would argue that the island ought to be a permanent and fixed feature but in practice a table or large trolley can serve as an island.

The work triangle in an island kitchen can be very compact as the various services can be located close to each other. You can position the cooker, fridge or sink at the island although often the need to bring the necessary services (gas or electricity, and water) from the sides of the room may affect the choice.

Finding the space Island kitchens are not suitable for very small rooms. Generally they are spacious, with room all the way round the island to allow cupboard doors both on the island and on the facing run of base units to open easily. A conventional island is about 1200× 1200mm square, and the minimum size is about 600×900mm. Too large an island can involve a lot of unnecessary walking, but if the kitchen isn't large enough to accommodate even a small island, it may be possible to enlarge the room, perhaps by combining the kitchen and scullery or larder.

However, an island can often be successfully fitted into a smaller room. Such islands generally serve as work-tops only, with no permanent services attached. While a large room can accommodate a standard square or rectangular island, a specially designed curved or irregular-shaped island may be more suitable for a room in which space is at a premium.

In addition to the actual surface of the island, it's important to think about the areas above and below. Both can be designed to enhance the 'look' of the room as well as providing useful and accessible storage space. It is also sometimes possible to slot an appliance underneath the island worktop, and a cooker hood above an island hob is extremely useful for removing cooking smells.

A classic island

The irregularly-shaped central island in this kitchen houses both the hob and a second sink. With a large work surface, storage below and a cooker hood above, such an island can become the focal point of the kitchen.

THE ISLAND WORKTOP

The top of the island can include a hob or a sink – or it can serve purely as an extra work surface, perhaps incorporating a breakfast bar.

Connecting the services almost always means that the existing floorcovering has to be lifted so that gas, electricity and water pipes and cables can be brought to the island from the sides of the room. The connections can be run across a concrete floor before the final screed is laid, or chased into the existing screed. So long as a timber floor has sufficient depth below, services can be installed underneath.

Electricity is the simplest service to install, and allows a fridge, hob, cooker hood, and small electrical appliances to be used on the island. In contrast, if you install a sink, it needs both a supply of fresh water and an outlet to remove the waste.

A simple island can provide valuable extra working space, perhaps with special features such as an inset chopping board or marble surface for rolling out pastry.

Most islands are made to the standard height of 900mm. But if you find that this is not always ideal when you are stirring the contents of a casserole or kneading bread, for example, you can install an island at a different height.

△ *A family kitchen*
Originally, this kitchen was very small – extra space has been created by knocking two rooms into one to accommodate an island and a family breakfast bar.

The hob is located on a side wall making room on the island for a barbecue grill and a large food preparation area. The space below the worktop houses a fridge and a wine rack along with drawers and cupboards.

△ **A worktop island**
Providing an island with a gas or electricity supply can be troublesome and expensive, so it's often best to use a new island only as a worktop.

Here, the breakfast bar in the kitchen on the far left has been replaced by a more substantial dining table and the island serves both as a serving area and a working surface. The wine rack below the island is particularly useful for dinner parties.

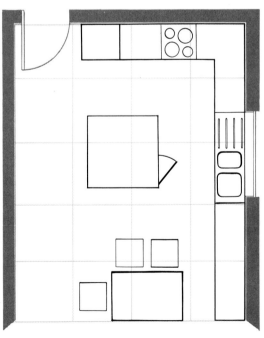

Scale: 1 square = 1 metre square

BRIGHT IDEA

A self-opening rubbish bin This ingenious rubbish bin is mounted on the inside of a cupboard door so that the lid is opened and closed by a cord when the door is opened or closed.

◁ **Country pine**
An island need not be custom-built. This pine island has been constructed from four single base units placed back to back and finished off with end panels. The worktop includes a gas hob and an electric deep fryer and hotplate.

▽ **A movable island**
The trolley in this kitchen makes a movable island, and it is ideal for small as well as more spacious kitchens. The solid maple chopping surface should give years of service, and the vegetable basket, drawer and storage shelf provide a useful place to keep fresh foods and implements. Mounted on four locking castors, the trolley can be moved out of the way when not required.

PLANNING A TINY KITCHEN

Squeezing equipment, storage and worktops into a small kitchen demands forethought and meticulous planning

Nowhere is planning more critical than when designing a tiny – as opposed to a restricted or small – kitchen. Squeezing in enough working and storage space can pose a real ingenuity test. While time-saving appliances are essential, they come in fixed sizes and no amount of wishful thinking can shave off extra centimetres!

So plan! Start with your priorities. How will you use your kitchen? For quick preparation of mainly pre-packed meals? Or are you a keen cook who enjoys home-cooked food? How many people must be catered for? Is entertaining a priority?

Next, list the appliances and utensils you already own and those you intend to buy. Then stand back and study the space available. Start at the door – get rid of it if you can, or install a sliding door to save vital floor space. Can you remove all or part of a wall so that the kitchen opens on to the dining area?

In all probability the majority of kitchen catalogues will set you dreaming but provide little practical help; every-thing is just a bit too big. You can order specially-designed and built units, but this solution is expensive.

So try a different approach. Buy some boating or caravanning magazines and write off for some of the sales literature on offer. You will be surprised at the space-saving ideas featured in their galleys.

From this study you will learn one critical lesson: everything in your tiny kitchen must have a purpose. There is no room for frills or frippery. But that does not mean that it must be a dreary room. Good design and good planning can make the tiniest kitchen a pleasant and attractive room in which to work.

An open-plan kitchen
Removing the door into a small kitchen saves space. The entrance to this kitchen, which leads on to a dining area, has also been enlarged.

STYLE ON A SMALL SCALE

Aim for clean, open lines in your tiny kitchen so as to create an illusion of greater space. 'Sleek' and 'streamlined' are good descriptions to keep in mind.

Keep colours light: dark wood finishes are fine in a large kitchen but can easily overpower a tiny space. Similarly, decorate the walls to blend rather than contrast with worktops and units. The room will appear larger as a result. Integral doors which fit over appliance fronts (except for cookers) are available in most ranges.

To prevent blandness creeping in, you can highlight the details (such as

handles or trims) in contrasting colours.

A fully-tiled kitchen is easy to keep clean – an important consideration as walls tend to get dirtier in a confined space. Avoid tiles with strong patterns – instead choose subtle striped effects or gently-mottled designs. Rectangular tiles laid widthways across a narrow floor will give the appearance of width.

Use lighting to increase the feeling of space: dark corners crowd in on you. Strong overhead lighting is essential but try to avoid casting harsh shadows. Wall-mounted spots concentrate the glow where it is needed and work surfaces can be lit by strip lighting

△ *Sleek and streamlined*

An all-white colour scheme creates clean and simple lines in this narrow, corridor-like kitchen. A space-saving, skirting-board-high central heating radiator warms the room without disturbing the streamlined effect.

hidden beneath wall units.

If your list of priorities includes the need for maximum worktops, covers for the sink and cooker hob can add vital work space. Again, such covers will add to the unbroken surfaces in your tiny kitchen, enhancing that all-important feeling of space.

△ Hi-tech kitchen

This kitchen breaks all the rules by using only strong, vibrant colours – apple green, buttercup yellow and vivid red – in a compact room. Although this bright colour scheme may not be to everyone's taste, there is no quibbling with the dramatic effect!

Rubber stud flooring provides an eminently practical worktop and wallcovering. The shelving, constructed from metal and plastic industrial systems, is infinitely flexible.

▷ Simple lines

Finding sufficient storage space is nowhere more important than in a small kitchen. Here, wall units almost to the ceiling make the most of the height of the room, and useful midway units keep spice jars and cooking utensils within easy reach.

STORAGE AND APPLIANCES

Fitting all the basic equipment into a tiny kitchen is a problem in itself; finding space for today's time-saving gadgets as well as a well-stocked larder is a real challenge!

Appliances and fittings A sink of practical dimensions is a must. An empty space-saving sink in a showroom or catalogue can look capacious, but will it hold even a modest number of pots?

If your tiny kitchen is a place for the preparation of quick meals you may well want to include a microwave. A combination oven – the latest microwave technology – can function as both a microwave and a normal convector oven. Some even have two hotplates on top, to replace a cooker hob.

Fridges in tiny kitchens still need to be roomy enough to store sensible quantities of food. Anything less than 133 litres of space is probably only sufficient for one person. Look for a fridge with a 3- or 4-star frozen food compartment. Carefully loaded, a fridge this size will store a surprising amount of food.

You may have to share your tiny kitchen with a washing machine. There's little choice in machine sizes, but most models will fit beneath the draining board. A combined washer/drier saves space. Although a dishwasher will take up valuable space, it is well worthwhile in a tiny kitchen, not least because it provides a place to store dirty dishes.

Time-saving small appliances are always tempting, but they only save time if they are readily to hand and they do occupy valuable worktop space. So keep temptation at bay and settle for the essentials: a food processor, electric kettle and toaster, say.

Storage will be a continual problem and every square centimetre must be utilized. Start by choosing units with pull-out racks, carousels and door-mounted storage space. Assess the height of items to be stored in wall units: extra open shelves can almost always be added to increase storage capacity.

Consider a waste disposal unit in the sink to do away with bulky rubbish bins and look, too, at midway units which store spice jars, mugs and other odds and ends.

Hanging utensils on wall-mounted racks in that midway space is another space-saving idea, leaving cupboards free for less-frequently used items. Ceiling racks are fine if ceilings are high, but they can cause claustrophobia and bumped heads in a room of only average height.

Above all, avoid clutter. Keep only what is absolutely essential near at hand. If you follow this rule your tiny kitchen will serve you well.

△ **A cover for a hob**
Conventional hobs disrupt the continuity of worktops, unless they are placed in a corner. One way of creating an unbroken line of working space is to choose a model which comes with an integral cover. On this electric model, the cover is hinged so that it can easily be pulled down when the hob is not in use.

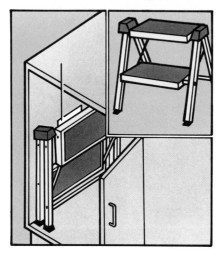

△ **Folding steps**
Steps are essential if the cook is to reach up to high shelves. These sturdy steps come with a fixing bracket so that they can be stored inside a base unit.

△ **Wall-mounting a microwave oven**
A microwave oven can be hung on the wall at a convenient height (using a specially-designed bracket) to free valuable worktop space below.

△ **Tidy cutlery**
A two-tier cutlery drawer such as the one shown here keeps cutlery and utensils tidy and gives you twice the storage space in a single drawer.

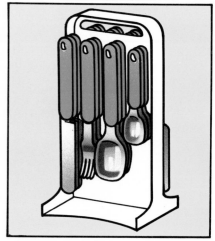

△ **Hanging cutlery**
A cutlery stand can hold a 24-piece cutlery set. Such stands are available in plastic or wood, and the cutlery handles come in various colours.

△ **Multi-purpose sink**
This sink incorporates a full-sized bowl and draining board; a second, water-saving stepped bowl; and a drainer which sits across the main bowl (above,

right) or in the upper section of the stepped bowl. A special chopping board can be slotted over the sink or draining board when these are not in use – its lipped edge protects the sink

from damage. To keep worktops uncluttered, the chopping board is stored flat against the wall. (Chopping boards which slot over standard sinks are also available.)

△ **Cup hooks**
Cups and mugs are difficult to stack neatly on a shelf – instead, screw a strip of cup hooks or individual hooks under wall units or in the wall itself.

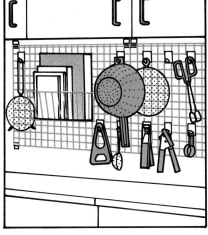

△ **Wall grid**
Made from strong plastic-coated wire, a wall grid fits into the space between wall and base units to keep utensils – even cookery books – close to hand.

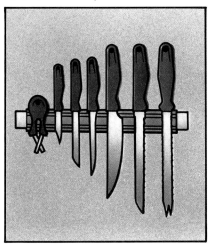

△ **Magnetic knife rack**
A wall-mounted magnetic strip stores kitchen knives neatly, near at hand and safely out of the way. Your knives will keep sharper than if stored in a drawer.

△ **Under-sink storage**
A metal basket which runs on sliding rails fitted to the unit door provides organized storage beneath a sink. Rubber wheels prevent scratching.

△ **A plinth drawer**
This neat, pull-out drawer makes use of the usually dead space in the plinth below base units by providing storage for small, infrequently-used items.

△ **Storage behind cupboard doors**
Pegboard fixed to the inside of a wall unit door can be used to hang utensils from hooks. In larger spaces, special plastic baskets can be used.

WAYS WITH DOORS

Hinged doors, by their very nature, take up space when open and in the tiny kitchen this can be a hazard as well as inconvenient. Dispense with them altogether wherever possible or consider installing sliding or bifold doors.

If you feel you must have a door into the kitchen, try to hinge it so that it opens out of the room. This saves valuable floor space in the kitchen and can prevent an accident if someone enters unexpectedly and bumps into the cook who may be manoeuvring hot pans.

A sliding door is a compromise, but the door must still go somewhere and this requires wall space to house it when open. (Sliding doors for base and wall units are also available.) A better choice might be bifold doors which are hinged down the centre. When opened, the door closes back on itself so that it takes up half the space of a standard door.

▽ **Sliding doors**
Sliding doors close off this kitchen (and the bathroom behind) and waste minimal space since the doors slide along tracks mounted in the corridor.

△ **A folding division**
Concertina-style folding doors can be kept fully closed or open, or partially closed to act as a partition between a small kitchen and a dining area.

▽ **Bifold cupboard doors**
Where sliding doors cannot be installed, bifold doors can provide a space-saving solution since the door can be folded back on itself.

KITCHEN STORAGE

One of the secrets of successful storage is to have the right space available for the objects you want to store.

KITCHEN STORAGE CHECKLIST
- [ ] Canned and packet foods
- [ ] Fresh and frozen foods
- [ ] Pots, pans, utensils
- [ ] Electrical equipment
- [ ] Ovenware
- [ ] China and glassware
- [ ] Table linen
- [ ] Cutlery
- [ ] Plastic bags, foil, clingfilm
- [ ] Tea and hand towels
- [ ] Washing up materials
- [ ] Empty jars and bottles
- [ ] Rubbish bin
- [ ] Cleaning materials/implements

Planning kitchen storage can be difficult. All too often, it's a question of trying to fit a quart into a pint pot so start by making a checklist of the items you want to store. This enables you to make the best use of the available space in order to create a tidy, well-ordered kitchen that is a pleasure to use and pleasant to look at.

All in all, there are four basic areas which can provide storage space. Wall units are hung on the walls above work surfaces. The space between these two can be filled with various forms of midway units and shelves. Below the worktop, base units contain cupboard and shelf space, often for bulky or heavy items. And finally, don't forget the ceiling. As long as it's high enough, rarely-used items can generally find a home here.

As a general rule, frequently-used items should be stored close at hand. Things which you use only rarely can be stored high up or low down, but avoid keeping bulky or heavy items too high up, too low down, or in very deep cupboards or shelves.

Combined storage
In a small kitchen, careful planning of storage is essential if everything is to be fitted in. Here a combination of cupboards, drawers and open shelves make use of all the available space. An entire wall fitted with shelves and cup hooks provides a home for decorative and everyday crockery.

△ *A place for everything*
This spacious and streamlined kitchen includes a well-chosen mixture of base and wall units, midway storage space and even a ceiling shelf, as well as several special features.

Look, for example, at the special corner shelves for both base and wall units. These take full advantage of space that might otherwise be lost and they are also rounded so if you bump into them it is less painful.

And doors fitted over the end of the base units in the foreground create a shallow cupboard – for storing spices, perhaps.

THE RIGHT COMBINATION

Whatever the size of your kitchen, careful planning can help you to find a home for everything. In fact, a huge kitchen isn't necessarily an advantage – think of all the extra miles you could clock up during the year! Rather, you should aim to make every single inch of space work to your advantage.

This way, you'll achieve a maximum of storage room without making the room look cluttered or too functional and clinical.

Wall and base units are the backbone of most kitchen storage systems. To accommodate pots and pans as well as small dishes, kitchen units should incorporate a mixture of shelves and drawers, both deep and narrow. Adjustable shelves allow you to change the structure of your storage system over time.
Wall units As most people can reach only the first and second shelves in their wall units, use this area to store everyday china and glass or frequently-used cans and packets of food. The higher shelves can be used for items such as

preserving jars in use only once or twice a year.

It's best to choose wall units which are slightly shallower than the worktop beneath so that you don't hit your head if you lean forward. Cupboards should always be installed over a counter, though, and never over an empty space – the danger of walking into such cupboards is all too real.

Where space is tight, narrow wire shelves can be attached to the back of wall unit doors and used to store small objects. The baskets must be fitted so that they slot into the space between the cupboard shelves when the door is closed. High baskets are difficult to reach into, so use only the lower half of the cupboard door.

Leaving some areas open to view makes the contents easy to get hold of but can mean extra dusting.

A grid system along the wall can incorporate such gadgets as a knife rack, somewhere to hang often-needed utensils, and perhaps even a useful paper towel holder.

◁ **Drip-dry storage**
The old-fashioned scullery idea of having a large built-in plate rack so you just wash up things and pop them straight into their drainage/storage place still has a role to play.

The drainage area is positioned over the sink, and is topped and flanked by open shelving. Cupboards and drawers below the work surface complete the storage system.

▽ **The right mixture**
All the wall units here are slightly shallower than the base units and worktop below. Note how the central shelves are even shallower than their neighbouring cupboards so that extra headroom space is created over the sink. They also make the run of units look less overwhelming.

MIDWAY UNITS

These are designed to make use of the space between worktop and wall units. Most manufacturers offer a range of midways; or you can adapt their ideas.

Wire grids are used with butchers' hooks to hang utensils. Some grid systems are fitted with baskets and shelves. You can make your own cut-price grid by hanging a wire cake cooling tray on the wall.

Hanging rail A chrome or wooden rail suspended under units can be used to hang utensils, wire baskets, sieves and other odds and ends. Make your own rail from a length of dowel or piping.

Shelves Narrow midway shelves are useful for herbs, spices and other frequently-used ingredients. Fix cup hooks under the shelves, or buy some slide-on under-shelf containers to make maximum use of space.

Boxes Manufacturers offer both open and closed midway storage boxes. Some have interior fittings, such as plastic compartments for storing ingredients.

△ A variety of solutions
The planners of this kitchen have incorporated several different types of midway units. Clear plastic storage drawers make it easy to find the right ingredient. Gleaming copper pots hang on a rail above the worktop, and knives are always to hand over the chopping block. A wire rack over the sink completes the range of midway units.

◁ Adding on
Midway units can often be added on to an existing set of wall units. Here ready-made shelves, complete with side brackets, provide a home for condiments, candlesticks and jars. Wooden pegs below can take mugs and cups.
 Such shelves can be very narrow. A depth of only about 10cm will take mugs and small jars; wider shelves can hold larger items.

◁ Custom-made shelves
Special-purpose midway storage is relatively easy to construct yourself, although some manufacturers do offer a wide range of units.
 Here, a midway shelf houses an electric mixer together with its attachments, as well as a useful cookery book holder.

BELOW THE WORKTOP

Kitchen base units house things of many different shapes and sizes, so it makes sense to have a combination of cupboards, drawers of different depths and open shelves, rather than a uniform row of cupboards and drawers.

Open shelves accommodate pots and pans in daily use, and if you have small children who play in the kitchen, a deep open shelf can hold a toy box. A narrow open space can be used to store serving or baking trays, or fit a telescopic rail for hanging towels.

Base cupboards Pull-out wire baskets mean that you can easily see – and reach – the contents of deep cupboards. There is a storage basket to suit most needs: under-sink baskets, vegetable storage baskets of different sizes, and bottle baskets. Deep shelves are not ideal for base cupboards as objects tend to get pushed to the back.

Corner base units generally incorporate a revolving carousel for storing things in the angle of the corner.

◁ *Shelve it*
Shelves of standard depth cupboards have to be fairly far apart to enable you to reach objects right at the back. But you can pack as much on to narrow shelves which are spaced closer together to allow for only a single pile of dishes or cups. This way, you gain more floor space.

△ *Below the plinth*
Enterprising kitchen manufacturers use the plinth space beneath base units as a miniature drawer. It is useful for storing tins, baking trays, shoe cleaning materials or a small 'essentials' toolbox containing, perhaps, spare fuses, fuse wire, a screwdriver and torch.

USING THE CEILING

Don't ignore the ceiling in your search for extra storage space. A hanging rack or rail, or a high shelf, can accommodate a surprising number of pots and pans.

Always check that it does not interfere with headroom.

◁ *Room at the top*
Here, utensils not in daily use stand on top of wall units and an extra shelf neatly stores a row of preserve jars. Keep a pair of folding steps handy – don't risk standing on chairs.

▽ *Hanging storage*
A rack suspended by chains from a crossbeam or joist provides valuable extra storage space. Ready-made racks are available, or you can make your own from lengths of piping or broom handles, plus butchers' hooks.

BASIC FITTED KITCHEN UNITS

The right combination of units is the key to a successful kitchen.

A fitted kitchen means that all or nearly all available space is used for storage, with no obvious gaps between units. It is a dramatic contrast to the old-fashioned type of kitchen which might have a sink, a table, a cooker, a refrigerator and one or two cupboards – all as separate items. A fully-fitted kitchen consists of matching wall and floor cupboards, incorporating a sink and oven with electrical appliances under a continuous worktop. (The most popular choice of cooking appliances in this type of kitchen is a split-level oven/grill in a tall housing unit and a separate hob set into a base unit.)

Base units The basis of a fitted kitchen is the base unit. This is usually 600mm deep (from front to back) and 600mm wide (side to side). This is known as the standard 600mm module.

Domestic appliances are now made to fit the 600mm module size as well, but when planning you often need to allow for a slight gap for washing machines and tumble driers (for vibration) and for refrigerators and free-standing cookers (for air circulation).

Apart from the 600mm module, there are many variations in size. For example, you can buy single base units 200mm, 300mm, 400mm and 500mm wide, double base units 1000mm or 1200mm wide, or triple width base units 1500 to 1800mm wide. These are all generally 600mm deep.

Once you have the basic unit you then need a worktop to go on top and a plinth for the units to stand on. The plinth is usually 100 or 150mm high although you can get lower or higher plinths if you are particularly short or tall. Once assembled, the unit (generally 850mm high) will give you a working area of around 900mm in height. Base units are floorstanding but should also be screwed to the wall and to each other.

Tall units These also stand on the floor, but are taller – designed to be used as broom cupboards, larder units or for housing appliances, especially split-level ovens. A typical tall unit suitable as larder/broom cupboard or for housing an oven stands around 2000mm high (600mm wide, 600mm deep).

Wall units should be fixed to the wall above the worktop and are generally around half the depth of base units so you don't hit your head on them when using the work surface below. They are available in widths and heights from 200-1000mm. Before buying wall units decide whether you want them to go right up to the ceiling – taller units are usually more expensive, whereas standard units may leave you with wasted space above.

If you have tall units in your kitchen, standard wall units are generally positioned so that all the tops line up. If there are no tall cupboards, you need a gap of about 450mm between the top of the worktop and the bottom of the wall units – for practicality's sake.

Both base and wall units come in versions which fit into a corner.

Materials There is a wide choice of materials for kitchen units. Generally, the carcases and shelves of units are made from chipboard faced with melamine. Doors and drawer fronts (fascias) and sometimes the exposed end panels are made of other decorative materials:

☐ Solid wood (mainly pine and oak, but other woods available).

☐ Wood veneer (thin wood strips glued to chipboard – less expensive than solid wood, but similar in finished appearance).

☐ Wood/plastic laminate mixture (mainly white, coloured or textured melamine laminate with wood trims and handles).

☐ Plastic laminate (white or coloured, plain, textured or wood-effect) such as melamine or the popular brand Formica. There are also lacquer, polyester and other special finishes.

Worktops Chipboard faced with plastic laminate is the most popular choice, but other options include hardwood, ceramic tiles, quarry tiles, granite, marble, or a solid man-made stone-like material such as Corian.

BASE UNITS

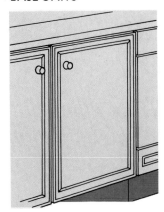

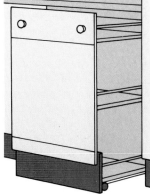

STANDARD UNITS
Style Floorstanding cupboards with one, two or three doors depending on the width of the unit.
In use Base units come in two styles – plain and drawerline. Plain units have full-height doors; drawerline units have drawers at the top. Single unit doors can be hinged on the left or the right.
Watchpoint High-quality units offer a choice of shelf positions, unit bottoms are coated with a sealant to prevent moisture swelling the chipboard, adjustable feet keep the carcase off the floor and there are additional supports in the centre of long shelves.

DRAWER UNITS
Style Available in the same sizes as standard units, drawer units consist entirely of drawers.
In use A good number of drawers in a kitchen is useful and a drawer unit should always be incorporated especially if plain – no drawerline – base units are used. Most drawer units have three or four drawers; pan drawers have two deep drawers – the whole unit including drawers, fascia, and sometimes the plinth fascia too, pulls out for maximum access – particularly suited for storing saucepans.
Watchpoint Check that the drawers open and close smoothly.

L-shaped corner unit

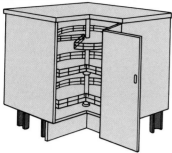

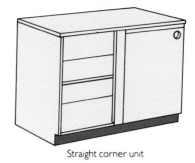

Straight corner unit

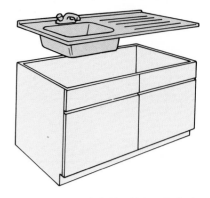

CORNER UNITS

Style A base unit which is designed to fit into a corner between two meeting runs of units.

In use There are two types of corner unit. The L-shaped corner unit has open shelves or a double-hinged door so the entire contents of the shelves can be seen. Often fitted with swing-out shelves. Alternatively there is a straight corner unit. This is a double unit with only one door – the other half of the unit is just open shelves. The adjacent units then fit against the open half. With the shelf removed, this type of corner cupboard is often fitted with a carousel (see opposite).

SINK UNITS

Style A unit for a kitchen sink.

In use Sit-on sink/drainers (usually stainless steel) are designed to sit directly on one of these units. Such a sink also incorporates a lip which runs along the front of the unit and a narrow 'splashback' along the back. A sink unit doesn't usually have a central shelf, as the space is needed for the plumbing. A drawerline sink unit has only one real drawer under the drainer, plus a dummy drawer in front of the bowl.

TALL UNITS

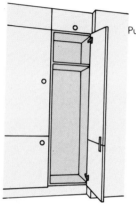

Pull-out larder unit

BROOM CUPBOARDS

Style A tall cupboard for storing cleaning equipment.

In use Broom cupboards are generally 300-600mm wide and may incorporate one or two shelves and have one or two doors. Usually tall enough for brooms and mops and often used for storing vacuum cleaners and small kitchen steps.

Watchpoint Some have two doors which both have to be opened to take out large items.

LARDER UNITS

Style A tall cupboard used for storing food.

In use Some look like a broom cupboard – only the shelves are closer together. Others are pull-out larder units which have wire racks attached to the door fascia so the whole interior slides out on runners.

Watchpoint They don't usually have any vents in them for fresh air to circulate, so should not be used for perishable food.

APPLIANCE HOUSING UNITS

Style A tall cupboard for domestic appliances – typically single or double ovens.

In use Although you can get housing units for 'single' ovens to 'slide under' a worktop, most people opt for a tall unit – 600mm wide – to take a single or double oven (and perhaps a microwave) so they are positioned further off the ground. Cupboards above and below the appliance provide space for storing pots and pans.

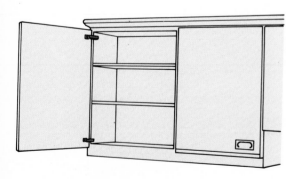

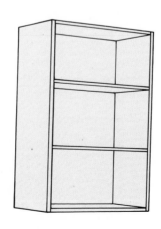

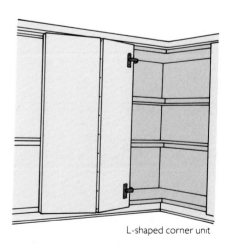

L-shaped corner unit

STANDARD UNITS

Style The standard wall unit is a single or double cupboard 500mm or 1000mm wide, fitted with one or two shelves and doors (plain or glazed).

In use Two heights of wall cupboard are generally available – standard (600mm high to match the tops of tall wall units) and extra-height (900mm), which are suitable to go right up to the ceiling. As with base units, other widths are available and single-unit doors can open either way.

OPEN SHELVES

Style Plain shelves designed to be installed in a run of wall units. Rounded shelves for the end of a run of units are another option.

In use They are also available with gallery rails which not only look decorative, but are also handy to secure display plates and special tableware.

CORNER UNITS

Style A wall unit that is designed to fit into a corner between two adjacent runs of units.

In use As with base corner units, two styles are available – straight and L-shaped.

Watchpoint Check which way the cupboard doors open and whether this is going to be convenient and safe in use.

KITCHEN UNIT EXTRAS

These additional fitments make a basic fitted kitchen more convenient.

Once your kitchen layout has been designed and the base, wall and tall units chosen, there is a whole range of extras which can be fitted in, on or under the basic units to make a kitchen easier or more efficient to use.

Most of these extras are additional compartments for storage of one sort or another; racks, drawers, bins, and so on. Others are hide-away fitments, such as ironing boards, tables, mixer support plinths or book rests.

Even matching cornices and pelmets are available to provide the finishing touches to your kitchen.

EXTRAS FOR BASE UNITS

TOWEL RAILS
Style The odd gap or space between cupboards in a run of base units is almost inevitable. Make use of this space by fitting a telescopic towel rail to the underside of the worktop over the space.
In use Ideally this should be positioned as close to the sink as possible.

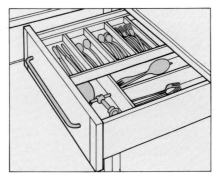

CUTLERY TRAYS
Style All ranges of kitchen units offer divided cutlery tray inserts to fit into drawers.
In use This helps you keep cutlery neat and tidy. Look out for the double-decker inserts – these are two-tier, allowing you to store twice as much without everything becoming jumbled together.

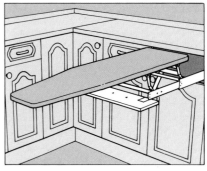

IRONING BOARDS
Style A pull-out ironing board for *in situ* ironing, hidden behind a dummy drawer-front.
In use Not usually as large or as easy to use as a freestanding ironing board.

WASTE BINS
Style In a fitted kitchen, there is often no space for a separate waste bin. A fitted bin positioned on the back of a cupboard door opens automatically when the door is opened. There is also one which fits into a deep drawer.
In use Takes up space within a cupboard.

BASKETS
Style There are many types of wire baskets and racks which fit on to the back of opening cupboard doors or into the cupboard itself.
In use Choose from those which hang like shelves, pull-out on runners like drawers, or just stack.

PULL-OUTS
Style A door-fronted unit which has all-wood, old-fashioned drawers – called pull-outs – in it.
In use These are much more expensive than ordinary drawer units.

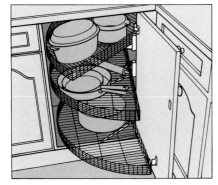

CAROUSELS
Style A semi-circular, plastic-coated wire tray which fits on the inside of the opening door of a straight corner cupboard (see Options 101-102).
In use Generally more suited to storing things which are light in weight.

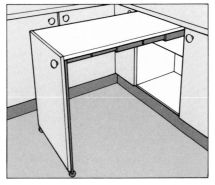

PULL-OUT TABLES
Style There are various styles. This one fits behind a dummy door fitted with castors. The whole unit pulls out on telescopic rails.
In use Provides a useful table or extra surface, pulls out to a maximum of the worktop's width.

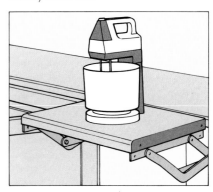

MIXER SUPPORTS
Style Full-size table mixers can be extremely heavy to get out of a cupboard.
In use A mixer support provides a solution – this is a spring-loaded table which swings up for use and away again into the base unit.

WINE STORAGE
Style Wine racks are often available as alternatives to base units.
In use Typically, one rack fits into a 300mm space – two fit side-by-side in a unit. Bottles are stored on their sides.

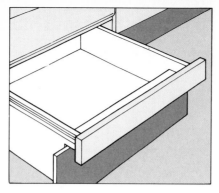

PLINTH DRAWERS
Style Special drawers which fit into the space under kitchen units.
In use Ideal for under-oven storage for baking tins and roasting trays.
   Also look out for a neat two-step ladder which fits into the plinth space – excellent for reaching high wall cupboards.

DECOR PANELS
Style Many appliances, such as dishwashers and fridges can be fitted with these fronts so that they blend in with rest of kitchen units.
In use They clip over the appliance's existing doors. Decor panels are only available for certain ranges of fitted kitchens.

OPEN SHELVES
Style A rounded open-shelving unit that fits at the end of a run of units.
In use These provide additional storage as well as being a neat way of finishing off the run.

SMALLER DETAILS
When planning a kitchen, don't forget to consider future requirements for the services and the smaller accessories which add the finishing touches.
- ☐ With the number of appliances in an average kitchen, it is a good idea wherever possible to have a separate socket circuit for the kitchen.
- ☐ Fit as many socket outlets as possible – certainly no less than eight (four doubles) for an average-size kitchen – not including switched spur outlets for fixed appliances such as an electric cooker.
- ☐ Under-cupboard lights to illuminate worksurfaces.
- ☐ Cooker hoods or extractor fans.
- ☐ Dummy drawer fronts to conceal pull-out fittings such as ironing boards or foldaway tables or to disguise gaps between units.
- ☐ Cornicing and architraves to match your units.
- ☐ Extras for worktops such as inset sinks or hobs, ceramic tile inserts for hot pans, or marble or Corian inserts as pastry slabs.

OTHER ACCESSORIES

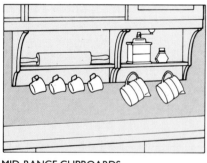

MID-RANGE CUPBOARDS
Style Designed to fit in the wall space between base units and wall units.
In use Can be open shelves or have sliding doors – very useful for small jars, bottles and items which would get lost in a large cupboard.

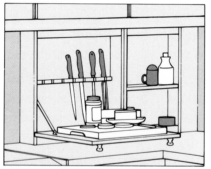

MID-RANGE CHOPPING BOARDS
Style A chopping board which folds away when not in use with a special rack behind for storing knives and cooking implements.
In use Handy – as these larger chopping boards are usually heavy and awkward to store.

TALL UNIT FITTINGS
Style Some of the most useful extras you can buy for a tall unit are purpose-made, plastic-coated wire brackets or hooks for storing ironing boards, vacuum cleaners and accessories, saucepan lids, etc.
In use Most of these are readily available from sources other than the kitchen unit manufacturer, such as hardware and cookware shops.

EXTRAS FOR WALL UNITS

OPEN SHELVES
Style Rounded shelves which are wall-hung and finish off runs of wall units.

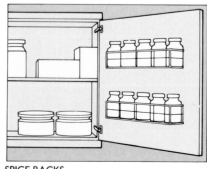

SPICE RACKS
Style Fitted to the inside of cupboard doors.
In use An easy-to-see way of storing small bottles and containers.

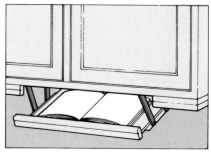

BOOKREST
Style A drop-down bookrest which, when closed, looks like part of the pelmet below a wall unit.
In use Somewhere to place open cookery books at eye-level – away from sticky worksurfaces.

WORK SURFACES AND SPLASHBACKS

Your choice of kitchen worktop should combine practicality with good looks.

Since kitchen worktops have to bear the brunt of most cooking activity, they must be able to withstand the heavy wear and tear that they will be subjected to without becoming shabby or grubby. Although splashbacks don't need to be quite so hardwearing, they should nevertheless be easy to clean.

Even if you always use a chopping board, a worktop will occasionally be subjected to nicks and scratches. So the surface must be strong and resilient. It also needs to be able to withstand at least moderate heat to prevent burn marks if a hot pan is put down on it.

And since you are bound to spill things on it, the ideal worktop is also easy to clean, stain-resistant and waterproof.

Lastly, worktops and splashbacks should be as attractive as possible since they are an important element in any kitchen design.

The dimensions Standard base units are 900mm in height since this is judged to be the most comfortable height for most people. But if you are taller or shorter than average, some kitchen manufacturers can alter the height of the plinth in order to raise or lower the worktop accordingly.

The normal depth of base units (from front to back) is 600mm and the worktop is usually a few centimetres deeper. It is possible to install a deeper worktop by positioning base units a small distance from the wall. This gives more room to range toasters, electric kettles and similar appliances neatly along the back wall without encroaching on work space – and also means that pipes can be hidden behind the units.

Materials Kitchen worktops can be made from many different materials, with differing visual and practical characteristics and, of course, different prices. The most common materials are plastic laminates, wood and ceramic tiles. Granite, marble and man-made materials which resemble natural stone are also available.

Farmhouse style

Wooden worktops and a tiled splashback provide practical surfaces which are in keeping with the natural style of this kitchen. A butcher's block acts as a chopping board and a marble slab on top of the worktop provides a cool surface for rolling out pastry.

PLASTIC LAMINATES

By far the most popular choice for kitchen worktops, plastic laminates are available in an overwhelming variety of colours and effects. These range from pale pastels to bright primaries, through imitations of natural materials such as wood and marble – even bold geometric patterns.

A plastic laminate is made up of a thin sheet of plastic bonded to chipboard, blockboard or plywood (in ascending order of quality and price). Formica is the brand name of one of the best known ranges of plastic laminates. Melamine is a cheaper alternative to plastic laminate and is made from plastic-impregnated paper.

Most fitted kitchen manufacturers offer a selection of laminate worktops to co-ordinate with their range of units, but laminate can also be bought separately in cut lengths for DIY kitchen fitting, or to replace an existing worktop.

Although boiling water and hot splashes will do no harm, a hot pan or iron should never be placed directly on to a laminate worktop. Similarly, laminates are generally resistant to knocks and scratches, but should never be used as a chopping surface.

△ *Cream and blue*
It is almost always possible to co-ordinate the plastic laminate worktops with the units in a fitted kitchen. A single line of patterned tiles on the splashback make a visual link with the grey-blue trim on the units.

▽ *Spoilt for choice*
The plastic laminate worktops shown below – speckled grey, plain pink and wood-effect – are just three of the huge variety available. The edge of the worktop can be square (in this case cleverly accentuated with a darker pink inset stripe) or curved.

CERAMIC AND QUARRY TILES

While most ordinary ceramic tiles can be used for kitchen worktops, tiles manufactured specially for this purpose will last longer. Quarry tiles, designed to be laid on floors, are also suitable and create a rugged, rustic feel. Although worktop and quarry tiles are thicker than ordinary ceramic wall tiles, they can be fixed to walls to create a co-ordinated splashback.

Look for ranges which include curved edging tiles for a neat finish. (Some manufacturers even produce mitred edging tiles for the corners.) Alternatively, a wooden edging will neatly frame worktop tiling.

Tiles are very easy to keep clean, are not easily scratched and are less likely to be damaged by hot saucepans than many other worktop materials.

A tiled worktop is noisy to work on. In addition, individual tiles can be chipped or cracked if something heavy is accidentally dropped, though this is less likely to happen with quarry or purpose-made worktop tiles. Replacing a single tile can be difficult.

Tiles can be laid over an existing – perhaps disfigured – worktop but it is important to ensure that the existing worktop is strong enough to take the weight of the tiles. If it is not adequately supported, a tiled worktop can begin to sag.

Grouting Since the tiles on a worktop are laid on a horizontal rather than a vertical surface, water is liable to collect on the surface, particularly in the grouting which is usually slightly recessed. This means that waterproof grouting is essential to prevent water seeping into the surface below the tiles. It is also important to ensure that there are no gaps between the tiles and the grouting, where crumbs and similar bits could collect.

Grouting can, with time, get very grubby and needs to be regularly cleaned with a stiff brush and a solution of domestic bleach. It may occasionally be necessary to rake out the existing grouting and replace it. White grouting has a tendency to go grey, so an off-white or coloured grouting may be worth considering.

MAN-MADE STONE

Although the various synthetic materials now available for kitchen worktops feel like smooth stone and can look like marble or granite, they suffer from none of their disadvantages (except price). Corian (the best-known man-made stone) is virtually indestructible – it is hardwearing, warm to the touch and completely heat and stain resistant. Small scratches are easily removed by rubbing down with ordinary kitchen cleaner. It can be moulded into almost any shape, to create an integral worktop, sink and draining board with no joins in which dirt and germs can hide. However, it is very expensive.

▽ *Shades of pink*
A tiled worktop and splashback add colour and interest to this all-white kitchen. The large expanse of tiles is broken up by mixing various shades of pink on the worktop and combining white and pink tiles and a border with a fuchsia design on the splashback. Grey grouting complements the pink tiles and won't discolour and look shabby.

WOOD, GRANITE AND MARBLE

These natural materials all produce elegant and attractive, though expensive, worktops.

Wood A wooden worktop is best made from a hardwood – teak, maple, oak and beech are common choices. Some wooden worktops are sealed with a clear varnish; others are treated with a special oil which must be periodically renewed. The types of wood used for worktops is hardwearing and will withstand moderate heat although very hot pans may scorch the surface. A tiled inset next to a hob or oven can be used for standing hot pans.

Solid wood comes in different thicknesses (and therefore different qualities); wood veneer (where a thin sheet of real wood is bonded to chipboard or hardboard) represents a cheaper alternative which can be equally long-lasting.

Marble and granite are undoubtedly elegant and virtually indestructible – but are also very expensive and heavy, so that the units (and the floor) may need to be reinforced in order to be able to bear the weight. Marble is porous and should be coated with a special sealant to help prevent it staining with alarming ease. Granite is less porous and also comes as a veneer.

△ *Granite splendour*
There is no arguing with the fact that the granite worktop and splashback add a touch of opulence to this kitchen. The shiny, mottled grey surface goes well with bright primary colours. Granite comes in a variety of colours which include dark and light greys as well as shades of green and pink. While some granites are very mottled, in others the colour is more solid.

◁ *A maple worktop*
Tough enough to be used for squash courts and dance floors, solid maple is an ideal choice for a worktop. Treated with respect, wood actually improves with age and use, unlike plastic laminate or tiles.

A custom-made wood worktop can replace an existing damaged worktop – or add the finishing touch to a new kitchen. The worktop's edge can be square, rounded or even chamfered – depending on your preference.

SPLASHBACKS

As the name implies, the splashback area above the worktop must be easy to clean so that splashes and spills from cooking can be removed without causing lasting damage.

The choice of material depends partly on your choice of worktop and kitchen units. Ceramic wall or worktop tiles, quarry tiles, laminates – even marble and granite – are all suitable.

In addition, of course, a splashback can be painted or covered with wallpaper. Although it is fairly easy to renew paint and wallpaper, it's best to use an oil-based paint or a washable wallpaper to give a reasonably longlasting finish. Instead of tiles, consider a tile-effect washable wallpaper which to all intents and purposes looks very like real tiles.

Visually, the worktop and splashback should not be equally dominant or the end result could be overwhelming. A bright or highly patterned splashback is best combined with a plain or pale worktop, and vice versa. Remember too that strong patterns – on either the worktop or the splashback – may conflict with the many utensils which find a home on most kitchen worktops, so creating a working environment which is over-busy and distracting.

△ *A personal splashback*
In a farmhouse-style kitchen, a fully-tiled splashback may look out of place. Here, a small tiled area of Victorian tiles framed in wood, provides a practical and sympathetic backdrop to an old, marble-topped sideboard.

Odd tiles, as opposed to a complete set in the same pattern, are easy to find in antique shops and markets. Choose tiles which have a theme – or a colour – in common.

▷ *Chequerboard effect*
Combined with plain units and worktops, an eye-catching splashback can form the visual focus of a kitchen.

Here, a simple arrangement of black and white tiles is reminiscent of the op art so popular during the 1960s.

A softer effect could be produced by using more subdued colours or patterned tiles.

A pull-out table can fit snugly into a drawer space and slide out to extend the available worktop space. Such an extendable surface could also double as a tea tray or occasional breakfast table.

When you choose a pull-out table, check that it is securely supported along its entire length when extended.

MAKING WORKTOP SPACE

Except for those lucky enough to possess an exceptionally large kitchen, most cooks would agree that they have insufficient worktop space for their needs. The most costly solution is to rearrange completely the entire room in order to squeeze in as much worktop space as possible. But there are less drastic solutions.

Start by trying to free as much of the existing worktops as possible. Rows of storage jars or tins may look attractive ranged along the back wall, but they do take up valuable space. Small appliances such as food processors can often be stored in cupboards rather than on worktops. Some kitchen manufacturers even offer pull-out shelves which allow appliances to be stored behind closed doors.

If there is room, a movable trolley can serve as an additional worktop (as well as providing extra storage) – but choose a version with locking wheels for safety. You may even be able to purchase an old butcher's block with a solid wood top which makes an ideal chopping board.

△ *A movable trolley*
A trolley with locking castors provides an extra worktop which can be moved out of the way when not in use.

▽ *Using the walls*
A spare wall can be made to work for its living by means of a securely fixed, collapsible shelf.

COLOUR
IN THE KITCHEN

The colour scheme you choose plays an important part in bringing the right atmosphere to your kitchen.

Creating a pleasing colour scheme for a kitchen can be more complicated than for any other room in the home as there are so many elements to consider. And kitchens generally contain expensive appliances and fitted units which cannot be replaced at a whim.

Fitted units come in a whole host of colours and finishes, ranging from the highly dramatic to the subtle. And since coloured facing panels are now available for many kitchen appliances, a degree of colour co-ordination can be achieved between appliances and units as well as surfaces such as walls and ceiling.

Kitchens contain, too, many small appliances and utensils that are always on show. If too many colours or patterns are involved, the result is bitty, busy and tiring on the eye.

The room's size and aspect always influence the colours chosen. A small, dark room benefits from light, airy colours and – in addition – the smaller the room, the greater the risk of fragmentation – so use plain, uninterrupted colours for a streamlined look.

These are just some of the considerations to bear in mind when planning your kitchen. Choose colours and patterns for the long term and – as you decide on the main colours – remember to consider the accessories which will add the finishing touches.

Fresh and simple
The colour of the wooden units in this kitchen is lifted by the crisp white contrast and a judicious use of clear primaries. The resulting atmosphere is both cheerful and relaxed.

LARGE AREAS OF COLOUR

When choosing the main colours or patterns which will predominate in your kitchen, it's a good idea to start with the fitted units and worktops. Then consider the elements that can be changed more easily and cheaply – wall and floorcoverings, or paintwork (and, of course, the accessories and details).

Apart from your personal preferences and the mood you're aiming for, be sure you can live with your choice over the years. A good choice, for instance, is fitted units in neutral white, beiges and creams, or natural wood.

The amount of daylight is an important consideration. Pale colours reflect light and can make a room feel larger, but too much white could be dazzling in a sunny, south-facing kitchen.

▷ *Formal stripes*
Strong patterns don't look their best broken up by shelves or racks, so keep them away from work areas – like this striped wallpaper above the wall units.

▽ *Coloured units*
Moss green kitchen units create a restrained background in this room. Stained floorboards, a rug and matching seating complete the co-ordinated look.

△ **Hand-painted units**
Wooden kitchen units can be painted almost any colour under the sun: here a warm cornflower blue with white detailing has been chosen. The dragged paint effect is protected by several coats of clear varnish to provide a longlasting finish.

The white, tiled worktop and splashback and the blue and white patterned blind emphasize the scheme.

◁ **High-tech look**
Glossy black kitchen units create a streamlined, modern look with the pale wood trim on the units adding a subtle note of relief to the stark black. Neutral walls and worktops, together with a black floor, complete the overall scheme.

COLOUR IN THE DETAILS

The kitchen, with small worktop appliances, utensils, storage pots and jars, table linen and crockery, affords great scope for using small areas of colour to highlight and break up the large expanses of worktops and units. Planning is important, however, both to stop the room becoming too busy and to prevent colourful accessories clashing with each other.

Having decided on the main colours for the room, choose accessories which blend or contrast with the overall scheme. If the background is pale and unobtrusive so that the main colour interest lies in the accesssories, try to select at least a couple of larger items in the accent colour of your choice – tiles, perhaps, or the tablecloth or window covering.

Then colour match the rest of the room's details as far as possible to avoid a fragmented look. Paint door and window frames to blend with the colour scheme. Although it may be difficult to find small electrical appliances in identical colours, you should be able to find complementary shades or discreet neutrals. Light fittings, pots and pans, chopping boards, oven gloves, tea towels, mugs on racks, the cutlery and crockery – even the kitchen sink – can all add to your colour scheme.

*△ ◁ **A whole new look***
The two kitchens shown here (above and left) are structurally identical, and have the same layout, fitted units and dining table. The difference lies in the clever use of coloured detailing that totally transforms the look of the room.

The kitchen above is enlivened by using plenty of red and white – from the wallpaper to the floor and a range of accessories.

In the kitchen on the left, a soft and sophisticated colour scheme has been created by retaining the same units and combining them with delicate pastel shades throughout the room.

*▷ **Bold primaries***
Some kitchen units allow you to choose from different coloured handles and trims above and below wall and base units. The glossy yellow ceiling echoes the colour of the window frame and reflects the plentiful natural light in the room.

BRIGHT IDEA

Electrical fittings come in many bright colours as well as standard white, and so can be used to enhance any style or colour scheme. They are also available in other materials and finishes such as brass and chrome.

◁ *Blue outline*
Simple white units are given a smart new look with a neat blue trim. To achieve this effect yourself, use masking tape to protect the surrounding surface when painting existing units.

◁ Open shelves

It is possible to brighten up a rather dull kitchen at minimal expense, simply by painting the walls. And paint is inexpensive and easy to renew if you feel like a change in the future.

Here blue and white china, together with a variety of kitchen necessities, are arranged on open shelves against a pillar-box red background. By choosing the colours carefully, the china and crockery displayed on open shelves make an important contribution to the overall look of a kitchen.

▽ A painted kitchen

In a kitchen which lacks fitted wall units, it is easy to introduce colour by painting the walls. Do beware, though, of creating an overpowering atmosphere if you opt for a strong colour. Here, for example, touches of red and brown break up the large expanses of green and tie in well with the cherry motif on the curtains.

STREAMLINING KITCHEN GAPS

Gaps between units and appliances can be filled to give your kitchen the fitted look.

△ **Adding an eating area**
A simple breakfast bar can be used to fill space between units or across the end of the room. A length of work surface makes a good, solid top.

FITTING ON A BUDGET

<u>Problem</u> When installing a fitted kitchen, a limited budget can make it impossible to afford the number of fitted base units needed. How can the kitchen be made to look fitted and streamlined without filling all the space with expensive units?

<u>Solution</u> Use a combination of fitted units and open shelves. Space the closed units to suit your needs, then fill up the spaces in between with inexpensive shelving. Contiboard comes in white, wood effect, primary and pastel colours.

You can even leave some gaps the width of a standard base unit. This allows you to insert a unit when you can afford it. Alternatively, choose a range where doors can be bought separately and simply cover the open shelves with doors when your budget allows.

Open shelves between units can be used in many different ways. Two deep shelves provide room on the bottom for a beer crate with a wine rack on top. Wire or wicker baskets can be used on narrow shelves for convenient and easily-accessible storage.

SPACE FOR TOWELS OR TRAYS

<u>Problem</u> What can be done with a narrow space too small for a kitchen unit?

<u>Solution</u> Gaps, at the end of kitchen units, or between them on a wall, that are the wrong length to accommodate an exact number of standard units are irritating and a waste of space.

You can use the gap to house trays, or you can buy a custom-made fitting to fill the space.

The most useful fitting is a telescopic towel rail. These are available with two or three arms. The rail can be fixed beneath the work surface above the gap, or to the back wall. The rails pull forward so that towels are easy to reach.

Another way to fill the space is to buy a set of folding kitchen steps. These measure around 90mm wide when folded and will slide into a narrow under-worktop space. It is also possible to buy steps which fit behind a removable section of the base plinth.

Alternatively, fit shelves across the gap and use them to store small jars of spices and other kitchen odds and ends.

ADD A BREAKFAST BAR

<u>Problem</u> What is the best way to deal with a long gap if you can't afford to fit units?

<u>Solution</u> Run a worktop or a narrow shelf across the gap and add a couple of stools to create an instant breakfast bar. If you want to make use of the space beneath the worktop, fill it with wine racks (available made-to-measure from good cookshops and some wine merchants), stacking plastic boxes or tiers of wire trays on castors.

You can link units across the end wall of a room by running a narrow breakfast bar between them. This works particularly well if the bar can be positioned beneath a window. Eating breakfast or a snack facing a blank wall is less appealing. The area beneath the bar must be left open so that the unit doors can be used.

◁ **Using open spaces**
Spaces can be filled with shelves at different depths to house a mixture of objects. Spacing units out with open shelf areas is a useful exercise if you can't afford as many cupboards as you would like.

MIDWAY STORAGE

<u>Problem</u> In a kitchen where storage space is limited, it seems wasteful not to use the area between the worktop and the wall units. What kind of fitting can be used here without obstructing the worktop space?

<u>Solution</u> Fitting baskets to the underside of wall cupboards doesn't obstruct the space below. Under-shelf baskets are available made from plastic-covered wire mesh with open fronts, or from rigid plastic with up-and-over doors. The up-and-over door type is useful for storing bread, biscuits and other perishables which need protection from the drying effect of air.

Cup hooks fixed beneath units are useful for hanging mugs and bunches of dried herbs. If your greatest need is for hanging storage, fix metal mesh grids to the wall between the units and the worktop. Use butchers' hooks to hang utensils from the racks. Some racks feature a range of accessories, such as hook-on baskets for cleaning materials, shelves and a circular container to hold washing-up liquid. These are useful above the sink.

Narrow shelves are another way to use the wall space. The shelves should be a maximum of 15cm (6in) wide and must finish at least 25cm (10in) above the worktop. Shelves wider or lower than this obstruct the worktop. Use the shelves for spice jars and other small containers.

◁ *Filling the gaps*
Gaps beside a cooker or between units can be filled with a useful telescopic towel rail. The rails are available from flat pack kitchen unit suppliers. You can buy a rail with a heating element to dry the tea towels. This type of rail must be fitted by an electrician.

GAPS AROUND THE COOKER

<u>Problem</u> Old cookers were not designed to fit in with modern kitchen units so there are often narrow gaps at each side. How can these gaps be filled to give a neat, streamlined look?

<u>Solution</u> Gaps beside the cooker are a collecting point for crumbs and food spills. You can fill the space with a piece of worktop, mounted on a batten at one side (the batten can be fixed to the wall or unit next to the gap) and hard up against the side of the cooker at the other side. This prevents food and crumbs falling into the gap.

The space below the worktop can be used as a tray recess, for a telescopic towel rail or filled with shelves for storing spices and other ingredients.

SPACE BETWEEN WALL UNITS

<u>Problem</u> Where a kitchen has been fitted in a haphazard way, with units at different levels and spaces between them the effect is visually disturbing and untidy. How can this higgeldy-piggeldy arrangement be given a neat, streamlined look, without fitting a completely new range of units?

<u>Solution</u> Where there are several units mounted at different levels, the easiest way to bring them together is to run a shelf across the top. The shelf should be

▽ *Space between units*
Spaces between both wall and floor units can be filled with open shelves set at different depths. Use shallow baskets on the shelves to keep small items in order and easily accessible.

△ *Around the cooker*
Narrow spaces around and above this cooker have been filled with open shelving to give a streamlined look.

positioned just above the highest unit. Use the shelf to display an attractive collection of jugs, pots or bowls and you'll draw the eye away from the cupboards. Run a second shelf across the bottom, starting beneath the lowest unit. Running shelves across top and bottom creates interesting spaces which can be used for display. You can attach cup hooks to the underside of the bottom shelf and use them for hanging mugs, jugs and utensils.

Wall cupboards can be linked by running open shelves between them. Space shelves wide apart for pans and other large objects, close together for spice jars and odds and ends.

LINING UP NEATLY

<u>Problem</u> Modern appliances are all a standard 600mm deep (front to back). If used with old style 500mm kitchen units, they jut out, spoiling the line of the units and causing awkward gaps.

<u>Solution</u> The easiest way to deal with this problem is to remove the worktop from the old units. Move the units forward, so that they line up with the appliances, then fit a new 600mm deep worktop to cover the gap at the back.

You won't be able to do this where an appliance is next to the sink as it would involve moving the water pipes and drains, but one area set back does not look as untidy as a wall of zig-zags. If you have a gas cooker, the supply pipe must be extended. This should be done by a gas fitter.

LIGHTING THE KITCHEN

Good lighting can transform a kitchen, making it a safe and pleasant place in which to work.

It's a curious fact that while people often spend considerable sums of money on a new fitted kitchen, the lighting of that newly-installed kitchen is often ignored. Yet lighting is possibly more important in a kitchen than elsewhere in the home, partly because of the varied activities that take place there.

Kitchen lighting needs to be conducive to more than just work. The lighting requirements of food preparation differ considerably from those of eating a meal at a kitchen table or breakfast bar. Many families find that their kitchen is the social centre of the home, where members of the family gather to chat and exchange news. Since many hours are spent in the kitchen, good overall lighting will do away with the eye strain and headaches which can be caused by time spent in an environment which is too bright or too dim.

Safety should not be ignored. If you work in your own shadow, or in a room where the level of lighting is too low, you are much more likely to suffer an accidental cut or burn.

Finally, there is the question of aesthetics. A beautiful kitchen cannot look its best if the lighting does not do it justice.

Glowing feel
In this kitchen, a tungsten downlighter provides overall light with a warm, golden quality. Fluorescent strips under the wall units cast bright, shadowless task lighting.

LIGHTING THE WHOLE ROOM

Good overall lighting in a kitchen creates the right mood – neither too bright nor too 'atmospheric' – and produces efficient working conditions.

The level of general lighting which should be installed depends on a combination of factors: the strength of the task lighting, the room's aspect, and whether it is decorated in pale or dark colours. Good natural daylight is a great boon; choose translucent coverings for windows if you need to screen them during the day.

A central strip light, though somewhat utilitarian, provides the best light for the least money. Fluorescent strips (even the modern colour-corrected types) tend to produce a rather harsh, white light which has a 'flattening' effect on fitted furniture; tungsten strips give a yellower, warmer light.

Pendant lights should not throw a glare into the cook's eyes. Match the fittings you choose to the style of the room, bearing in mind that simple shapes which won't act as dirt and grease traps are best in a kitchen.

Spotlights fixed either singly or on a track are flexible as you can angle them more or less where you please. They do create shadows, however, and can cause glare on shiny surfaces.

Downlighters are neat and inconspicuous, particularly if they are recessed into the ceiling. Downlighters direct light

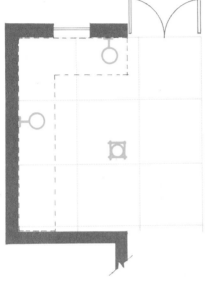

◁ Classic pendant lighting
A series of pendant lamps fitted with classically simple shades provide illumination for the whole room and specific task lighting over the worktops. Such lights need to be carefully positioned: if these lamps were any lower, the cook would be forced to work in a disturbing glare of light.

The single spotlight is fitted with a crown-silvered bulb to reduce glare; it is angled to direct light on to the movable trolley.

▽ Uplighting the kitchen
A pair of elegant tungsten halogen uplighters direct their beams on to the ceiling and bounce light back into the room. Uplighters work on the principle of reflected light so the ceiling must be white or at least pale. Dimmer switches control the light level.

The trolley is lit by a tungsten halogen downlighter. The fitting which has been chosen incorporates a swivel movement allowing the direction of the light to be altered.

Scale: 1 square= 1 metre square

downwards with a broad or narrow beam, depending on the fitting chosen; some types can be angled.

Wall lights which bounce light off a pale ceiling give good overall illumination and help to avoid shadows. Although tungsten halogen fittings are expensive, the quality of the light they produce is excellent. Since the fittings take very high wattage bulbs, only one or two tungsten halogen uplighters will be needed to light an entire kitchen.

BRIGHT IDEA

Concealed strip lighting can be installed below wall units or open shelves so that the light, but not the light fitting, is visible. Installing such fittings is one of the easiest ways of improving kitchen lighting. (Either make a baffle to conceal the light or buy one from kitchen specialists.) Fluorescent strips cast very white light; tungsten strips give a warmer and yellower light.

△ *A hand-painted kitchen*
The lighting in this custom-made kitchen, hand-painted in shades of old rose, shows off its delicate lines and glowing colours to advantage.

Concealed tungsten strip lighting below the wall units provides task lighting and casts a warm, yellowish glow. (Fluorescent strips would give off a colder, whiter light and would make the delicate pink appear bluer in colour.) Recessed downlighters fitted into the ceiling provide inconspicuous overall lighting; the gold-effect reflectors enhance the warm quality of the light.

▷ *Varied lighting*
A combination of fluorescent strips and tungsten downlighters light this all-white kitchen.

Fitted both below and above the wall units, fluorescent strips throw a white light down on to the work surfaces (including the sink) and upwards on to the ceiling. The ribbon of light around the top of the room which the strips create adds a definite touch of drama. The recessed tungsten downlighter lights the rest of the room.

◁ **Modern and streamlined**
Concealed tungsten strip lighting above and below the wall units casts a yellowish glow on to worktops and ceiling, balancing the cool colour of the kitchen units. The miniature eyeball-type recessed downlighters sparkle and glitter, but leave the floor in relative darkness. Neither the hidden strips nor the downlighters disturb the streamlined look of the room.

TASK LIGHTING

Efficient kitchen lighting must be shadow-free. This means that any task lighting you install must be positioned so that you do not stand between the light source and the worktop, so casting shadows. Beware, also, of the glare which can be caused by bouncing over-bright light off shiny tiles, work-tops and appliances. Either direct the light away from reflective surfaces, or use lower wattage bulbs.

So long as there are wall units (or shelves) above the worktops, the best way of providing task lighting is to install strip lights beneath. But if your kitchen has no fitted wall units, suspend a number of pendant lamps over the worktops. Positioning them above the outside edge of the worktop will ensure that you cast no shadow as you work. Alternatively, one or more angled work lamps on a shelf or the worktop itself provide good task lighting.

Even if the sink is located beneath a window, it will need its own light source. A downlighter on the ceiling should do the job well (it's best to avoid spotlights since they produce a very strong, glaring light). Another alternative is to install hidden lighting behind a pelmet. Similarly, the hob needs a separate light source. Many cooker hoods incorporate an integral light; if you need to install a light, choose a fitting in which the bulb or strip is enclosed to protect it from heat and grease splashes.

▽ **Alternative arrangement**
The two large recessed downlighters which replace the miniature eyeballs in this lighting scheme ensure that light reaches the rather dark floor. They throw a wide beam and so create two, overlapping, pools of light.

An additional strip light installed below the display shelves highlights the collection of ornaments. It has been hidden behind a baffle (painted to match the walls) for safety as well as style.

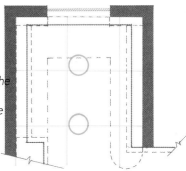

Scale: 1 square = 1 square metre

THE BEDROOM

In the small homes of today, bedrooms need careful planning to be more than just a place to sleep. Storage, leisure pursuits and study must be catered for as well, and working out how to achieve these aims, especially on a limited budget, is a complex task – and one which is surprisingly often neglected.

The following chapter is full of bedrooms of every conceivable style, including bright ideas for decorating newborn babies' and children's rooms, and how to cater for their needs as they grow into independent adults.

It starts with basic planning – where to position the bed, how much storage space to allow, where to install lighting – and progresses to the planning of an efficient storage system for clothes and other items, whether it is the popular built-in type, or individual cupboards and shelves. The ideal bedroom is created in easy, affordable stages and drawings illustrate possible options to several basic schemes.

Here too are designs to exploit awkward-shaped rooms such as attics or lofts, and particular attention is paid to space-saving ideas such as sofa beds and other items of furniture that can have a double function in the bedroom.

PLANNING YOUR BEDROOM

Your bedroom may not be on public view but it still merits care and attention to detail.

Good bedroom planning helps make the most of what is often a smallish space; clever storage simplifies your daily routine. And an eye for decorative possibilities helps to create a stylish, welcoming room.

Which room For some people, the bedroom is just a place to sleep. Others like a retreat where they can relax, read, listen to music or watch TV. In some homes, the bedroom may be the only area for quiet activities such as sewing, studying or writing letters.

The first step in planning a bedroom is to choose the most suitable room. Most houses are designed with the bedrooms near the bathroom and away from the living area, but if the existing layout does not work for you, there is usually an alternative. If you like to sleep late, for example, avoid a room which overlooks the street or gets the full glare of the morning sun. If you just want somewhere to lay your head for eight hours, opting for the largest bedroom would be a waste of space. It might be more sensible to give children the biggest bedroom, equipping it with toy storage and desk space, thus easing the pressure on the rest of the house.

Fitted or furnished The layout of your bedroom depends essentially on how you tackle the problem of storage. Fitted or built-in cupboards decrease usable floor area but can be tailored exactly to your requirements. Traditional storage furniture, such as a chest of drawers, wardrobe, blanket box and dressing table, can create awkward dead spaces, but are often attractive in their own right.

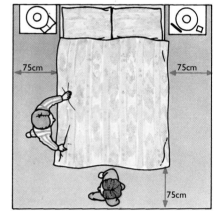

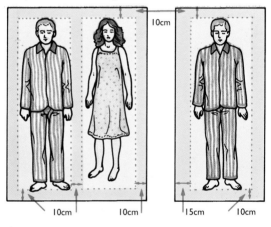

Bedroom space
Far left: 75cm is needed around a bed for changing sheets, circulation and vacuuming, fit castors if the bed is against a wall. Slightly less space will do between two single beds.
Left: the minimum allowances around and between two people sharing a double bed and around one person in a single bed.

MAKING A PLAN

Start by drawing a diagram of the room on graph paper, marking on all existing features, such as windows, doors, alcoves, radiators and cupboards. Include the position of all services, such as telephone or TV aerial points, electric sockets and switches. Then, working to the same scale, draw the shapes of the furniture you own or intend to buy on a separate piece of paper, cut them out and arrange the pieces on the room plan to find the best arrangement.

Bedrooms are not subject to heavy traffic but access is still an important consideration. Beds should have enough clearance to allow for circulation and changing sheets. If space is tight, fit castors to the bed to make it easier to move. Make sure there is enough room for cupboard or wardrobe doors to open fully, that drawers pull out without obstruction and that there is a clear route between the bed and the door.

Note any aspects that could be changed to increase space or practicality. You might want to rehang a door to improve access, move a radiator or add a new electric socket or switch.

LIGHTING

Work out the lighting you need on your room plan. General overhead lighting is flexible if controlled by a dimmer switch, preferably operated by the door *and* the bed.

In addition to general lighting, you probably need some task lights. Direct lighting from a table lamp or spotlight is essential for a study or hobby area. Fit a light inside a deep wardrobe with a small switch in the door jamb (rather like a fridge door).

Mirror lighting A dressing table mirror illuminated by a pair of tall candlestick lamps or a row of Hollywood-style bulbs to either side, as shown on the right casts an even, shadowless light across the face which is ideal for putting on make-up.

For a full-length mirror, an overhead bulb casting enough light to illuminate you from head to toe without shadow is ideal, especially if you are dressing for artificial light; daylight-balanced fluorescent strips either side of the mirror give a closer reflection of true daylight.

Bedside lighting A bedside lamp should be adjustable, so that it casts a direct beam on to your book without shining into your eyes. In a double bedroom it is best to have two bedside lamps, so that one person can read in well-directed light if the other wants to sleep.

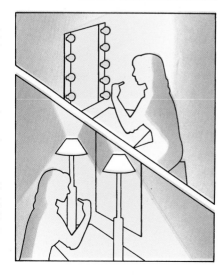

STORAGE SOLUTIONS

Although bedrooms tend to be small, the demands for storage are often high. If you don't want to disappear under a pile of clutter, every inch will have to count.

Start by making a detailed, specific list of what you need to store:
- [ ] winter and summer clothes
- [ ] evening clothes
- [ ] outdoor wear
- [ ] suitcases and handbags
- [ ] bedlinen and blankets
- [ ] laundry
- [ ] shoes and hats
- [ ] cosmetics and jewellery
- [ ] books
- [ ] sports or exercise equipment
- [ ] items relating to specific activities, such as a sewing machine.

Once you have made your list, see if you can find a home for some of the items elsewhere, Suitcases, for instance, could go in the loft; bedlinen in an airing cupboard; the laundry basket in the bathroom. Winter clothes could be packed away during the summer months and vice versa. Consider fitting a box room or part of a hallway with cupboards and shelves to take the overflow.

Whether you are planning to have built-in or free-standing furniture, there are many space-saving ideas.
- [ ] Hang ties, belts and beads in a row over a rail fixed to the back of wardrobe or cupboard doors.
- [ ] Store shoes, tights and socks in tiered wire baskets or pocketed shoe tidies.
- [ ] Blankets and linen could go into an ottoman at the foot of the bed or in pull-out drawers underneath.
- [ ] A laminate countertop could serve both as a work surface and dressing table.
- [ ] Fit a second rail halfway up a wardrobe or cupboard to double the hanging space for jackets, skirts and shirts.
- [ ] Extend built-in cupboards right up to the ceiling to make full use of the wall area.
- [ ] Fit roller blinds to cover shelving or cupboards and save the space needed for door clearance.
- [ ] Use a shop rail for hanging clothes if there isn't enough room for a wardrobe or cupboard – but keep clothes in bags to protect against dust and fading.

Above all, don't skimp on space. Allow room for expansion – don't jam your wardrobe so full of clothes that dressing becomes a chore. A cupboard should cater for specific needs: evening dresses are 45-50cm longer than standard daytime dresses; and small items get lost in deep drawers.

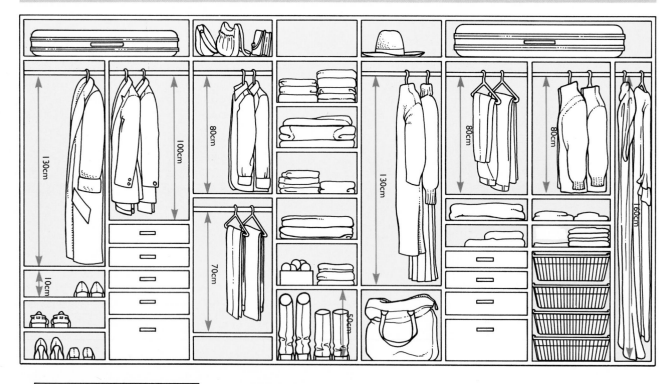

WARDROBE PLANNING

People vary in size. So, obviously, do their clothes. The dimensions given above are for an average adult man and woman sharing a wardrobe.

The overall height of the cupboard can vary according to the height of the room. The depth should be about 60cm, enough to accommodate a bulky coat on a large hanger. The main hanging rail should be slightly above eye level, at about 180cm, allowing clearance above of 6cm to hook and unhook hangers. Clothes are heavy, so long hanging rails must be supported from above by strong brackets.

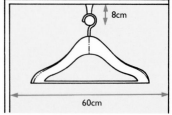

BEDROOM STYLE

Bedrooms are where you begin and end the day, so they should be decorated and furnished to provide a peaceful, comfortable atmosphere that will set you off on the right foot.

To create a general feeling of calm, avoid too bright, insistent colour schemes and busy patterns. Keep it simple with light, pastel shades and small patterns. Increase the feeling of space by co-ordinating patterns and colours for bedlinen, curtains or blinds, and wall finishes. Mirrors are also useful, maximizing natural light and giving an illusion of depth.

Don't neglect the personal touch. An armchair, or even a sofa if there is enough room, will promote a feeling of comfort. Fresh flowers and decorative objects provide accents of colour.

STORAGE IN THE MASTER BEDROOM

No matter how tidy you are, an efficient storage system will transform your bedroom.

Whatever its size, a master bedroom should be a calm haven from the hectic activities of the rest of the house. But if it's strewn with clothes, shoes, magazines, jewellery, sports gear, make-up and all the other bits and bobs that seem to have no home, it will never feel like a peaceful retreat.

The way to create a feeling of space *and* ensure that all the personal clutter that lives in the bedroom is safely out of sight is to give yourself sufficient, well-planned storage. With careful planning, you might even find you have room for a TV, so you can watch the programme of your choice for a change – a real luxury.

FOCUS ON FURNITURE

Make your bedroom furniture work for you. If, after deciding where to put your bed and dressing table, you are left with one clear wall, uninterrupted by a door or window, you will be able to have a range of floor-to-ceiling wardrobes built in along the entire length of the wall – and enough storage space for clothes and shoes, and possibly for the rest of your possessions.

Free-standing wardrobes and chests give you less storage space than built-in ones but, if you are considering moving fairly soon, this may be a more sensible option.

Roomy chests of drawers, beds with drawer divan bases and bedside tables that incorporate small cupboards all provide vital extra storage space.

A low chest or trunk at the foot of the bed provides extra storage without taking up a lot of space.

Make the most of every inch of space inside wardrobes. It is unlikely you will need an entire run of full-length hanging space, so consider adding a low rail in one section for shirts and racks for storing shoes. And incorporate drawers, open shelves, or wire trays – perhaps even a linen basket – into the cupboards. Store suitcases and seasonal or holiday clothes which are not often needed in overhead cupboards.

Classical elegance
Built-in wardrobes look less overwhelming when the line is broken with a bed or dressing table. Here off-white double wardrobes with a period feel are topped by a row of high cupboards, creating an alcove for the bed. The built-in headboard has a shelf along the top for lamps and books, and for displaying photographs and ornaments. A matching dressing table and drawer unit gives storage space for smaller items.

SPACE AT A PREMIUM

In a small bedroom, storage space is at a premium – and so is floor space. The best solution is one that looks good, works well and gives you room to relax.

Before committing yourself to new furniture, work out a budget. There's no point in spending a fortune on getting every last detail perfect in an elaborate fitted wardrobe if you plan to move in a couple of years. Remember that improvements like these may not necessarily always add their full value of your property.

Whatever type of furniture you choose, plan it carefully so that you end up with the best combination of hanging and shelf space.

Equally important is to make sure that the style of storage is in keeping with the character of the room itself. Think about the design, finish and colour, not forgetting final touches such as knobs and handles that can affect the whole look.

In an older building, the room may still have many of its original features. If the picture rail and ceiling mouldings are in good condition, it would be a pity to cover them with fitted cupboards. Of course, you may have to, in which case, matching up the lines of these features with the wardrobe doors will help to preserve the room's character.

Bedroom storage isn't just about wardrobes, of course. There may be odd corners that can be used for extra drawers or shelves.

The space underneath the bed is often wasted – consider a drawer divan base, or a free-standing drawer unit that slides under for packing away winter blankets or summer clothes that would take up precious space in a wardrobe.

Free-standing This is the most flexible option. It is a positive advantage to be able to move things around if you feel like a change. And, of course, you can always take it all with you when you move. The disadvantage is that free-standing furniture tends to take up more room than built-in cupboards.

With free-standing furniture, make sure you give the room a sense of unity. Choose second-hand pieces made of the same type of wood, for example, or items from one of the many ranges of modern bedroom storage units that are designed to mix and match.

If you find yourself with a rather

unrelated mixture of pieces, painting them all the same colour will help to achieve a unified look.

Built-in For a really neat look that maximizes storage space while taking up minimum room, it's hard to beat built-in, wall-to-wall wardrobes.

Ranging from simple shelf and rail arrangements to versatile modular units and very sophisticated systems of shelves, drawers, hanging rails and compartments, fitted wardrobes come in a wide variety of styles.

There are many off-the-peg systems available, or doors and rails can be bought from a DIY supplier, ready to fit yourself. Alternatively, you could get a carpenter to build in the wardrobes for you – this is a particularly good solution for an awkward-shaped room.

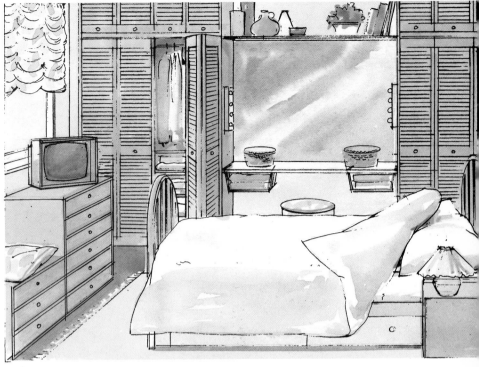

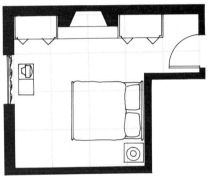

Scale: 1 square = 1 metre

◁ **Country simplicity**
Natural wood was chosen for the free-standing furniture in this attractive bedroom – a good choice to go with the pine fireplace. The full-length wardrobe has a concealed storage area in the base. There is a tall chest of drawers for clothing, with room for a mirror, lamp and pictures on top, and there is plenty of space to keep make-up in a two-drawer table.

△ **Fitted out**
In the alternative arrangement, fitted wardrobes with bi-fold, louvred doors are built in to the recesses on either side of the chimney breast. These fold-back panels slide on tracks and come as narrow as 30cm – useful if you are short of floor space. Louvred pine helps to provide texture and break up a large expanse of wood.

Wardrobes need to be 60cm deep – deeper than the recesses – so a slim dressing table fits neatly in between. It has wire trays on both sides for make-up, while film-star style bulbs on either side of the recess provide perfect light for making up.

Notice how the line of the picture rail continues across the front of the units. Above picture rail level, top cupboards with matching louvred doors provide space for rarely used items or out-of-season clothes.

BRIGHT IDEA

A small wall safe disguised as an electric plug socket is a cunning place to hide jewellery, documents or other valuables. Fitted into the skirting board – or anywhere else where a normal socket would look right – the heavy-gauge steel safe hides behind the false plug socket front and is locked and unlocked through one of the 'plug' pin holes. Install following the manufacturer's instructions.

CONFUSING THE BOUNDARIES

If your main bedroom is small, probably the last thing you want to do is to steal yet more floor space for large wardrobes. But you can have the best of both worlds – lots of storage and, at the same time, create the illusion of space by using clever colour schemes and mirrors.

Using colour As a rule of thumb, the paler your colour scheme, the more spacious the effect. Steering clear of using too many colours or large patterns helps too.

If you decide on built-in wardrobes, choose a light wood rather than a dark one, otherwise you will have a dark wall of doors dominating the rest of the room. And remember that louvred doors have a lighter feel about them than solid ones.

Another solution is to paint the doors so that the wardrobes melt in with the surrounding decoration. Or you could cover them with wallpaper to match the rest of the room, sealed with a protective coat of clear varnish.

Mirror effects Mirrors make space seem larger. A mirrored surface not only provides a looking glass for dressing but, if it is adjacent or opposite a window, increases the amount of light in the room.

◁ **White space**
Mirrored wardrobes and an almost white scheme make this small room seem spacious and airy. As it is not overlooked, sheer festoon blinds are used to maximize all available light. Continuous surfaces – rather than lots of separate pieces of furniture – help to streamline things. Here, one top links three chests of drawers, creating a dressing table. One chest overlaps the window alcove and the top continues along the side of the bed, and incorporates a bookshelf.

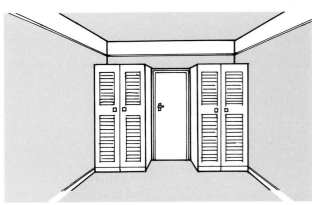

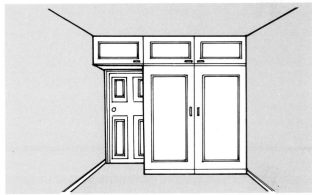

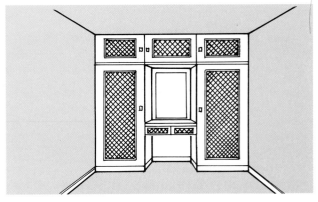

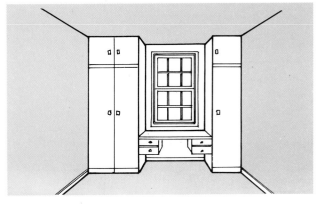

▷ **Space-saving ideas** Top to bottom:
☐ Tall cupboards placed on either side of the door are neat and unobtrusive.
☐ In this room the door is to the side so a wide wardrobe with top cupboards and extra storage above the door is a good choice.
☐ An arrangement of cupboards and overhead storage to incorporate a dressing table and mirror.
☐ A window wall of cupboards and dressing table; mirroring the sides of the cupboards makes the window appear larger and gives more light.

△ **Pull down**

When space is really tight, open doors are a nuisance. These venetian blinds across one short wall are a neat solution. Behind them there is a flexible arrangement of hanging rails, shelves, drawers, and racks of wire vegetable baskets that can be wheeled out easily. Pleated paper or pinoleum roller blinds are cheaper alternatives to venetian blinds while, for a softer look, curtains hung from a ceiling track could be used.

BRIGHT IDEA

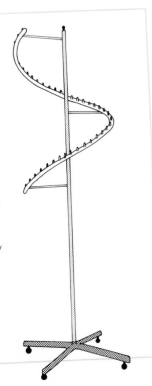

A spiral rail like those used in clothes shops is a good way to store shirts, dresses, jackets and trousers in a very limited space.

The spiral version will fit into a much smaller space than the more usual straight dress rail. It is 2m high but only 60cm in diameter and will take up to 60 garments of varying length.

This is not the sort of item you can buy from any high street outlet. Look in your Yellow Pages under the heading of Shopfitters.

△ **Drawer space**

You may have no space to fit a chest of drawers against a wall, perhaps because there is a radiator or door in the way, or you may simply need lots of drawer storage. A low chest positioned at the end of the bed like an ottoman gives you plenty of room for clothes and doubles as a seat or a convenient place for a TV.

BEDROOM LIGHTING

Bedroom lighting needs to be practical as well as able to produce an inviting atmosphere.

Bedroom lighting should be adaptable enough to combine good overall illumination with bright task lighting and softer, mood lighting to create a cosy atmosphere.

General principles At least one light should switch on from the door so that you don't have to stumble across a dark room. And it is much better if general lights can be controlled from the bed as well as the doorway.

Whether or not you are an avid reader-in-bed, you need good bedside lighting for getting into and out of bed. If you have to get up in the night it is more convenient, and less disturbing for anyone else in the room, to switch on a bedside lamp rather than the main light.

Dimmer switches are a valuable addition to bedroom lighting as they enable you to change the level of light to suit your mood.

Bedtime reading
The arc of light cast by a bedside lamp depends on the height of both the lamp base and the table on which it stands. Below, a short lamp on a high table provides just enough light for comfortable reading in bed. Above, if you have a lower table you'll need a taller lamp for easy bedtime reading.

CHOOSING THE FITTINGS

Most light fittings are perfectly suitable for bedrooms; your choice depends on your taste and needs.

A central pendant can give reasonable – but fairly inflexible – general illumination. One problem, however, is shadows; if you undress standing between the light and unlined curtains or a blind you may provide your neighbours with an interesting spectacle!

Wall lights strategically positioned round the room create warm pools of light. Two can be used as bedside lights, helping to give unity to your lighting scheme.

Downlighters Recessed downlighters provide good overall lighting, although you may have a problem with glare; the eye tends to be drawn towards the ceiling when lying in bed. You can overcome this by choosing downlighters with louvres or try the adjustable eyeball type. These can be angled towards the walls to highlight pictures or objects on shelves, or directed towards wardrobes or dressing tables. Wall-mounted spot-lights can also be used in this way.

▽ *Fold-away*
This swing-arm wall light is classic enough to work in both a period setting or a more tailored room. It is an excellent choice for the bedside as it can be folded against the wall or pulled round for reading.

△ *Classic lamp*
Wall lights are a particularly neat solution to the space problem in a small room and there are numerous styles from which to choose. The design of this lamp is based on an old-fashioned gas bracket fitting.

▽ *Flexible arrangement*
Downlighters unobtrusively complement the decor in a tailored bedroom. The ceiling lights and the two lights over the bedhead are each switched separately, and dimmers allow for changes of mood.

△ *Standard lamps*
If there is not enough space for a bedside table, a standard lamp provides a practical alternative. Its extra height gives a wide spread of light.

BRIGHT IDEA

Clamp-on lamp The simplest way of lighting the bedside is to use a clamp-on lamp attached to the bedhead. To prevent the clamp from damaging the bedhead, insert a piece of foam between the two.

LIGHTING THE BED

Table lamps to match the room's decoration are a popular choice. If you intend to use them as reading lamps, they need to be on fairly tall bases so as to shed light on your book.

Sometimes, however, there is not enough space for even the smallest bedside table or a lamp as well as all the necessary clutter. Wall-mounted fittings are one answer; pendants suspended over bedside tables are another space-saving idea.

△ *Double direction*
If you have space for large tables beside the bed you can choose imposing lamps with big shades. Little light is diffused through these opaque shades but, because of their height and the width of the bottom opening, they give excellent illumination over a wide area. They also cover the wall with light through the top aperture.

▷ *Versatile work light*
The no-nonsense lines of this adjustable task light suit this modern interior. Such a lamp is also extremely practical. Its jointing – based on that of the human arm – makes it easy to move into a variety of positions. It can be angled over the bed and adjusted up and down. The head can also be turned round to give indirect background illumination.

BEDROOM FURNITURE

Take your time choosing furniture and your bedroom can become something more than just a room to sleep in.

If the bedroom were used solely for sleeping, it would be the simplest of rooms to furnish, needing no more than the best bed money can buy. But it is also the place for storing clothes and personal effects, where you dress and make up, drink early morning tea, and read or watch television late at night. More than that, it often has to double up as a study/workroom, a children's playroom and, in small 'studio' flats, as the living room as well.

Furniture that performs so many roles must be flexible: in a bedroom/study, for example, a desk with drawers and a wall-mounted mirror above would be more useful than a specialized dressing table. For those who eat breakfast, write letters, or watch TV in the bedroom, an additional table is needed. Good storage is always essential and you should never underestimate the space you will need for out-of-season clothes, blankets and linen, as well as books, records and other odds and ends. Space must also be found for those items – such as a radio, reading light, alarm clock, toiletries and so on – which are best kept on view.

If you are starting from scratch, you are free to choose from either built-in or freestanding ranges. Built-in furniture, which can be fitted into odd corners or angles, is often a good buy for small and oddly-shaped bedrooms. Larger or more regularly-shaped rooms can take advantage of the flexibility that a freestanding arrangement can offer. Combining the two options can give you the best of both worlds, particularly if you have existing pieces to incorporate.

Before buying, shop around for sizes and shapes to suit your bedroom, and colours and finishes to complement the look you want to achieve: stripped or varnished pine for a cosy cottage bedroom; rich polished mahogany in a large Victorian home; cool white melamine or pale blonde ash for simple masculine rooms; pastel drag-painted wood for a more romantic, feminine air.

Fitted elegance
Modern fitted wardrobes in plain white with a gold trim combine well with an old-fashioned brass bedstead.

BEDS AND SEATING

Beds are by nature conspicuous and cumbersome objects. There's no way really to prevent the bed dominating the room, especially when it is a double that needs space at either side for both occupants to get in and out.

The type you choose depends on the style and use of room – a simple divan for a modern interior; a brass or wood bedstead in a period home; bunk beds for children; a sofa bed for guests.

A practical and pretty headboard can be added very cheaply. A pair of piped foam cushions mounted on a pole or a padded fabric 'sleeve' to cover an old wooden headboard can be made to match the decor. Buying a headboard with a new bed makes it easier to match the style; the choice ranges from classic button-back upholstered headboards to cottage-style pine, natural or painted wicker, tubular steel, or sleek laminate.

Seating The minimum you need is a stool or chair for the dressing table and perhaps a small button-back 'lady's chair' on which to leave clothes over-night. A small sofa or armchair will turn a large bedroom into a haven for quiet moments away from the family.

△ *An imposing style*
Carved hardwood furniture suits this period bedroom, echoing the beamed ceiling. Two bedside table lamps allow one occupant of the bed to read while the other is sleeping, and an antique towel rail is both decorative and useful.

◁ *A choice of bedside tables*
A practical bedside table should have spacious drawers or shelves as well as generous surface space. A balustrade stops things slipping off and a pull-out surface forms a handy tray for early morning tea. A bedside table which is an integral part of the headboard makes for clean lines, while an extra-tall table makes reading in bed easier.

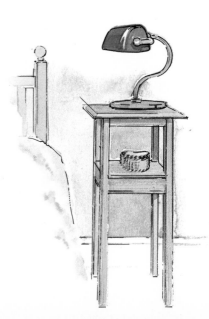

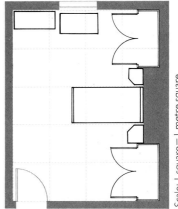

◁ **A successful mixture**
One advantage of freestanding bed-room furniture is that various styles and materials can be combined. Here a pine wardrobe and chest of drawers go well with a colourful modern sag bag, white bedstead and bedside table and a low, antique-looking table for pot plants.

▽ **A bold design**
A wardrobe fitted into an alcove makes excellent use of space, while a blanket box provides storage as well as seating. The vibrant colours in the bedding are picked up in the carpet and blind.

Scale: 1 square= 1 metre square

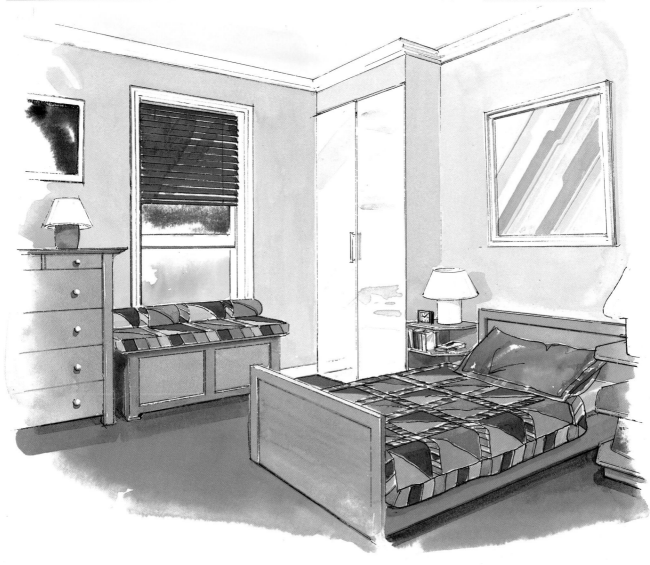

WARDROBES AND STORAGE

If you plump for built-in wardrobes, and have the space, you could dispense entirely with additional furniture, making the dressing table and bed an integral part of the design. A fitted bed surround can incorporate the headboard and tables, with high cupboards above for extra storage.

While freestanding wardrobes offer less storage space, they can be a better choice in an older home with fine original mouldings which would be obscured by built-in furniture. With the increased popularity of fitted furniture, there are plenty of second-hand bargains — junk shops and newspaper ads are great sources of well-made wardrobes in need of no more than a wash-down, polish or coat of paint. Look out for old doors, too, that a carpenter could build in as a cupboard door across an alcove.

A traditional storage item, such as an ottoman or blanket box, is a worthwhile addition for housing clothes and linen. Placed at the end of a bed, it can also double-up as an extra surface for a portable television or tea tray.

△ *Airy and light*
The clean, uncluttered design of this fitted furniture makes a relatively small bedroom seem spacious, yet manages to accommodate a surprising amount of storage space at the same time.

The line of the low drawers and cupboards is continued around the bed by a single shelf, with integral bedside lights. Although they are in fact separate pieces of furniture, the bed and split-level night table appear to be a single unit.

▷ *Bed alcove*
By using built-in furniture in this bedroom, it has been possible to create a whole wall of wardrobes, with a separate 'his' and 'hers' combination flanking the bed. High cupboards frame the bed and provide additional storage for out-of-season and rarely-used clothes.

ATTIC BEDROOMS

As well as providing much needed additional space, a bedroom in the attic has its own special advantages.

An attic room tends to have a different feel from other bedrooms. It is usually the warmest place, as heat rises, and has a degree of privacy not possible in the rest of the house. It is rarely overlooked and often has an attractive bird's eye view of the surrounding area.

An attic bedroom must have a fixed staircase – a folding ladder leading to a hatch will not do. But the stairs can be narrow and twisting, or even spiral, check your local planning regulations.

DECORATION

Choose a scheme which makes the attic bedroom look more spacious. In general, small patterns work best and light colours are more suitable than dark – unless you want a dramatic effect.

Whether you treat the sloping areas as walls or ceiling depends largely on what proportion of the room is pitched. A large expanse of flat ceiling can be treated separately from slopes and wall but if there is little true ceiling, both areas are best handled as one. If there is a low area of flat wall below the slopes you could treat this as a dado and paint or paper it to accent the main pattern or colour.

If you want to carry the same wallpaper up one wall, across the ceiling and down the other side, choose a random or abstract pattern. If a design has a definite right way up on one side of the room it will turn disconcertingly upside down on the other and you may get a jarring effect where a flat end wall meets the ceiling. Instead, choose an allover design of flowerheads, a mini-print or a small geometric pattern.

Romantic roses
Here a floral wallpaper has been used for walls and slopes with a simpler, complementary design on the ceiling. The two areas have been clearly separated by adding a cornice in an accent colour. The window is pretty and high enough to be left uncurtained.

CONVERSION

If you need an extra bedroom, a loft or attic may be ideal for conversion. Some types of roof construction easily lend themselves to conversion, others make the job more difficult or even impossible.

You may need planning permission and, in any case, you are subject to building regulations which set down minimum standards as to headroom, size of windows, access and so on.

Windows The most easily installed windows are those which follow the roof profile. These can take the form of flush windows let into the roof slope, often with a central pivot for opening. Or fit windows in the vertical gable ends – casement, sash, pivot, round portholes or even triangles echoing the gable – to suit the exterior style of the house.

Dormers have the advantage of giving you extra headroom but involve a little more structural work. They also need careful handling in order not to spoil the overall look of the house. One small dormer, roofed and gabled to sympathize with the existing structure can be a very attractive feature; a long dormer incorporating windows and flat areas of wall needs more thought to avoid giving the house a top heavy appearance.

USING THE SPACE

Part of the attraction of an attic bedroom is its irregular shape – sloping ceilings, unusual windows and interesting nooks and crannies.

Often the usable area is long and rather narrow which offers several options. You may decide on two bedrooms, or one larger bedroom together with its own bathroom.

Another possibility is to have just one long bedroom incorporating a seating area or study.

You may find there are existing features which naturally split the room, perhaps a chimney stack or beams. Alternatively, you can use the windows to create a division; a window midway along one sloping wall could separate a seating area from a sleeping alcove.

Storage Because of their low, sloping ceilings, attics often have wasted space where there is not room to stand upright. But this space can make useful storage; cupboards built into the eaves have the advantage of being unobtrusive.

If you need taller hanging space than is possible with an eaves cupboard, you could build in cupboards along a window wall, with low cupboards under the windows and ceiling height wardrobes for the rest of the run.

◁ *Working space*

In this bedroom/study the sloping walls and the ceiling and floor have been close-boarded and painted gloss white to make the most of the available light.

Generous built-in cupboards, which accommodate the slope of the ceiling, separate the sleeping and dressing area from the desk and chair.

The bed fits neatly into the space between the two runs of tall cupboards under one window; its headboard incorporates a wide shelf for a lamp, books and so on. Under the far window there is a cupboard to sill height for papers and office clutter.

▷ *Teenager's den*

The same attic with one of the built-in wardrobes removed has been transformed into a bed/sitting room, ideal for a teenager. A small desk with an angled work lamp and chair under one window provides a study, while inexpensive modular seating under the other window creates an area for entertaining. Tubular steel shelving for books and TV is a neat storage solution.

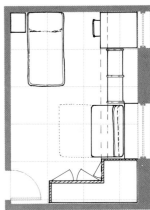

scale: I square = I metre

◁ *Under the eaves*

To overcome the height problem of a floor-to-ceiling slope, a cupboard is built into the lower part of the wall. The attic is painted to match the sky – the walls, ceiling and woodwork are bright blue for bold impact. Crisp white is used for the chair, bed, table, cupboards and wall lights.

The curtains are made of white voile, cased top and bottom and threaded on to white-painted rods. The bedlinen is hand decorated: fabric paint was sponged on to plain white sheets and pillowcase to create clouds.

WINDOW DRESSING

One advantage of an attic bedroom is that it is rarely overlooked, so the window treatment can be purely decorative.

Dormers can be an attractive feature but, as they are often quite deeply recessed, some daylight is cut out of the room. Conventional curtains, even when drawn right back, still cover part of the window, cutting out even more light.

A roller blind is a practical choice but, used on its own, even a patterned blind looks quite severe and is best suited to tailored schemes. Frilly festoons, or roman blinds are softer looking. If there is space above to hang the blind, this will help make the window look taller.

Conventionally hung curtains and blinds are no good for sloping windows. Roller blinds on side runners are a neat solution, as are lengths of sheer fabric threaded on to curtain wire or rods, or curtains hung in the normal way at the top and held against the wall with a horizontal pole.

▷ **Tailored look**
Clear pastels and geometric designs create an unfussy setting for wooden furniture. A striped white roller blind reinforces the crisp, tailored theme and pale grey paper in the dormer recess makes the most of the available light.

◁ **Soft drapery**
As this attic room is not overlooked, the curtain is solely for decoration. A length of sheer fabric is hung across the window from a brass pole and then caught up at one side and allowed to spill liberally over the floor. Together with the leafy houseplant, this creates a pretty focal point without cutting out any daylight.

BRIGHT IDEA

Full length curtains Sloping windows can present difficulties when hanging curtains. Fix a curtain pole above the window and a second just below the slope. Hang the curtains from the top pole and tuck them behind the other one so that they follow the sloping lines of the wall.

△◁ Jagged edge

Hanging curtains on swivel rods on pivoting brackets is an excellent idea for a dormer window.

Here, salmon pink, green, grey and white striped fabric has been used. The curtains are taken right up to the ceiling and the space above the window is covered in the same fabric. Pink and green are alternated for the lining and the unusual saw tooth edging.

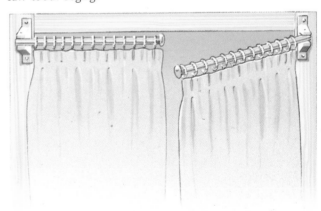

△ Swivel rods

Curtains are slotted on to the rods or hung from runners. Each rod is swivelled across the window at night, opening back against the sides of the recessed window during the day. They can meet at the middle, as above, or cross over for a more luxurious effect. The curtains can be caught back with ties to follow the shape of the recess.

CORNERWISE

The steep slopes of a bedroom in the roof often create unusual corners which, at first glance, seem too awkward to be of any great use. Have another look and you'll find all sorts of ways to handle them.

Fitting in shelves is extremely easy and a display area does not need parallel, or even symmetrical, sides to look attractive. A sloping space too low for a chest of drawers, could house a blanket chest, toy box or even a child's desk and chair.

▷ Desk space
In this child's room, a sloping corner space has been turned neatly into a tiny study. A raised platform defines the area, the back is hung with shallow shelves, and a small wall-hung desk and stool take up the rest of the space.

▽ Boldly bordered
Painting the dado the same deep colour as the carpet and keeping the sloping wall above light gives a more spacious feel to a cramped space. A positive feature is made of the room's steep slope and angles by outlining each wall with a wallpaper border.

Mitring a border

1 Paste a length of border along one edge to within 25cm of corner. Extend unpasted section beyond corner and fold extending edge away from but following the angle of the next edge so you get a crease across the apex of the corner.

2 Cut along creased line, using a metal ruler and craft knife.

3 Fold and cut the next length in the same way, matching pattern on the fold.

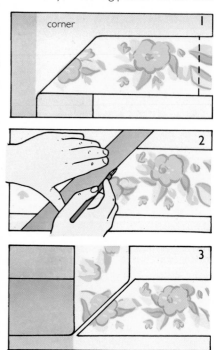

ROOM FOR A GUEST

With forethought, a spare bedroom can be warmly welcoming for guests and serve family needs at other times.

Having friends or relatives to stay can be a great pleasure for all, but careful thinking through is necessary in order to make the visit welcoming for your guests and worry-free for you. Most houses haven't space for a room specially set aside for visitors; often the spare room has to be put to use at other times, too. But with a little preliminary thought, these different roles can be successfully combined.

The atmosphere of a guest room is important. To provide a fitting welcome, the room should be fresh and inviting without being overwhelmingly forceful in style. Creating pleasantly comfortable surroundings needn't involve a heavy financial outlay. You don't have to buy expensive new furniture, though do avoid using the room as a dumping ground for ill-matched bits and pieces discarded from other areas of the house.

Your guests have chosen to spend time in your home, so don't feel you have to eradicate all traces of person-ality from the room. A dreary, hotel-like atmosphere, anonymously bland, may offend no-one but it won't actually give much pleasure, either.

It's the little touches which so often make guests feel especially welcome, rather than luxuries such as an en-suite bathroom. Pander just a bit to regular visitors. If children frequently stay you could collect together a surprise toybox or a drawer of modelling clay, crayons and puzzle books. For guests who rise earlier and retire later than the house-hold, provide tea-making facilities and the loan of a TV or radio.

A big bowl of sweet-smelling flowers (especially if they are from your own garden) will make guests feel really very special.

A temporary haven
A fresh and inviting environment thoughtfully kept clear of the clutter that can so easily collect in a spare room. If you have space, twin beds provide the greatest flexibility of sleeping arrangement for guests.

AND SO TO BED

The bed can make or mar a visit for the guest, and it will almost certainly be one of your first considerations. Will you normally be having couples to stay? Do children often visit? Would you be better off with a double bed, or two singles? Single divans are generally more flexible as they adapt easily to different arrangements.

Experiment with the positioning of single beds, perhaps by placing them at right angles rather than side by side. Some single divans zip together for double comfort, and there are two-tier trundle beds; the lower one pulls out when needed.

Dual-purpose sleeping arrangements include sofa beds that sleep one or two people and chair beds that convert to sleep one. To keep floor space clear consider beds that fold up, or pull-down beds that store flat against a wall. Futons can fold up for seating, and roll out to form a bed. A regular shake will keep them loosely comfortable. Remember, though, elderly guests may have problems with a low bed.

Some sofa beds use the matching duvet as a daytime cover, but arrange convenient storage if bedding has to be removed during the day. A blanket box is ideal as it could hold extra blankets for chilly nights and also be used as a bedside table. Provide a light for bedtime reading, with a switch near the bed.

△ *Doubling up*
Single divans placed at right angles leave more floor space free than side-by-side positioning. With cushions and a cover, they adapt easily to a daytime seating arrangement.

▽ *Two into one*
Single beds that zip-link can be used as two singles or one double, whichever your guests prefer. It's a good idea to provide a radio or television, particularly if the stay is lengthy.

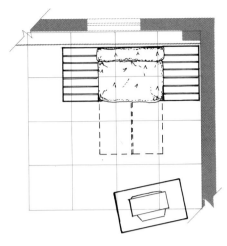

Scale: 1 square = 1 metre square

▽ ▷ **A welcoming home**
The inviting room shown below cheerfully reflects the personality of the household. A chest is a particularly versatile piece of furniture for a spare room, and little extras such as the plants make it all a very cosy temporary home.

   As an alternative to the cane bed, a futon (shown right) could flexibly meet sleeping or seating needs. A light with dimmer switch has been thoughtfully positioned so that it can be used for bedtime reading or general lighting. And a television is bound to please.

DOUBLE PLEASURE

If you haven't the space to set aside a room specially for guests, consider furnishings that are flexible enough for double-up use. Beds for guests can provide daytime seating which will serve family needs at other times.

If the room has a dual role you may not want to fill available space with a wardrobe and chest of drawers. For guests' clothes you could partition or curtain off a wire storage system providing hanging space and trays for sweaters and so on. If you want to retain some storage for family use, keep it clearly defined in one area. For small rooms, a bentwood hatstand or a good supply of hangers for a series of coat hooks behind the door will be adequate for overnight visitors.

Choose versatile furniture for other purposes – a blanket box could be used as a bedside or occasional table, or convert a desk into a dressing table by adding a table-top mirror.

It's unlikely that many households will be able to offer guests the luxury of an en-suite bathroom. If they are to share family facilities, let them know the off-peak times so they can use the bathroom at leisure. A wash basin, screened from sight in the spare room, would ease pressure on the bathroom, and would doubtless be used at other times by the family. Keep guest towels warm and aired on a rail clipped to the radiator in the spare room.

Finally, before welcoming guests, put your spare room to the test by sleeping in it yourself for a night or two.

△ ▷ *Bedding down*
A sofa bed is particularly appropriate for a dual-purpose room as it converts quickly when guests come to stay and provides useful seating at other times. The mechanism of modern sofa beds is usually easier to operate than that of earlier models. If space is tight, look out for a sofa bed with storage for bedding built under the seating.

△ ▽ Ship-shape
Another versatile scheme that converts smoothly from night to daytime use. A ship-style bunk makes an attractive sleeping area and incorporates useful drawers for tidying away bedding during the day. This arrangement provides an unobtrusive sleeping area when guests stay the night; when visitors depart, it converts back for family use.

▽ Single style
Sleeping arrangements needn't dominate a room. Here furniture handsome enough for a study or second reception room can also meet the needs of an overnight guest.

◁ *Traveller's rest*
A colourful welcome awaits the guest who comes to stay in this home. Your visitors are less likely to feel that they are living out of a suitcase if a space for bags and cases is provided. Here a high bedstead means they can be tucked neatly away under the bed.

▽ *Basin boon*
A wash basin in a spare room can be a boon for guests and ease the bathroom rush hour for the rest of the household. A screen or partition will keep wash facilities separate for visitors, and enable the room to be used for general family purposes.

A READY WELCOME

Often small things rather than luxuries will ensure a happy stay for your guests. Apart from the essentials – a comfortable bed with spare blankets, bedside light, clothes storage – a thoughtful hostess will have ready some of the following hospitality measures:

☐ facilities for making drinks – a small travel kettle or element and teabags; coffee, sugar, hot chocolate and creamer sachets; fresh water and milk
☐ mineral water and glasses
☐ a soluble analgesic
☐ a small sewing kit and scissors
☐ tissues
☐ a clock
☐ guest towel and soap, plastic shower cap, sachets of shampoo and foam bath plus toothbrush and toothpaste for emergency use
☐ a tin of biscuits
☐ a few general interest magazines and paperback books; short stories, cartoons, crossword puzzles
☐ folder with writing paper, envelopes, pen
☐ hot water bottle/electric blanket
☐ loan of a radio or TV

THREE STAGES TO A PERFECT BEDROOM

Let the bedroom of your dreams evolve gradually.

Considering the importance of a good night's rest to our general well-being, it's surprising that the bedroom is so often neglected. Yet it's a rare individual who hasn't some notion of an ideal bedroom – whether crisp restraint or a cocoon of romantic bedhangings – but how to work towards that end?

What can't be achieved all at once is often possible in well-considered stages – and there's no reason why you shouldn't have a comfortable bedroom at each stage. In a new home other things may take precedence, but draw up long-term plans so the room doesn't lose direction along the way. Shed

things in an established bedroom that don't add up to a pleasing whole.

There are some basics common to every fine scheme. A good bedroom, and a good night's sleep, begins with a comfortable bed. In an existing bedroom, review your bed critically: is it due for retirement? If you need to buy a bed, buy a good one and make it a priority at an early stage.

Sweet dreams
A bedroom can be a perfect retreat from the rest of the world, but it's rare that a scheme that exudes luxury can be achieved all at once. Meticulous planning has gone into details of this room. A clever idea is the concealed lighting – which must be installed before soft furnishings are made up – to emphasize the corona and bed drapes, while a fine quilt and swags and tails combine to make a very special room.

PLANNED OPERATION

Stage 1 If your budget won't stretch to a top quality bed, sink your funds into a really good mattress and sleep on that, on the floor, for the time being. Improvise on a top cover: candlewick or a wool travelling rug, perhaps. Find a temporary way of dealing with storage: perhaps a screened clothes rail or curtained alcove, with hanging sweater and shoe holders to keep things tidy.

Buy a bedroom-quality carpet or a generous rug and sand and varnish the floorboards. A venetian blind softened by sheer side hangings is simple but effective for windows. Choose temporary lighting at this early stage – free-standing lights, and table lamps at the right height for bedtime reading. Freshen walls with a neutral colour until you decide what to do next.

Stage 2 Add a bed base for your good mattress if necessary. Storage needs should be obvious by now, so settle on a permanent plan – good fitted or freestanding wardrobes and drawers. Once the lighting is chased in – perhaps wall-mounted over the bed – repaint or paper walls in your favourite scheme. For low-cost softness drape windows with cheesecloth or muslin.

Stage 3 This is the point to surround yourself with whatever you feel makes life more comfortable. If you like, spend money on good soft furnishings – dress the bed with generous swathes of fabric. Give windows a top dressing of swags and tails.

If you prefer understated elegance, search out real quality in the details. Concentrate on one feature of the room: an antique iron bedstead or a distinctive old chest, perhaps. Replace plain venetian blinds with equally plain but rather more stylish roman blinds.

Find neat housing – possibly fitted cabinets – for a plethora of bedside electrics: lighting, a clock-radio, tea-maker, telephone. A TV on a trolley or swing-out shelf is unobtrusive when you don't want to view.

Country stages

A room that's grown in character is at first kept manageably simple (above). A good bed and carpeting are first-stage basics, with off-white painted walls for a low-cost, neutral background. A tied-back curtain uses fabric sparingly, with the same soft apricot on a candlewick spread – a colour that works well and is used again in later stages. A blanket box for stowing clutter has a temporary home under the window.

Stage 2 (below) introduces more furniture to evoke a country spirit: a sturdy washstand and the old chest of drawers – a junk shop find – that holds promise in spite of a covering of thick paint. The print that livened up a dull corner is replaced by a needlework sampler which exactly suits the mood.

At Stage 3 (left) the chest – now stripped and polished – lives up to its potential, with stencilling, brass handles and a mirror to complete the transformation. Finishing touches include soft furnishings. A rug softens the floor, and – a nice personal touch – a handpainted screen fronts the fireplace. The sampler is such a favourite that it takes a prime wall site.

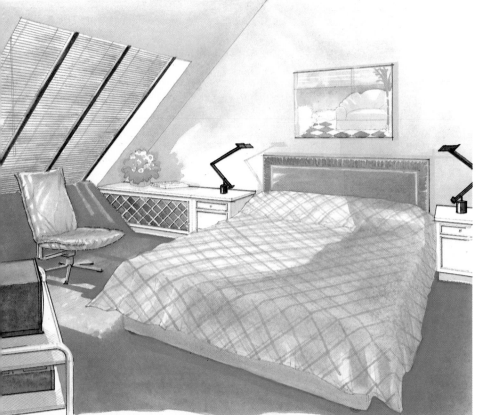

△ ◁ **Minimal flair**
With the basics in place Stage 1 (above)
is elegantly spare rather than sparse.
The best mattress money will buy,
handsome plain blinds and a carpet
that's soft underfoot are the main
first-stage expenses.

Stage 2 (left) has similar flair but with
some extra comforts. Now the
mattress has a bed base and headboard.
Modern angled lights, ideal for bedtime
reading, sit on units which run the length
of the wall, encasing the radiator. An
extra treat is the television which can be
wheeled out to view from the bed or
the comfortable new armchair.

With temporary curtained-off
storage giving way to built-in wardrobes
and the possibility of roman blinds at
the window, in Stage 3 the room will be
complete. Planned this way, there has
been no compromise at any stage over
looks or comfort.

Tranquil transition
After laying down the essentials – a good bed and soft flooring – in the first stage, a bedroom that's used in the daytime has been turned into a pleasant retreat with an armchair and fine old desk (above). The room is on the dark side so white bedcovers add a crisp freshness.

To relieve the subtle browns, another colour is introduced in the final stage (below): the rich green of the rug and corona makes the bed a distinctive centrepiece. A cheval mirror reflects light in a dull corner, brass swing-arm lights add extra style and pictures have been rehung to create focal points about the room.

BRIGHT IDEA

Well handled If you don't like the handles on a chest of drawers or cupboard, you can transform furniture quite easily by adding a set of new handles. Choose from a wide selection of plain or decorated ceramic, wood and brass styles to suit a modern or traditional setting.

△ **Mediterranean mood**
If you know you'll take a
while to build up from the
basics, go all out for
wholehearted simplicity. The
clearest of green paint with
pink-washed walls work
together like a dream here.
Comforts – a rug on the
floor, more permanent
lighting – can come later.
Unless, of course, you've
been won over by the bare
essentials!

▷ **Dual-purpose**
A bedroom that's used for
several purposes has smart
modular furniture that fits
awkward spaces and can
expand with possessions.
A judiciously placed blind
screens different functions.
Finishing details like the
roman blinds at the window
can be added as time goes
by. Harmony of colour has
evolved through the stages
to a particularly effective final
result.

NURSERIES: NEWBORN TO TWO

Babies and toddlers thrive in a warm, safe and attractive room of their own.

It isn't essential for a very new baby to have its own room, but after the first few weeks most people prefer to give him or her a separate nursery. This is best positioned close to the parents' room and away from the noise of the main living areas. A baby alarm in the kitchen or living room is a great help if you want to make sure the baby is sleeping without having to race up and down stairs.

People are inclined to think that a baby needs only a very small room, but your baby will not stay tiny for very long. The nursery needs to be adaptable to changing needs, and furniture and storage should be flexible. Miniature furniture may seem irresistible at first but is soon outgrown. A cot that can be converted into a bed, or a wardrobe with adjustable hanging rails for different sized garments is much more useful.

Decoration Plain colours or small print patterns for walls won't lose their appeal as quickly as a special nursery pattern that will be branded childish in a few years. Cushioned vinyl or cork flooring is warm to the touch, quiet to tiptoe across and easy to clean, and babies seem to prefer to crawl on a shiny surface.

Visual stimulus Babies are fascinated by colourful things and objects that move. You could make a mobile to hang over the cot, or hang pictures in view of it – change them regularly to make the display more interesting (see overleaf).

Playroom

This comfortable nursery has space for an armchair and has plenty of storage fitted into a wide alcove. There is room for a highchair and playpen and there is also lots of crawling space. The low cupboard can be turned into a toy store later.

ESSENTIALS

A crib, moses basket or removable carry-cot is cosier than a full-sized cot for a tiny baby. A moses basket or carry-cot is easy to carry and can be placed inside the big cot for convenience. This will also help to get the baby used to its future surroundings.

When buying a cot, choose a reliable make from a shop with a good reputation. Check its stability and make sure the dropside mechanism is safe and can't be worked by a toddler. A cot with an adjustable mattress position is a good idea. When the baby is very small, the cradle can be placed on the mattress at high level, saving parents' backache. Later on, the mattress can be lowered to prevent an active toddler from climbing out over the sides.

Once out of bed, small babies like to be propped up to see the world. A bouncing cradle or moulded plastic recliner with padded interior does this job well.

△ *Versatile room*
A well-planned nursery needs plenty of storage space. Here there is a small wardrobe with matching dresser – the top doubles as a changing table. A tall bookcase is used to display eye-catching toys, and later can be fitted with doors and used as clothes storage space.

▷ **Cot bumper**
Patterned padded bumpers securely tied to the cot protect a baby's head from the bars and draughts.

Parents spend a lot of time in a baby's room so, if there's space, add a comfortable old armchair.

Changing You need a surface at waist height for nappy changing, with storage to hand for all the essentials such as pins, powder and creams. There are purpose-made units available or use a changing mat on a table or chest, with a box or plastic cutlery tray close by for all the bits and pieces.

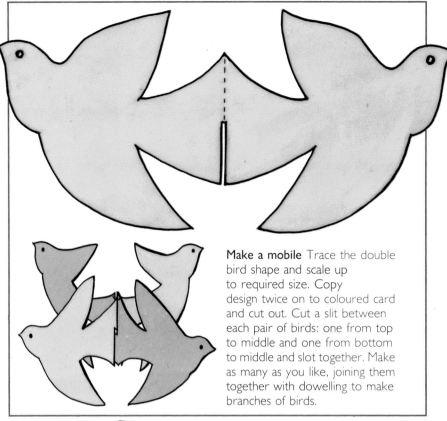

Make a mobile Trace the double bird shape and scale up to required size. Copy design twice on to coloured card and cut out. Cut a slit between each pair of birds: one from top to middle and one from bottom to middle and slot together. Make as many as you like, joining them together with dowelling to make branches of birds.

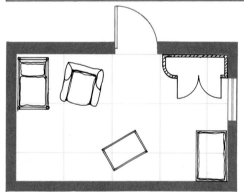

scale: I square = I metre

▽ *Adaptable furniture*
An old built-in wardrobe has been refitted with extra drawers and hanging rails to suit nursery needs. The top of the wooden chest-of-drawers is a good spot for the changing mat and the drawers beneath provide more storage. Both pieces can be painted the same colour for co-ordination.

STORAGE

For such small people, babies have a vast quantity of possessions. You need well-planned storage to stop the nursery, and indeed the whole house, becoming cluttered.

Most baby things are folded flat rather than hung, so in the early days a cupboard with drawers is more useful than a wardrobe.

Fitting out an alcove with shelves is less expensive than buying a new chest-of-drawers and more versatile: you can choose the depth and spacing to suit changing needs. Or you could transform a drab second-hand chest-of-drawers with a new coat of paint.

If you decide on a wardrobe or already have a built-in cupboard, it is probably more useful at this stage to remove the rail and fit the interior with shelves. You can adapt it later to suit the needs of a growing child, removing the lower shelves to take a toddler's toy box, clothes rail and so on.

A blanket box is another option and makes a good toy store and seat as the child grows older.

HEATING AND LIGHTING

Babies need to be kept warm; a room heat of 18-21°C is recommended. These days many houses have central heating, but if not, an approved electric convector heater is a suitable alternative.

A dimmer switch is very useful for a soft glow of light during night-time feeds and for checking on the baby. Out-of-reach wall or ceiling mounted lights are a better choice than plug-in table lamps with trailing flexes.

Getting a baby or toddler to go to sleep on light summer evenings can be a problem: lining curtains in an opaque, dark-coloured fabric, interlining them with a thick material, or supplementing the curtains with a light-obscuring blind are all good solutions.

△ *Room with a view*
There is plenty for a baby to look at in this nursery: a variety of objects on the shelves and a mobile in view of the cradle. A large, securely fixed mirror creates changing interest by reflecting the room.

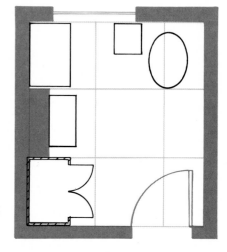

scale: 1 square = 1 metre

◁ *Changing needs*
With the addition of a large cot that transforms into a bed and a few modifications, a child can use this room well into school age.

SAFETY
☐ Don't use pillows for babies – they might smother
☐ Don't put bars on windows – in case of fire
☐ Use safety glass in low windows or cover with safety film
☐ Use window locks to stop children falling out
☐ Never put cot or bed by a radiator
☐ Use proper guards for all fires (including electric and radiators)
☐ Never leave a baby (lying or in a seat) on a table or worktop
☐ Put furniture in front of socket outlets or, better still, use safety covers
☐ Don't have trailing electric flexes
☐ Fix a gate to the top and bottom of the stairs

BRIGHT IDEA

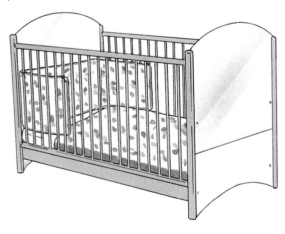

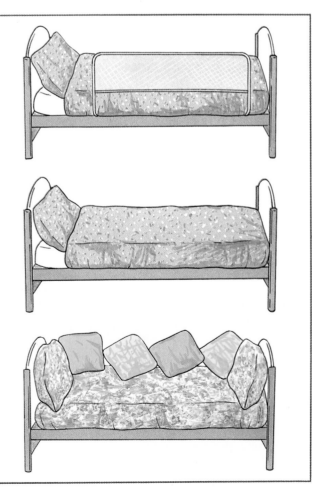

A **convertible cot** which has more than one mattress height is a good choice. This one is larger than average and converts into a bed which fits the child for several years.
☐ After the very early days the mattress is lowered, leaving the sides attached to stop an adventurous baby climbing out.
☐ For the first few months in a bed a soft mesh bedguard stops a toddler falling on to the floor.
☐ Eventually, with piled-up cushions, you can make it into a child-sized sofa. If you have more than one child, you probably won't want to convert the cot until the youngest is ready to sleep in a bed.

△ **Painted scene**
Small children like to look at interesting things. Here a fake open window painted on a blank white wall gives a view of a tropical sky and exotic birds.

◁ **Cut outs**
This decorative border just above the skirting is at the right height for a child to enjoy. Cutting out some motifs and grouping them on the wall gives an individual touch.

TODDLERS' ROOMS AND PLAY AREAS

Two- to five-year olds need bedrooms that are stimulating for play as well as peaceful for sleeping.

A good time to reassess the sleeping arrangements of toddlers is when they are ready to move from cot to first bed, at around the age of two, especially if the original nursery is too small to accommodate a full-sized bed. While proximity to the main bedroom is a priority with a new baby, parents of an early rising toddler may prefer to put some distance between them for the sake of a few more minutes' peace in the mornings. Depending on the layout, the bedroom should ideally be situated away from the noise of the living room.

If you are planning a toddler's room from scratch, your main concerns should be safety, practicality and visual appeal – in that order.

Safety first Fearless toddlers can easily hurt themselves, turning innocent everyday items into potential hazards.

The same care you exercise when buying safe toys, non-toxic paints and crayons and so on, should be taken when choosing the furniture and furnishings for their bedrooms. Choose fitted or heavyweight furniture which cannot be pulled over and has no sharp edges; lead-free paint for re-vamping an old chest, bed or chair; child-proof locks for cupboards the contents of which you prefer left intact; safety covers for electric sockets; non-slip mats and floor-coverings; safety gates for adjacent stairways; and safety catches for windows so they don't open too far.

Make sure that toddlers' playthings are well within reach, or they may turn into mountaineers as they try to overcome the challenge of high shelves and cupboards. If you want to protect books and other precious or breakable items, try to store them in another room; if they have to go on high shelves in the room itself, provide a stable step or stool for an older child to reach them in safety.

A magical bedroom

Apart from its obvious charm, this enchanting hand-painted mural provides stimulation for a child's imagination and a starting point for stories and games. A similar, if less original, effect can be created with stencils.

DOS AND DON'TS

The guidelines below will help your toddler's room resist rough treatment.

Wallcoverings A toddler's room is no place for expensive finishes which can be heart-breakingly ruined at the stroke of a felt-tip pen. Washable vinyl paint is much more likely to keep its good looks and does not date in the same way as childrens' patterned wallpapers. Pictures, pinboards or murals can all introduce an element of pattern.

Floorcoverings Fitted carpets or carpet tiles are best for warmth and comfort, though not perhaps the most durable floorcovering for a toddler. An inexpensive carpet (a 'room-sized remnant', perhaps) with a high proportion of synthetic fibres, should wear well and some are treated to resist spills. Cork or vinyl tiles or sheet vinyl are more practical and can be warmed up with washable rugs, but avoid high-gloss

finishes and use a non-slip backing for the rugs.

Furniture 'Building-in' is a wise investment, as it is both secure and space-saving. One floor-to-ceiling cupboard should provide all the hanging space needed for small clothes; a series of shelves below for shoes and toys can be removed as the clothes become longer.

If the budget won't stretch to fitted furniture, choose sturdy freestanding pieces with a combination of hanging and drawer space. Nursery furniture is soon outgrown; re-vamped old furniture is practical and cheap.

Buy a standard-sized bed with a sprung mattress and safety guard rather than an uneconomical 'child bed'. And if you want a second bed for occasional visitors, trundle beds (where the extra bed is stored below the main bed) or perhaps a futon rolled up to become a sofa are preferable to bunk beds.

△ *A shared playroom/bedroom*
This room is decorated in primary colours – bright pictures and paper kites liven up the sunny yellow walls, and a rug protects the carpet.

Bunk beds save space where two children share a room, but it's best to allocate the top bunk to the older child. Low drawers and a miniature table and chairs complete the combined bedroom/playroom effect.

Storage A tidy toddler is a rare being indeed – but providing ample, accessible storage helps maintain some order. Open cubes and shelves, and plastic or wicker baskets are a good combination.
Lighting which is permanently fixed to the ceiling or wall is safest. Table or night lights should be used only if the flex is concealed or permanently attached to the wall and the socket is as child-proof as you can make it.

△ Circus stripes

In this shared bedroom, roomy cupboards below the bunk beds keep toys tidy, leaving the floor free for games.

The decor is simple but effective – the panelling recreates the stripes of a circus tent and the furniture is painted a darker shade of blue. The varnished floor is tough and easy to clean.

▷ An alternative to bunk beds

Trundle beds are a practical space-saver where two children share a room; all that is needed is space for the extra bed to be rolled out. The window pane is covered with a clear plastic film which holds broken glass in place should an accident occur.

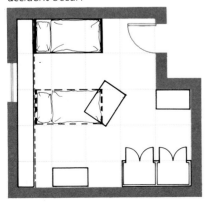

Scale: 1 square = 1 metre square

△ A room to grow up in

Children's tastes change as they grow up, and making drastic alterations to a toddler's bedroom to fit in with these changes can prove expensive!

This bedroom is eminently practical. The basic decoration is simple and will suit older children as well as toddlers, while the bright colours give it a cheery feel. Similarly, the furniture is adaptable – the large wicker chair is comfortable for a teenager or adult although the cushions make it cosy for a small child, and the chest under the windows can be turned into a dressing table. The low plastic table provides a spot for painting, jigsaws or tea parties.

▷ Woodland animals

Bedlinen designed specially for children makes a toddler's bedroom special and is not very expensive. There is a huge variety of designs and colours to choose from, often incorporating famous story book or television characters – it's a good idea to let toddlers choose their own. That way, they might be more willing to go to bed on time!

A PLACE TO PLAY

As toddlers begin to make friends, they are usually quite happy to spend more time playing with them in their own rooms. Making the room a pleasant and stimulating place to be will encourage this newly-discovered independence.

Growing toddlers may want to contribute their own decorative ideas, insisting on the presence of favourite book or TV characters. But since their tastes are bound to change, these are best kept to the cheapest elements (such as pictures and lampshades) with a fairly plain, though bright, background.

To be congenial, toddlers' bedrooms need to cater for the many activities likely to be crammed into a day. Allocating separate areas for different pastimes encourages children to move naturally from one to another. While messy activities are best confined to the kitchen, children like to display their creations on a pinboard or cork-covered wall. (Sticky tab fixings are safer than drawing pins.)

▷ *A practical arrangement*
Below the dado rail, Anaglypta wallpaper, painted with water-resistant paint, protects the walls of this tiny room. An attractive washable rug covers the hard-wearing carpet.

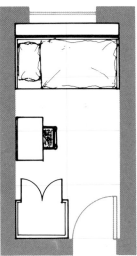

Scale: 1 square = 1 metre square

◁ *Space at a premium*
Often, the only way that toddlers or small children can be given their own room is by dividing a large room into two tiny ones. Here, a desk under the window provides a bright spot for painting or colouring and the bed ranged along one wall is matched by storage cupboards along the other.

▷ Keeping tidy

An adjustable storage system such as this is bright, attractive and likely to encourage toddlers to keep their possessions reasonably tidy. It is also sturdy enough to have a chance of retaining its good looks.

Stacking crates or vegetable racks, or wire trays in a metal frame are other cheap and cheerful alternatives to practical, see-at-a-glance storage for toys, games and books.

▽ Improvised storage

A wipe-clean melamine worktop (intended for kitchen use) has been installed in this toddler's room to provide an activity centre for painting, drawing and modelling.

A sturdy storage box mounted on castors is easy to roll out from under the worktop. Washable borders liven up both the worktop and the box.

BRIGHT IDEA

A safe stool is a boon wherever toddlers' legs simply aren't long enough. A stable but light plastic stool enables toddlers to step up into the bath or wash their teeth at the basin by themselves. It also has many uses elsewhere in the home – to sit on when drawing or painting at a low desk, as a stool for watching television, or to encourage toddlers to put away toys that belong in a high drawer.

CHILDREN'S ROOMS: FIVE TO TWELVE

This age group needs a well-designed space in which to grow and pursue a variety of activities.

Like everyone else, there are times when children need to get away from the rest of the family; to escape to a place which they can truly call their own.

In the average-sized home, two children sharing will often have to make do with a smallish room, while a third child may well have a room no bigger than an old-fashioned box room. And usually a child's room has to double up as a playroom.

This means available space must be utilized to its fullest extent. There will need to be places for hanging clothes, keeping toys, games, books and other paraphernalia, as well as for a bed. Ideally, there should be a work surface or table and a chair.

Furniture for children should be service-able but attractive and of a size to fit a child's needs for some years. It's no use spending money on tiny furniture for a five-year-old which will be quite inappropriate by the time the child is eight or nine.

A full-height fitted cupboard is a good choice as the interior can be adjusted to suit changing needs. In the early days a double tier of hanging rails on one side means that the bottom rail is within a young child's reach. The other side can have storage boxes or baskets at floor level for toys, with shelves above for clothes, bedlinen and so on. Later on, remove the lower rail and the child can take over some of the shelves.

Small beds specifically designed for little children are rather a waste of money – a full-sized one is a far better investment. Bunk beds are very popular. They allow more play area in a shared room and are handy for an occasional guest in a single one.

Safety first Never put a child under five in a top bunk. At any age an adequate guard is necessary, and the ladder must be secure.

Large expanses of glass and active children do not go together. Try not to put a child in a room with windows below waist height; if this is unavoidable then use safety glass or hardboard for the low-level panes and add a single bar across at, or above, waist level. Don't position furniture so that adventurous children can climb up and fall out of windows.

Install safety guards over radiators and never use a free-standing heater in a child's room. Obviously, any fire should be well guarded. Trailing electric flexes are dangerous as they act like tripwires and wall sockets should be protected with safety covers or positioned where a small child can't get at them.

Light and bright

A single room with a light and airy colour scheme in clear pastels. The large wardrobe gives plenty of storage and there is a roomy desk with drawers for papers, pens and pencils.

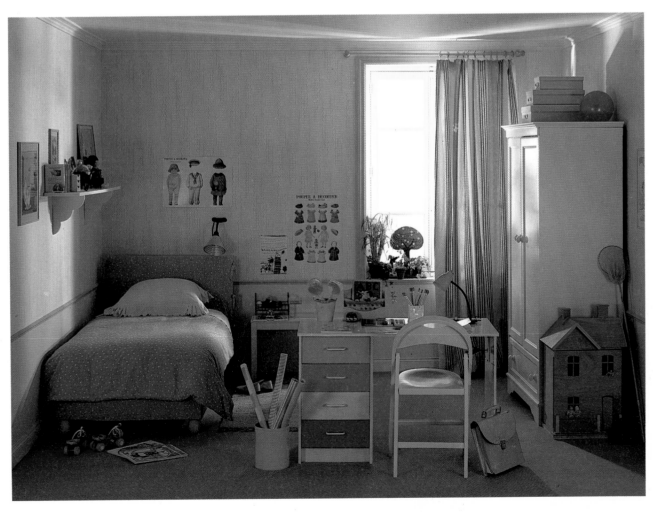

△ **Room to dance**

A large wardrobe with mirrored sliding doors takes clothes and clutter for this ballet enthusiast. Plastic hooks screwed to the wall on either side support a removable practice barre.

The colour scheme is a sunny yellow and white, accented with a strong blue.

An unusual feature is the bed canopy. A casing at one end of a length of fabric takes a pole which is tied to screw eyes fixed to the wall above the bedhead. Screw eyes fixed to joists in the ceiling above the four corners of the bed support poles hung from them with strong cord. The fabric is then draped over the poles and tucked into the bed end.

PAINT AND PAPER

Decorating a child's room is an enjoyable exercise and one where you can be bolder than in other parts of the house.

It may sound obvious, but do consult your child on his or her own decorative ideas. It's very easy to get carried away and to forget that it is not you who will be using the room. If the child has a particular hobby or interest you can use this as a theme. Don't overdo it – he or she might soon grow out of that particular craze.

Another pitfall is to make the scheme too finished and co-ordinated, leaving no scope for the child's own personality. **Decorative ideas** Whatever sort of decoration you choose, go for wipeable surfaces for peace of mind all round. There are any number of well-designed wallcoverings and borders which are specifically for children, and many adult ones are also acceptable.

An area of black or white board with chalks or felt pens allows free expression which is easily wiped away, and a pinboard will hold drawings or posters.

▽ *Art gallery*
The same basic layout has been given a new slant based on a strong geometric fabric which covers the headboard, divan base, and disguises an old armchair. Colours from the fabric are used on one wall, desk and chair and bedlinen. Another wall is covered in cork tiles to picture rail height and becomes an ever-changing art gallery.

BRIGHT IDEA

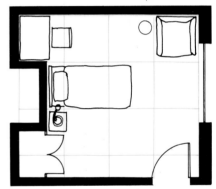

Cover a divan base with strong furnishing fabric to match your room scheme. Use a staple gun to fix it to the underside of the base. This is a tailored alternative to a loose valance.

scale: 1 square = 1 metre

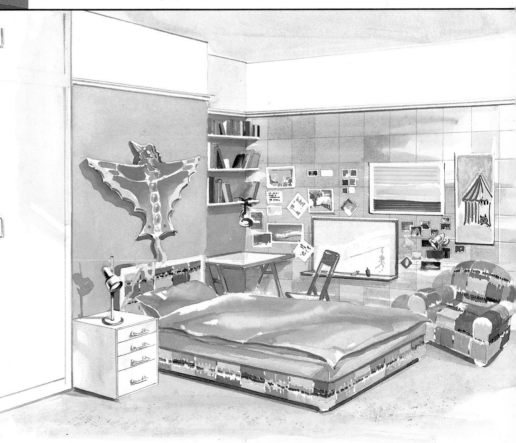

CLEVER BED ARRANGEMENTS

In most households with two or more children, bedrooms have to be shared. Even if the room is large, bunks may still be the best option where the room is used by both occupants for playing, reading and working, as well as for sleeping.

▷ *Off the floor*

There may seem no point in bunk beds if a room is for the exclusive use of one child, but there are advantages with an arrangement like this one. Here, bed, wardrobe, desk and bookcase take up the floor space of a single bed. This is a great plus in a small room, and leaves space for spreading out or, in a slightly bigger one, for a second bed.

▽ *Thinking of sharing*

Here the table is big enough for two to use at once, alternatively there is ample space for one child to be playing on the floor while the other is working or curled up on the settee reading a book.

The tubular metal furniture and clear colours chosen for this otherwise plain room help create an illusion of even greater space.

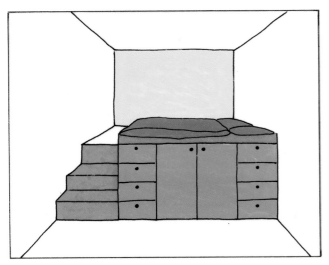

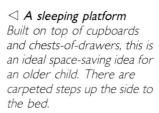

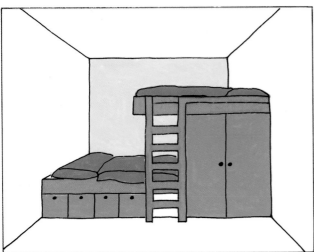

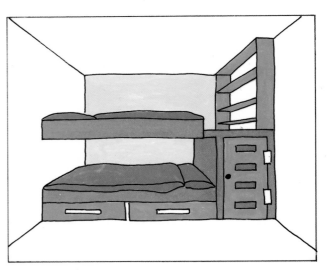

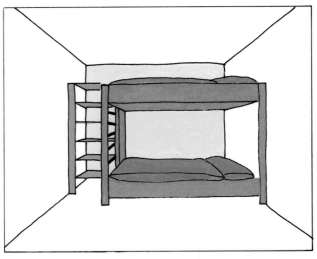

◁ **A sleeping platform**
Built on top of cupboards and chests-of-drawers, this is an ideal space-saving idea for an older child. There are carpeted steps up the side to the bed.

▽ **Wardrobe storage**
The sturdy cupboard door, with strong hinges, carries rungs to make a ladder. Additional shelving is arranged behind and along the bunks.

△ **An overlapping set-up**
For a room that is not wide enough to take two beds foot to foot, this system provides two sleeping platforms as well as a wardrobe and under-bed storage.

▷ **Strong metal framework**
A system of bunks, access ladder and shelving using scaffolding. An idea for the sure-footed only. (It is essential to make sure heads can't get stuck between bars.)

◁ **Bed-sit**
Low platform-based beds set at right angles to one another create a cosy corner for sleeping or idling. Quilted fitted covers give the neat look of a tailored sofa and lots of cushions add to the comfort.

An all-over scheme of blue and white mini-print paper and fabric gives a more spacious feel. Accents of pattern and colour come from the appliqué hanging, cushions and patchwork quilts.

The beds are rather close for more than one child for general use but are fun for sharing with an occasional visitor.

▷ **Occasional guest**
Most children love having friends to stay the night, but with a small room like this attic, a sociable soul has a problem. One answer is to choose a space-saving trundle bed like this one with another underneath which pulls out easily when it is needed. When not in use, it tucks neatly away to leave valuable play space.

◁ **Toy tidy**
There should be no arguments about putting away toys at night in this household; they are all simply pushed out of sight behind this cheerful threefold screen. During the day it makes a splendid display board or play house. It is simple to make and fun to decorate – with a painted scene or images cut out from a border or frieze and protected with several coats of polyurethane which can be easily wiped clean.

▷ **Book store**
A neat way to house books and oddments is by building plenty of shallow shelves beside and above the doorway, using those higher up for less favourite ones and for display. In this room the built-in cupboard finishes short of the doorway and this space would otherwise have been wasted.

Interest is added by outlining the cupboard mouldings with a colour from the wallpaper border and cutting out motifs to decorate the top door panels.

A YOUNG PERSON'S BEDSITTING ROOM

A young adult needs space to develop an independent lifestyle within the family home.

High life
An attic makes the perfect setting for a multi-purpose room. The inset shows a stylish sitting room, with storage units that hold everything from books to hi-fi equipment.

This modular system even comes complete with a fold-away bed, seen in the main picture, to gain valuable floorspace during the daytime.

There comes a time in a young person's life when the chance to take steps towards independence is welcomed. At the late or post-teen stage, young people need space to run their own lives, with the family at hand for support if necessary. A bedsitting room within the family home will give a student or first jobber the privacy needed for self-sufficient living.

Negotiation with your son or daughter will be necessary, as a young person won't appreciate being presented with a *fait accompli*. Taste at this age is likely to be more sophisticated than in the early teens, though some tactful steering away from stylistic extremes may be necessary if the space is to be easily reclaimed once the occupier has moved out. But a mutual respect is important. A first jobber may well want to supply some witty details as personal finishing touches or even make a financial contribution to the decorating cost.

△ Great divide

A combined sleeping and living quarter needs careful thinking through if it's to produce a workable whole. A divider can be used to separate different functions in a room. This one successfully closes off the sleeping area while open sections give an impression of space and provide shelving for an attractive display.

SETTING THE SCENE

To encourage a sense of independence, the bedsitting room should ideally be at a remove from the rest of the family. Attic rooms are often a good shape for one-room living; the garret ambience will doubtless be relished, and young legs can take stairs in their stride. For a room that is some distance from communal quarters, you may want some form of communication, such as a bell, to keep in touch. If the accommodation is within the family complex, it should be a no-go area for younger brothers and sisters.

Conventional furnishing may not be necessary or appropriate. Keep the overall design simple. The young person will of course be responsible for tidying and cleaning the room, and uncluttered lines will help to encourage good practice.

To live, sleep and eat in a small area requires skilful planning. Consider a versatile sleeping/seating arrangement, such as a futon which can be rolled or folded to form daytime seating. Fold-up or pull-down beds may make the most of a tight space, or a divan bed with storage under could have huge cushions for additional seating when friends are in. For a high-ceilinged room a more ambitious project to save floor space could include a tubular platform bed with storage below the raised sleeping arrangement.

SELF-SUFFICIENT LIVING

Though the occupant will probably be putting in frequent appearances at mealtimes to eat with the family, separate catering facilities will help encourage self sufficiency. Equipment could range from a basic hotplate and kettle for snacks and hot drinks to a complete mini-kitchen, screened or curtained from view.

Provision of a separate bath or shower would be ideal. There is a range of tiny bathrooms and fold-away showers on the market which would take up little space in a multi-purpose room. And an extra shower or bathroom would certainly prove useful once the bedsitter has been vacated. If the provision of separate facilities is not possible, and the youngster has to share the family bathroom, try at least to provide a wash basin in the bedsitting room.

Your young son or daughter is likely to be a more civilized being than during the early teenage years, but sidestep possible conflict through anticipation of problem areas. Lay down strict house rules regarding noise levels from the very beginning. A well-fitting, draught-proofed door, thick curtaining, wall-to-wall carpets and insulating mats on electronic equipment will all help to deaden unwelcome sound. Music fans should be encouraged to use earphones when the family wants peace and quiet, as the base element is not contained by the usual sound-deadening properties of fitted carpets, bookshelves and soft furnishings.

Expensive wall finishes may not be appropriate, particularly if posters or theatre programmes are likely to be stuck to the wall. Choose a satin-finish oil-based paint for the greatest resistance to damage.

▽ **Designs on space**
Storage is a critical factor in a multi-purpose room. A vast built-in wardrobe is one of the cheapest ways to provide cupboard storage, and can also be used as a dressing room. By painting furniture and walls in the same muted tones, the room is given a measure of co-ordinated restraint.

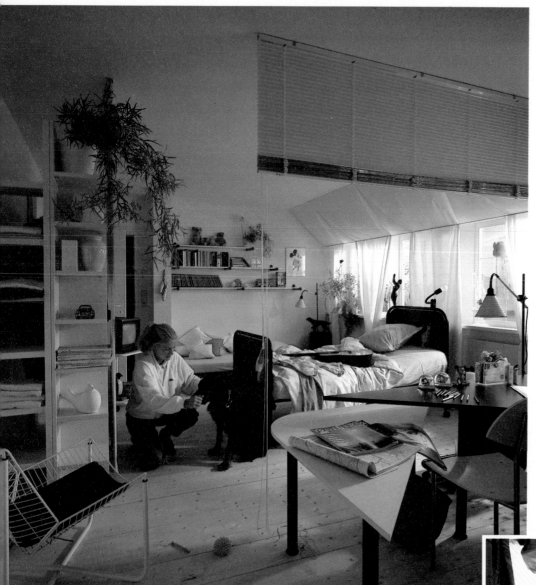

◁ *Youthful panache*
A loft conversion that cheerfully reflects the personality of the young occupant. Open storage displays everything from books to bears, as well as holding more practical necessities. Venetian blinds can be pulled down to screen the bed when dining, and raised to create a feeling of space. The use of sunshine yellow makes the room a happy base for independent living.

▷ *Changing places*
A row of tall office cabinets provides invaluable storage and is also cleverly used to partition off a dressing area which includes a hanging rail for clothes. Big, bold cushions and a vibrant bedcover make a lively impact in the sleeping/ seating area.

STOWING THE GEAR

Finding the best way of organizing storage of possessions in a bedsitting room is quite a challenge. Even if the lifestyle is casual, a sense of order is important, or informality can collapse into chaos. Plan an overall storage system from the start, so that floor space isn't crowded with bits and pieces all housed separately.

Look first at the layout, and consider how the room is likely to be used. Discuss the possibility of establishing areas for different functions – living, sleeping, catering – and plan the storage accordingly. If space is tight, you could gather together everything that needs to be stored in a large, walk-in cupboard.

Adjustable shelving can be inexpensive; open shelves are useful for books, hi-fi equipment and ornaments, and you could screen off a section to hold less sightly goods. Wire systems with hanging space for clothes provide inexpensive storage.

Modular units are a flexible choice for one-room living as they can be built up along a wall or used as freestanding dividers. The young person could investigate innovative storage, such as the tough, workmanlike units featured in the catalogues of firms supplying fitments for hospitals, shops and offices. For example, filing cabinets are now available in vibrant colours. A small cabinet could be used as a bedside table, while two or three larger models, holding general possessions, could serve as a room divider. House heavier belongings in lower drawers to keep cabinets stable.

▷ *Futon flexibility*
A futon is a versatile choice for one-room living, and is often popular with the young who relish an informal and unconventional approach to furnishing. A blanket box or old pine chest could be used for storing bedding during the day, and double as an occasional or bedside table.

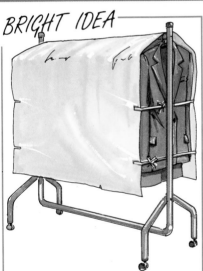

BRIGHT IDEA

Clothes cover-up A wardrobe is often too large and cumbersome a piece of furniture to fit easily into a multi-purpose room. A flexible and inexpensive alternative is to use a hanging rail, such as those found in clothes shops. To protect the clothes from dust and give a neat finish, drape a loose cover over the stored garments, and secure the open ends with ties.

△ *Colour galore*
This brilliant extravaganza of colour and pattern has been put together with tremendous verve and conviction. Careful use of blue throughout calms a blaze of colour. The room includes a wealth of imaginative detail that a young person could use to good effect – old furniture can be covered in handsome fabrics, and painted floor tiles and garden chairs can match the overall scheme. The room joyfully reflects the exuberance of youth, but definitely isn't for the faint-hearted.

▷ *Self sufficiency*
The complete mini-kitchen: occupying a space of only 600mm by 1000mm, the unit incorporates a sink with drainer, two-ring hob, small refrigerator and cupboard for storage. For more ambitious catering, consider fitting a multi-function microwave to the wall above the unit. The whole ensemble could be neatly screened from the rest of the bedsitting room.

BEDROOM FURNITURE

Consider your bedroom furniture carefully, for both looks and practicality.

Bedroom furniture is principally a means of storage, a neat and convenient way of keeping clothes, toiletries and sometimes luggage and study materials tidy, yet easily accessible. Looks are important as your chosen pieces will influence the whole style of your room, but shape and size must be carefully considered too. Often bedrooms are not large so you might have to be selective to ensure you get maximum storage in the minimum of space without losing out on good looks.

If space is very tight it might be worth considering fully fitted furniture. Models available include high chests of drawers (for wardrobes, see previous chapter), low-level units and built-in dressing tables that can be installed round corners. They can look very smart and come in a range of styles, materials, colours and finishes. However, fitted furniture tends to be more expensive than freestanding, though the price is usually inclusive of full design and fitting.

When choosing your bedroom furniture remember that it can be as traditional or as modern as you wish. Apart from pine, which is very popular, you can also find rich mahogany, cherry-wood, oak, elm and maple finishes.

Even the newly popular special paint effects like sponging, dragging and rag rolling have found their way into the bedroom ranges. A full range of styles is available going from a classical to a modern look.

Colours can range from traditional white and cream melamine with gold trim for the classical look to soft pastels and bright primary colours for a more modern look.

Style is something you should decide firmly before you buy. Your chosen furniture should reflect not just your personal tastes, but also your lifestyle and the purpose of the room – whether it is to be just for sleeping, or something more as well.

If you are trying to create a feminine and romantic atmosphere then a pretty, turned-leg dressing table and ornate cupboards could fit in. A child's or teenager's room will have to serve more than one purpose and you will need to consider shelves and cupboards for storing toys and books as well as clothes, and a dressing table that doubles as a desk.

For complete flexibility, there are several furniture ranges which you can put together yourself in any combination of components to create cupboards, chest of drawers and cabinets. These come in timber or metal and are generally of a high quality.

But beware when buying self-assembly furniture as the general rule is that you get what you pay for, and bedroom furniture at the very cheapest end of the range may not look quite as good as you hoped, however carefully you put it together. You may well find, too, that it is rather less sturdy in the long run.

DRESSING TABLES

MODERN
Style Low-level drawer units linked by matching top create a neat run.
In use Ideally suited to a modern style room. Useful for children's rooms as it makes a good desk.
Watchpoint You can improvise with filing cabinets and a worktop.

INTEGRATED CORNER
Style Corner-shaped dressing table built into the corner of the room and integrated with a run of other fitted furniture.
In use An excellent space-saver providing both drawers and a surface in an area that is usually wasted. This type of dressing table can also stand alone.
Watchpoints It can be difficult to get sufficient daylight behind the dressing table, so you may have to consider an artificial source of light such as lighted mirror or a wall lamp directly above.

COVER ALL
Style Kidney-shaped dressing table supplied with a rail for a curtain which runs around the dresser to cover its contents.
In use Provides lots of storage space. The curtain keeps all the drawers out of sight.

CLASSIC
Style Classic style freestanding dressing table which normally has a large integral mirror and little drawers or shelves above for jewellery and small items and one or two drawers below for hankies, underwear and other small items.
In use Makes a good focal point in a traditional setting. Usually available in a solid wood.
Watchpoint Like any dressing table, it needs good light behind and is traditionally positioned in front of the window. This style of dressing table can also be rather imposing in a small room and some designs provide little storage for the size (though there are models with drawers next to the knee hole to provide more storage).

BUILT-IN
Style Dressing table area built into a run of floor-to-ceiling cupboards.
In use A very neat option in a fully fitted bedroom. The winged mirrors can be useful for looking at the back of your head. Watch out for some of the special facilities such as slide-out cosmetic trays and spaces large enough to hold bottles for storage.
Watchpoints Because the style is fully fitted giving a more modern look, you may be restricted in style. Artificial lighting is essential as the dresser cannot normally be positioned in front of a window.

THE BATHROOM

If you are planning a complete bathroom refit or just want to update what you have, this chapter will help you get the best results, whether your preference is for a delightfully nostalgic, period look or the super-modern, ultra-streamlined style.

To begin with there is all the information you need to get the basic planning right, followed by a wealth of ideas for bathrooms to suit every taste and pocket. There are tips for making the most of small bathrooms, imaginative ways to give an old bathroom a new look, and very detailed, annotated photographs showing you precisely how to create different style bathrooms to suit your needs.

Complementing the design ideas is clear, practical information about choosing the best materials to cope with the rigours of water, steam and condensation. Walls and floor coverings are of vital importance so here you will find creative but practical tiling schemes, for example, as well as instructions for finishing touches which enhance at minimal cost, such as boxing in the sides of a bath.

Brimming with bright, practical ideas to help you make the most of your bathroom, this chapter will bring out the designer in anyone planning to redecorate or refit one of the most important rooms in the home.

ORGANIZING YOUR BATHROOM

Think carefully about plumbing, heating and ventilation when planning your bathroom.

The bathroom should be one of the most inviting rooms in your home. Try to make it a combination of warmth and luxury with the practical plus points of easy-to-clean fittings and splashproof wall and floorcoverings.

Relaxing in a hot bath, or enjoying an invigorating shower are both wonderful ways to unwind after a difficult day, but a chilly, badly decorated bathroom is no place to linger. Often a coat of paint, some thick, foam-backed carpet, fluffy towels and the addition of a heated towel rail can make the difference between discomfort and welcoming warmth. If the suite is old and in poor condition or the plumbing is antique and the space badly planned, more radical improvements are needed.

FIRST STEPS

Look through manufacturer's brochures to find a style you like. Although many of the rooms shown are larger than the average family bathroom, there are plenty of good ideas on how fittings can be arranged. Some bathroom manufacturers offer a free fitting kit.

Specialists If you can, it is worth visiting some specialist bathroom shops. Here, there are bath, basins and fittings in many different shapes and colours. Specialists are a good source of non-standard size baths, such as continental sit-up models. You'll also see unusual finishes, such as fake marble and metallic effects. Some specialists sell showers, including the latest 'environmental enclosures', complete with soft rain effect and piped music. All specialists have a

range of taps, tiles, towels, flooring and accessories, so it is possible to do all your bathroom shopping under one roof.

Colour choice When looking at brochures, remember that colour printing can be deceptive. Most sanitaryware manufacturers supply colour samples which can be matched up with wall-coverings, flooring and tiles. Take the colour sample with you when you shop and ask if you can compare colours in natural light – shop neon changes tones.

Plumbing If you are unsure how changes might affect plumbing – and whether or not restrictions would make your plans possible, ask a plumber for a survey.

Ventilation Lack of ventilation causes condensation in bathrooms. An extractor fan fitted to the window disposes of steam without bringing in cold air. If the bathroom does not have a window, it must be fitted with a ducted fan which switches on when the light is turned on.

A ducted fan wafts steam out through ducting which travels between walls to the outside air.

STARTING FROM SCRATCH

Installing a brand new bathroom is an opportunity to get everything right. A new suite, flooring, lighting, heating and decoration give you the chance to plan a room to suit both your tastes and your lifestyle. Use the checklist below to decide what you would like in your new bathroom before you make a plan and choose the fittings.

Make a plan Measure the room in metric as sanitaryware is sold in metric

sizes and draw the shape of the room on to squared paper, allowing one big square per 25cm. As well as the length, width and height of the room, mark the following on the plan.
- ☐ The position of the door and the direction in which it opens.
- ☐ Size and position of windows.
- ☐ Position of the hot and cold water supplies.
- ☐ Hot water cylinder and airing cupboard.
- ☐ Radiator or heated towel rail.
- ☐ Cold water tank.
- ☐ Electrical fittings.
- ☐ Anything you want to keep.

CHOOSING FITTINGS

Re-planning your bathroom need not mean buying new fittings. If the existing suite is in good condition but badly placed, it may be worth moving it around. Alternatively, if you hate the colour, think about having the bath and fittings re-surfaced. There are several specialist companies who offer this service. The work is done on site, there is a good choice of colours and the cost is about a quarter of the price of a new bathroom suite.

If your suite needs replacement, look through bathroom manufacturer's brochures and make a shortlist of suites which appeal to your tastes. If the house is modern in style, concentrate on the new soft, clean pastels. If you live in a period home, look at Victorian style and decorated suites.

Before you make the final plan, it is worthwhile thinking about the plumbing, space around fittings and the best way to position them.

Plumbing The WC needs to be linked to the main stack (the big pipe which goes down the outside of your house). Moving this is very difficult, so try to keep the WC in the same place.

It is cost-effective to have the WC, bidet, basin and bath in a line, so that there is one straight run of water pipes. The pipes can be hidden away behind a partition (called a plumbing duct). It may be possible to position the duct across the room so it makes a low dividing

BATHROOM CHECKLIST

Before you begin any sort of bathroom equipment, list what is wrong with the current room, and what you would like to have.

☐ **Facilities** How many bathrooms, showers and WC's do you need? If the family have left home, would you be better off with en suite facilities in the master bedroom, and a separate

shower and toilet?

☐ **Position** Is your present bathroom in the right position?

☐ **Hot water** Does your present system provide enough hot water?

☐ **Who uses the bathroom?** Do you need to make safety provisions for old people or children?

☐ **The fittings** Are they in good condition or do they need replacing?

☐ **Your budget** How much can you afford to spend?

☐ **Heating** Is the bathroom warm?

☐ **Ventilation** Does the bathroom suffer from condensation?

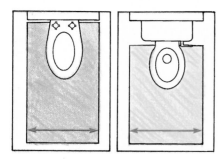

△ **WC and bidet space**
There should be enough space around the WC and bidet for comfortable use – about 70cm wide and 110cm space in front.

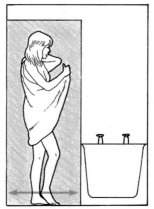

△ **Beside the bath**
Allow enough space (70cm minimum) beside the bath for users to climb in and out and to dry themselves.

△ **Around the basin**
Space around the basin is important, allow 70cm wide and 110cm in front. Avoid siting deep shelves above basin.

wall. Position the bath on one side and the WC, basin and bidet on the other. If you want to hide pipes in ducting, choose a wall-hung WC, basin and bidet designed for use with ducted plumbing.

Space around fittings Sufficient floor space around fittings is important if the bathroom is to work efficiently. There should be enough space around each fitting for it to be used comfortably. At the side of the bath, allow room for the user to get in and out easily and dry himself in comfort. A standing area 70cm wide at the side of the bath is the minimum comfortable space.

Space at the front and sides of the washbasin, WC and bidet is equally important. Allow an area 70cm wide and 110cm long in front of the washbasin. Don't position a shelf or cupboard over the basin where someone could bump their head. The WC and bidet should be set in an area about 70cm wide, with 110cm of space in front. If the WC and bidet are side-by-side, the space between them can be decreased as it is unlikely that both will

▽ **Build a plumbing wall**
If you site the basin, bath, bidet and WC along one wall, piping can be hidden in a duct. Shaded areas show the space needed for fittings.

be used at the same time.

If the bathroom has a separate shower cubicle, make sure the entrance is not obstructed and that there is enough space for the door to open fully. If space is limited, choose a cubicle with a sliding door. Allow about 70cm of standing space in front of the shower.

POSITIONING FITTINGS
The way fittings are positioned can help to make your bathroom practical and pleasant to use.

The bath The usual site for the bath is with one side and one or both ends hard up against a wall, but if space and plumbing permit, it is possible to achieve a more interesting layout by centring the bath along a wall, or in the middle of the floor.

If the bath is positioned with the side centred in the middle of a long wall, you can build a plumbing partition duct along the tap end and site the washbasin or WC on the other side of it. The plumbing duct wall should end at about waist height. The space above can be left open, or can be filled with shelving

or a display of plants. The advantage of doing this is that the bath is screened from the rest of the room, so more than one person can use the facilities at a time.

Another idea is to build a floor-to-ceiling tiled partition at each end of the bath so that it is enclosed in an alcove. Put the WC at one end and a shower cubicle at the other.

The washbasin If there is space, install two washbasins to ease the strain on the bathroom at peak times. Make sure that there is enough space for two people to stand at the basins. If the WC is in the bathroom, site the basin close by. Make sure, too, that there is a towel rail close to the basin and wall space for a toothbrush holder and soap dish.

WC and bidet Ideally, the WC and bidet should be separate from the bathroom, but in many homes lack of space makes this impossible. You may have very little choice on position as it depends on the location of the main soil stack, but if possible, site the WC close to a window or ventilation. The bidet should be beside the WC.

BATHROOMS FOR CHILDREN
☐ A step up to the bath makes climbing in and out easier.
☐ A shower cubicle fitted with a thermostatically controlled shower means that children can wash safely, unattended.
☐ As children have a habit of locking themselves in bathrooms and toilets, fit a lock which can be opened with a screwdriver from the outside.
☐ A plastic box on wheels makes a good home for bathtime toys.
☐ Install a locking cupboard for medicines.

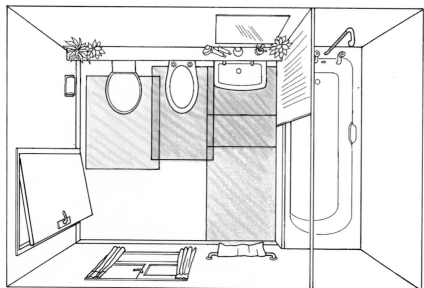

MAKING THE MOST OF SMALL BATHROOMS

A small bathroom can be very cosy, but there's usually room for improvement.

Although catalogues from manufacturers of bathroom suites illustrate larger-than-life settings, most of us have to deal with much smaller rooms.

THE OPTIONS

If the rest of your accommodation is generous, you can make a separate shower room or toilet, freeing valuable space and reducing pressure on the bathroom itself. Or, if a room next door is large enough, you can 'borrow' some of that space and enlarge your bathroom. These solutions, however, are expensive, involving both major

plumbing works and building expenses.

More realistically, you can try to work with what you have. In terms of re-arranging the plumbing, it is relatively easy to change the position of the basin, more difficult to change the position of the bath, and hardest of all to move the toilet.

A cheaper alternative is to replace large, and perhaps outdated or ugly fittings with smaller, more compact and modern ones.

The easiest and least expensive solution is to use colour, pattern and mirrors to create an illusion of space.

High-level ideas Many small bathrooms are too high in proportion to their floor area. Transform some of this high-level space into storage: cupboards above the bath are one possibility; building a narrow shelf between the top of the door and the ceiling another. Or try continuing the ceiling colour a short distance down the walls to the line of an imaginary picture rail to improve the proportions of the room.

Neat boxing in of any messy plumbing work and clever conversion of awkward areas into concealed extra storage space will help to streamline a small room.

Cool and pretty

Crisp white panelling, fresh florals and pale blue tiles give an air of sophistication to this ordinary, rectangular bathroom. Notice how the skirting has been continued around the bath panel and into the kick recess of the vanity unit. A pretty festoon blind in a charming flowery print disguises the frosted glass window; the same fabric is used for the chair cushion. A row of flower-pattern tiles, the houseplants and prints all echo the floral theme.

△ Stunningly simple
Palest pink fittings with candy-striped tiles make the most of this elegant bathroom.

Clever positioning of two large sheets of mirrored glass opposite each other carry reflections to infinity and create the impression that the bath is set into an alcove. As there is no shower attachment, and the bath is set a tile's width in from the wall, shelves could be built above the end of the bath. These could be used for storing towels and other essentials.

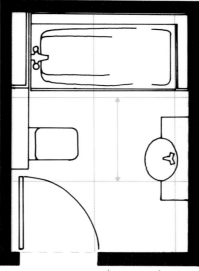

1 square = 1 metre

▷ Off the floor
For a really sleek effect, wall-hung fittings make for a spare, uncluttered look (floor plan above).

There wasn't enough room for a separate shower, so one has been built into the wall at the end of the bath. The strongly patterned shower curtain co-ordinates with the wallpaper border. There are glass shelves above the built-in cistern while the solid shelf next to the basin has been tiled.

SMALL AND STYLISH
Used cleverly, mirrors can appear to double the size of a room, while the clean lines of modern, wall-hung fittings, together with a sophisticated colour scheme, will help to create a sense of space.

Reflections Bathroom mirrors have far greater potential than being used just for shaving or brushing your teeth.

Mirror tiles come in all sizes, from tiny mosaic squares to huge glass panels, and range from the traditional silver to smokey grey and warm, pink-tinged tones. Tinted mirrors and small mirror tiles are kinder to less-than-perfect naked bodies than large panels of silvered mirrors.

In poorly ventilated bathrooms, condensation on mirrors can be a problem,

BRIGHT IDEA

Double shower curtain If you want to use a shower curtain but can't find a ready-made one to go with your colour scheme, use a co-ordinating fabric. Punch holes in the fabric, re-inforce them, and clip on plastic rings to attach a waterproof lining.

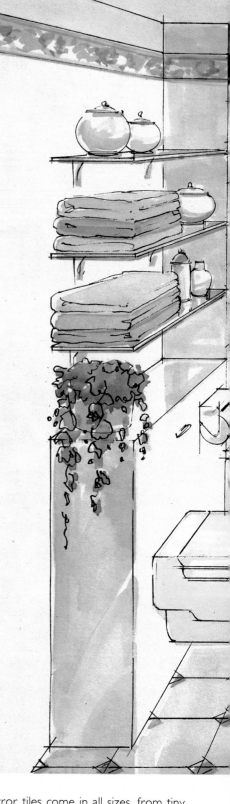

and glass mirror tiles feel cold to the touch. Acrylic mirrors and tiles are slightly better in this respect and are lighter in weight but are easily scratched. Make sure any mirror you buy is suitable for bathroom use, or the mirrored backing may come off.

Like ceramic tiles, mirror tiles need to be fixed to rigid, even surfaces, and large mirrors need strong, sound walls.

Fitting solutions Whether making a new bathroom or replacing existing units, remember that wall-hung basins and toilets take less floor space than conventionally supported bathroom fittings and that cleaning under them is simple. Be careful of weak internal walls; basins weigh least, but an occupied toilet is very heavy. If in doubt, consult a reputable builder or surveyor.

Although there are no scaled-down toilets, there are models with slim-line cisterns, ideal for ducting. There are also small basins, usually advertised as being suitable for bedrooms, but equally useful in tiny bathrooms. Steer clear of basins sold specifically for cloakrooms. These are too small to be useful for anything other than washing hands.

◁ **Tiling interest**
An interesting pastel scheme
gives a spacious feel to a
small room. Woodwork and
tiling are in the same grey
and are a good contrast to
the pale pink walls. Tiling
interest comes from the
diamond pattern, which is
continued around the
mirror, creating a border.

▽ **Streamlined unity**
A narrow bathroom with a
period feel is fitted into
an area no more than
3 m by 2 m. The vanity basin
unit has roomy cupboard
space and the boxing in
around the cistern is
continued up to the ceiling
to make an open-shelved
dresser.
    The uncluttered feel is
created by building in the
bath and the basin in a
continuous line, matching up
the line of the skirting with
the bottom of the panelled
fittings.

CLEVERLY CONCEALED

The smaller the bathroom, the more
important it is that dull or unattractive
items are kept out of sight.

If you are replacing bathroom fittings,
go for the sleekest ones you can find –
suites that have been designed so that
the plumbing can be concealed or
ducted. Alternatively, you can combine clean lines with hidden storage
space by boxing in your fittings.

If the toilet and basin range along one
wall, and the supply and waste pipes are
laid in a single line, the whole lot,
including a slimline cistern, can be
hidden behind a purpose-built false wall,
finished to match the scheme of the
bathroom. The top of the wall can be
used as a narrow shelf for accessories
or ornaments. (Make sure you can open
a panel to gain access to the pipes and
cistern.)

Storage If the cistern is on a long wall,
boxing it in could include shelving on
either side or above.

Boxing in the basin is a smaller scale
project, and there are ready-made
vanity units available from manufacturers. If the front is fitted with a door,
you will have the perfect hideaway for
shampoo bottles, cleaning materials and
spare toiletries.

TIGHT ON SPACE

If you have a really small bathroom, perhaps where you have 'borrowed' space to make it en suite with an adjoining bedroom, you may not have the room to fit in a conventional bath.

The obvious answer is a shower but, for those who prefer a bath, a sit-down model provides an up-to-the-neck soak. In the room on the right this arrangement enables you to have bath, toilet and basin without overcrowding.

To avoid a small room becoming claustrophobic, keep your colour schemes simple – go for clean lines, either with light, neutral backgrounds to help create a sense of space, or choose a single clear colour for a brighter effect. This is not the place for unnecessary clutter, so keep it all out of sight; built-in storage is a definite bonus in this situation.

A real plus in a small bathroom is that you can splash out on a few more expensive materials than usual – tiles, fabrics and flooring – without breaking the bank.

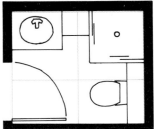

I square = I metre

△ Deep water

Where there is no space for a conventional bath, consider a sit-down model. Using pale wall and floor tiles gives a quiet, restful mood to this very small room. The neutral scheme also helps blur the boundaries between the floor, walls and sides of the bath, lending a sense of space.

◁ Mellow yellow

The alternative solution is a shower cubicle to replace the bath (floor plan above). This time the colour scheme is simple but stunning – all white fittings and tiles in the shower contrasted with bright yellow vinyl wallpaper, rubber flooring and accessories. A corner opening shower door is the best choice for this tight space.

◁ *Country look*
This bathroom in an older house has been given a country feel by taking easily cleaned gloss-painted tongued-and-grooved boarding up to windowsill level. This is higher than a normal dado but is very practical in a bathroom. The bath has been set 15cm in from the window wall, thus creating a useful shelf.

The 'dead area' above the toilet is taken up with a roomy kitchen cabinet, painted to match the boarding with a front panel covered in the same paper as the walls.

A wide and wonderful wallpaper border defines the perimeters of the room and outlines the fairly small window.

△ *Hidden storage*
Sliding mirrored cupboards not only double the apparent size of this compact room, but give plenty of storage space. This very neat solution does, however, have a snag; the mirrors really must be kept immaculate or the whole effect is spoilt. There is a special liquid available which can be applied to mirrors to help minimize misting in a steamy bathroom.

◁ *Bright primaries*
There is no reason why you shouldn't use colour boldly in a bathroom. Here, areas of primary red and blue are teamed with a greater amount of white — fittings, paintwork and walls — and the wallpaper above the dado picks up the primary colours in a small stylized design.

NEW LOOKS FOR OLD BATHROOMS

If you are not happy with the way your bathroom looks, think about how you can make it more stylish.

If your existing bathroom is looking tired and outdated, it is not difficult to improve on what you have. Even if you find it is too small for your family's needs there are ways round the problem.

Better use of space Rearranging the fittings can make a surprising difference to the usable area, particularly if you

New look

A dilapidated bathroom (right) can be revived simply by redecorating. Bringing the ceiling colour a little way down the walls and covering the top of the window with a festoon blind are both ways of visually lowering the ceiling.

A great transformation has taken

rehang a door that opens into the centre of the room so that it opens back against a wall. If the existing layout is really not making the best use of the available space, it is obviously well worth replacing the fittings at the same time as repositioning them. Experiment with squared paper and cut-outs of

place in a similar room (below). Large mirrors add a much needed illusion of space and actually do multiply the level of light in the room. The windowsill has been built up by two tile widths, the bath is placed under the window and a new vanity unit updates the old basin. Crisp white with blue tiles and blind make the room light and airy.

your bath, basin and so on to find the best arrangement.

If a new layout is not viable, one answer could be to knock a bathroom and next-door toilet into one. This larger space may allow you to include two wash basins and/or a shower cubicle to help with the morning rush.

Other possibilities are to take in an adjacent passageway to make a bigger bathroom or to take some space from a next-door bedroom by moving the partition wall.

An extra bathroom If you have one large bedroom, it might be a better plan to sacrifice part of it to make a small en suite bath or shower room to relieve pressure on the main bathroom.

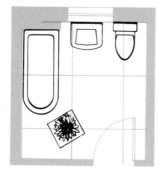

△ *Austere original*
This rather grim bathroom in an Edwardian house is in desperate need of redecoration. Although the original roll-top bath has been painted and has lost its claw feet, and the bath taps are beyond repair, most of the period fittings are in good condition and suit their setting far better than modern ones.

scale: 1 square = 1 metre

NEW VERSUS OLD

Before you start ripping out all your old bathroom fittings and replacing them with brand new ones, look at them carefully. If they are in good condition you might only need to change the decoration – new tiling, paint and wallcovering and possibly some new taps can be enough to effect a complete transformation.

You may find that your old bath is of better quality than most modern ones around today. Cast iron baths, for instance, were once commonplace but are now fairly difficult to find, as well as being expensive. If the only thing wrong with the bath is worn enamel or calcium deposits, it is possible to have it re-enamelled.

When renovating older properties, many people go to great lengths to track down period bathroom taps and fittings which have been thrown out by 'improvers'. If you live in an old house, or would like to create a traditional bathroom, there are a growing number of architectural salvage companies who deal in all sorts of period fixtures and fittings. There are also many manufacturers of reproduction sanitaryware, taps and accessories.

◁ **Authentic mood**

Here the atmosphere of the period has been recreated and the room given a homey cosiness. The bath has been renovated and the floor and woodwork are coated with glossy mahogany varnish. Plain dark green tiles were chosen for the area below the dado, with an edging of hand-decorated green/brown/white ones.

The Edwardian love of green plants is acknowledged by a leafy wallcovering and a hanging potted fern.

▽ **Modern setting**

The same room adapts well to a more modern treatment. The outside of the bath is painted grey with a black and yellow stencilled border to match the painted dado. The same three colours are used for the vinyl tiled floor.

BRIGHT IDEA

Border design Make a border to match your own colour scheme by painting the relief design of an anaglypta border wallcovering. On this geometric pattern the background was painted grey and the raised design was picked out in the same yellow as the walls. Make sure you use an oil-based paint to protect your hard work from condensation.

QUICK CHANGE

The least expensive way to change the look of a bathroom is to add new accessories such as a matching mirror, tooth mug holder and soap dish. Pale or neutral coloured fittings set against plain walls and floors are the most versatile bases from which to work.

In a white or cream room you can add a flowery festoon blind, pick out two or three of the colours for towels and add a wooden toilet seat and towel rail for a country look. Alternatively, you could choose a roller blind with a strongly coloured geometric design and take one colour from this to use as an accent.

Stylish setting

A classic white suite, a black and white tiled floor and chrome fittings are set against creamy walls (left). The look is spacious and smart but the mood is rather bleak.

The introduction of just one strong colour – a bluey-green – immediately makes this a more interesting scheme (below). The chrome trolley, mirrors and the pictures well-placed over the basins and bath further improve it. A couple of dramatic plants are the perfect finishing touch.

BATHROOM SURFACES

Surfaces need to be practical as well as attractive to survive the extreme conditions in a bathroom.

Extremes of temperature, steam and moisture all take their toll on a bathroom surprisingly quickly. Surfaces need to be tough, waterproof and easy to maintain if they are to survive bathroom conditions and look good.

The most common materials are paint, wallpaper, tiles, or a combination. The colder, harder and shinier the surface, the more it will suffer from condensation. Mirrors and windows are the first to mist up and steam will turn quickly to water against a tiled wall.

CONDENSATION

Unless a bathroom is kept warm and well-ventilated, moisture in the air from a steaming hot bath or shower condenses, streaming down the walls and misting up mirrors and windows. In a small bathroom or in one without a window, the problems are multiplied.

The two basic ways to deal with condensation are to install an extractor fan for ventilation and to keep the bathroom at a constant heat.

Ventilation To stop the bathroom mist-ing up, it is essential to allow the moisture-laden air to escape. Fans that rely on convection should be positioned high on the outside wall, removing the warm, wet air as it rises. Motorized extractors are more efficient, sucking the moist air out.

Warmth There are several kinds of instant heater if you don't have central heating or want to boost the temperature during the winter; wall-fixed fan heaters or radiant fires warm up a room quickly and, although inadequate on its own, a heated towel rail gives some background heat.

White practicality

Wall-to-ceiling tiling is, perhaps, the ultimate answer to the need for a waterproof and washable environment. Here, not only the walls but also the bath and basin surrounds are covered in classic white tiles. Red detail and a scarlet vinyl floor break up the otherwise stark and shining whiteness.

WALLCOVERINGS

Wallpapers, vinyl and foil wallcoverings are perfectly suitable for bathrooms, and patterns are great disguisers of uneven surfaces.

Wallpaper requires a sound smooth surface that has been well prepared and sized before it is hung. For best results, always use a fungicidal adhesive. Wallpaper can absorb a small amount of moisture but in really damp conditions it may start to peel and curl at the edges and joins, although sealants are available which provide a clear protective coat. Always test a sealant on a small area first to check that your paper is colour-fast.

Although washable wallpaper cannot withstand repeated scrubbing, it can be washed down fairly vigorously.

Vinyl is more expensive than ordinary wallpaper, but more robust due to the layer of vinyl fused on to a stout paper backing. It is also tough and moisture-resistant.

Plain textured vinyls can be used to simulate those fabric coverings which would be unsuitable in a bathroom – silk, hessian, grass-cloth, for example. Others convincingly mimic the appearance of ceramic tiles at less cost; they are also warmer to the touch than ceramic.

Foil wallcoverings are steam-resistant and highly light-reflective, making them excellent for dark rooms that don't get much sunlight.

▷ *Opulent looks*
An attic bathroom can appear poky but this one looks good and is also practical.

Most of the available surfaces, including the airing cupboard doors, are covered in a mini-print paper, offset by patterned tiles which protect the splashback areas around the bath and between the basin and mirror. Bold floral curtains either side of the bath give extra height to the sloping ceiling.

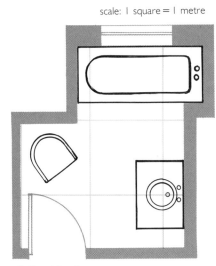

scale: 1 square = 1 metre

◁ **Seaside theme**
The walls in this pale bathroom are
covered in a practical vinyl wallpaper,
resilient enough to withstand splashes
and drips. The woodwork is painted in
white gloss and the bath panel is
covered in matching wallpaper
protected by a coat of clear
polyurethane.

▷ **Pastel alternative**
A different vinyl wallcovering is the basis
for this ice-cream coloured scheme.
Pale pink tiles in the alcove around the
shower, under the window and behind
the basin make a practical splashback.
Beaded wooden panels, painted pink,
blue and green, are now fitted along the
bath and under the basin.

PAINT

The cheapest and easiest way to decorate bathroom walls is to paint them with an oil-based paint, either eggshell or silk finish. Gloss is not advisable on walls as it tends to highlight the effects of condensation, can cause glare, and shows up imperfections on uneven wall surfaces. Emulsion is easy to apply and is a good disguiser of surface defects but is not so easy to wash.

Traditional paint effects such as sponging, rag-rolling and marbling work well in bathrooms. The durable coloured glazes used in many of these techniques make them particularly suitable for steamy environments.

TILING

Glazed ceramic wall tiles are the most practical work surface of all and can be used from floor to ceiling, up to dado rail height, or just around splash areas. Tiling a whole room can be costly, but it is a once-only investment that is usually worthwhile in terms of durability.

The variety of patterns, sizes, colours and textures available has largely dispelled the cold and clinical image of tiles, and there are prices to suit most pockets. Tiling a bathroom is a straightforward job and, if you are a DIY enthusiast, one that you can do yourself.

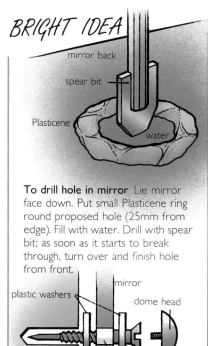

BRIGHT IDEA

To drill hole in mirror Lie mirror face down. Put small Plasticene ring round proposed hole (25mm from edge). Fill with water. Drill with spear bit; as soon as it starts to break through, turn over and finish hole from front.

Fix mirror Use screws with dome covers. Fit plastic washers either side of mirror. Protect hole with plastic sleeve. Don't overtighten screws in case mirror cracks.

△ **Totally tiled**
The white tiled floor and walls and large mirror by the bath are a good choice in this small, high-ceilinged bathroom. The hard-edged effect is softened with plants, shells and fluffy towels.

   Plain or patterned tiles can be used to equally good effect in a modern or, as here, a more old-fashioned bathroom.

◁ **Special effects**
Practical tiling to dado height is combined with the sophisticated marbled paint technique on the walls above. This effect is achieved by blending pastel green, pale cream and grey paint with a fine paintbrush and a sponge. Use a glaze or vinyl matt paint if you use special paint effects in a bathroom and protect your hard work from steam with a coat of clear matt varnish.

▷ **Diamond design**
A tiled surface on a vanity unit is a useful and practical place to put bottles of shampoo and dishes of soap. Extending the diagonals up the splashback makes these plain white tiles look more distinctive. The two small mirrors continue the diamond pattern and are emphasized by an edging of wooden beading to match the louvred cupboard doors and window frame.

▷ *Classic simplicity*
*Veneered wood has been
stained and varnished for the
bath panel and for the
surround of the unusual inset
brass basin. A matching dark
wooden, slatted blind over
the window directly above
the bath is easy to wipe clean
and preserves privacy while
allowing light into this small
room. Splash-resistant,
rag roll-effect vinyl wallpaper
gives an interesting texture
to the walls.*

◁ *Half panelled*
*Tongued-and-grooved
panelling in a bathroom feels
warm, is practical and
provides a good level of
insulation. In this traditional-
looking bathroom, panelling
up to the dado rail conceals
the poorly plastered walls.
To protect it from steam and
water, the wood has been
painted in a creamy coloured
vinyl matt paint.*
   *Above the rail, the uneven
walls are disguised by
marbled wallpaper in cream,
pale green and peach.*

CREATIVE BATHROOM TILING

For the adventurous, imaginative use of tiling will add flair and originality to your bathroom.

Ceramic tiles have long been recognized as one of the most practical surfaces for a bathroom, particularly in areas likely to come into contact with water. For practical reasons, it's a sound proposition to half- or fully-tile a bathroom wall as well as tiling the casing and surrounds of fitments such as bath and basin.

Much modern tiling is of course pleasing to the eye as well as practical, and in recent years the options for creative use of tiling have rapidly expanded. For the adventurous, this wide range of tiles presents a challenge to put creativity to work on designing a tiling effect uniquely suited to individual bathroom requirements and personal taste.

There certainly is no shortage of possibilities, with a splendid array of vibrant colours and unusual shapes, such as diamond, hexagonal and octagonal. The actual surface of a tile can be plain, raised, embossed, or incised. Patterns range from the prettily floral to modern geometric designs, with some also borrowing inspiration from a past era – there are many good copies of Victorian and Edwardian styles. Others, for example the high tech metallic finishes, are distinctly futuristic. Mural tiles or richly-decorated tile panels can create a focal point, and a range of attractive borders adds to the possibilities of creative tiling.

Before you let your imagination run riot, however, you must first sort out the practicalities. Start your initial planning by examining the shape and size of your room. Clever tiling can help to conceal flaws and highlight strengths. Which areas do you want to enhance, which encourage to fade into the background?

You must also study the surfaces. Are the walls square? Tiles produce such a perfect grid that flaws can be obvious. Use a spirit level to trace any fault, and plan so that a row of cut tiles falls in the least obvious place.

With such a wealth of ideas to choose from, remember mistakes can be costly. Spend time planning your tiling designs; it's too late to change your mind once the tiles are finally up. When looking for inspiration, find pictures of finished rooms, rather than making decisions based on a small section of tiling: what can be pleasing in small measure may be overpowering on four walls.

Draw on graph paper a plan of the walls and tile positioning; pin this up, with variations, in your bathroom and live with the idea for a while, until you are quite certain about your choice.

If you are using standard-sized tiles and your design is complex, invest in a grid which fixes to the wall, providing a framework for arranging and rearranging the design so you can see the result before you finally cement your tiles in place. Alternatively, lay the tiles down on a large flat surface to check the positioning.

Plain and patterned
A combination of different small, chunky tiles has been grouped to provide an attractive patchwork effect around a wash area. Note how they have been symmetrically arranged to give an unobtrusive sense of order to the overall design.

△ **Linear point**
An attractive and inexpensive way to add a dash of colour to budget-priced plain tiles is to use coloured grouting. The same colour can accent other features of the bathroom: here bold lines of red pull together different aspects of a room which, without special treatment, could have remained nondescript.

◁ **Tiling partners**
Two complementary methods of finishing off a panel of plain tiles: a pretty floral border echoes wall and curtain pattern, while a top layer gives a neat zigzag finish. If you want to create a similar effect, take care when cutting diagonals to ensure they are the same size as the square tiles, as a diagonal cut through the centre will obviously be longer than the outside edge.

MAINLY PLAIN

Very handsome effects can be produced by imaginative use of plain tiles, either on their own or combined with more decorative styles. Ordinary whites and neutrals are generally less expensive than vivid hues, but if you are tempted by anything particularly vibrant make quite sure you won't tire of the result after a while.

Tiles can be prohibitively expensive. If you want to keep costs down, consider budget-priced plain tiles for most of the area with the addition of more extravagant special effects such as borders or decorative inserts of single tiles, panels or even a tiled mural. Remember, though, if you use tiles from different ranges make sure they are of equal thickness.

With clever positioning, plain tiles on their own are subtly pleasing. Square and rectangular tiles can be laid stepped, in bricklaying fashion, while square tiles laid diagonally look handsome – they often create a more spacious effect than those laid in the conventional, straight method.

For good looks at low cost, consider using coloured grouting with budget-priced plain tiles which gives a very effective fine grid of colour. Grouting can be bought in a range of colours, or you can buy pigment if you want to colour it yourself.

△ *Blue mood*
Overall tiling in deep colours can produce dramatic impact, but to avoid too dense a result introduce variations on your theme. Here different tones of vibrant blue tiles are laid diagonally on walls but conventionally straight on other surfaces to add interest.

◁ *Tiled panels*
As an alternative to the overall scheme of rich blue tiles pictured above, a more neutral background can be used to give a lighter result, with the addition of distinctive panels and borders. The panels, large or small, can be designed to suit the size and shape of your room.

BORDER STORY

One of the most attractive ideas to give a fine finish to tiling is through introducing a border. These can range from delicate bands of fine pattern to bold, wide friezes. Borders can be added at ceiling or dado level, or can round off a partly-tiled surface.

Running a border or frieze around the room at dado height can help draw together aspects of an awkwardly-shaped room, and may give an impression of more pleasing proportions. A border can also frame attractive features – a pretty mirror, perhaps, or a window.

Tiles specifically designed as borders are frequently manufactured to complement a whole tiling range. They are often narrow rectangles, flat or raised. Modern versions of Victorian dado tiles are available, with the tiles ending in a raised sill.

You could experiment by creating your own borders. Coloured or patterned tiles can border contrasting styles, or you can build up a chequerboard effect with coloured tiles. The cumulative effect of a broad band of several rows can be dramatic, or consider swooping diagonal patterns across a large field of tiles on one or more walls. These more original creative ideas can give a great deal of satisfaction, but they do need conviction and careful thinking through at the planning stage before you commit yourself to any expenditure.

△ **Sunny spots**
Splashes of yellow on tiling and accessories cheer the starkness of pristine white. Note how disparate elements can be drawn together through careful use of accent colour.

▷ **Simply classic**
A subtle variation in tile positioning: large off-white wall tiles are stepped in brick fashion rather than laid conventionally in straight vertical rows. A black and white chequered border adds interest at dado level, and white floor tiles bordered by black complete the sophisticated effect.

◁ *Tiling trim*
As well as breaking up plain runs of tiling, contrasting colours or patterns can be used to draw the eye towards focal points in the bathroom. Here a mock dado in white and pink is extended to border the mirror, making a pretty feature of the area.

▽ *Plain and pattern*
There is a wide variety of different plain and patterned tiles on the market which can be arranged to suit your individual specifications. In this alternative arrangement of the wash-basin area pictured left, the tile section under the mock dado has a trellis pattern. The floral-edged border is also used to frame a mirror.

▽ *Dashing dado*
To relieve a large, bland stretch of tiling, decorative tiles can be added to provide interest at dado height. This border undulates round the room adding a cheerful dash to an otherwise muted colour scheme.

Diagonal tiling can add a subtle dimension to plain tiles. Blocks of diagonals bordered by rows of straight tiling can create stylish geometric patterning.

Tiles laid on the diagonal take up more space than those laid straight, so work out the positioning of adjacent diagonal and straight tiles carefully. Plot the whole panel on squared paper before you start. If necessary, trim the centre tile, as shown above, for a neat finish.

△ **Tiling framework**
Clever positioning of plain tiles can produce a very distinguished result. Here a window with a blind is made a decorative feature by skilful use of a soft green tiled surround – the tiles are built up above the window to form a handsome centrepiece within the framework provided by the gently contrasting wall.

Elsewhere in the same room the effect of long stretches of floor-to-ceiling tiling on facing walls is partly relieved by an ornate bamboo frame and decorative fan.

△ **Proud border**
Attractive raised borders can be used to create a dado on a plain run of tiles, or to highlight points of interest in a bathroom. This border is available in a range of subtle colours.

▷ **Fitment details**
A novel way of introducing pattern to plain tiled walls: these stylish tiling details make a decorative feature of bathroom fitments such as towel hooks and soap dishes.

BOXING IN THE SIDES OF BATHS

You can give your bathroom a new look by changing the panelling down the side of the bath – or create a luxurious and dramatic effect with a new surround.

Modern baths come complete with moulded panels that clip into place to hide the underside of the bath, and the supply and waste pipes. They are convenient and easy to fit, but may not fit in with your decor. In older homes, there may be problems. Flimsy hardboard panels round the sides of the bath may have deteriorated, or perhaps you want to change an existing panel.

You can buy matching shaped plastic or glass fibre side and end panels for almost every modern bath these days. And there are even curved panels to cope with corner baths. However, if you want to decorate the sides of your bath enclosure in some other way, you can achieve dramatic effects by boxing in the side yourself.

The principle is the same, whatever material you choose to use for the cladding and decoration. You start by building a simple framework of softwood posts and rails along the sides and end of the bath, and then attach the cladding material to this.

CHOOSING A FINISH

The cladding material can either be a finish in itself, or a surface to which you can add your chosen finish. For example, a purpose-designed mahogany panel or an old pine door can be fitted round the sides of a bath for a traditional look. For a more rustic effect, tongued-and-grooved boards, either varnished or painted, are a suitable choice. If your bathroom has a carpeted floor, you can even run the carpet up the side of the bath, though a better choice might be sheet vinyl to match existing flooring, or ceramic tiles to match the bath surround.

You could use hardboard if you plan to paper the panels, but the best bet (and the only choice if you want to tile the panels) is plywood. Don't use chipboard in a bathroom because it swells and bursts if it gets wet. For the same reason, any hardboard you use should be the oil-tempered variety, and plywood should be at least moisture-resistant (MR) grade. Ideally, water and boil-proof (WBP) board should be chosen.

ALLOWING FOR ACCESS

A vital point to bear in mind when boxing anything in, is that you might need access to it at some time in the future. For example, you may need to get at the waste trap of a bath if you have a blockage. If you think about this point at the planning stage, it's generally a simple matter either to make the panelling easy to remove, or to incorporate some sort of access hatch.

Tiled panel
This bath has been boxed in with a plywood panel which has then been tiled over. Similar panels are built in at the end and side of the room.

PLANNING THE JOB

Once you have decided that you want to panel in your bath and what type of finish you want on the panel, you have to start planning the job in a little more detail. It is simplest to fit a panel flush with the side of the bath, but if you have the space and have some experience of woodwork, it is attractive to build a shelf at the same time as the panelling, so that the panel is about 15cm out from the side of the bath. You need to measure up the bath so you can sketch out the framework and work out how much timber you'll need for it, what sized cladding panels will be required, and how you will make the various fixings.

CHECK YOUR NEEDS
☐ Softwood battening in 50×25mm and 50mm square sizes for bath panel frameworks
☐ Cladding material – ideally 6mm plywood
☐ Oval wire nails for assembling bath panel frameworks
☐ Screws and plugs for fixing support battens to walls and solid floors
☐ Screws for fixing cladding
☐ Mirror screws for fixing removable panels
☐ Tenon saw for cutting battens
☐ Panel saw or electric jigsaw for cutting cladding panels
☐ Electric drill plus twist drills and masonry drills
☐ Retractable tape measure
☐ Try square
☐ Handyman's knife
☐ Screwdriver
☐ Hammer
☐ Large spirit level
☐ Small spirit level
☐ Plumb line
☐ Knotting, primer, paint, varnish, wallcovering and paste, tiles and grout etc as needed for the finish you have chosen

HALVING JOINTS

To make up the framework supporting the bath panel described in this chapter you have to make a fairly simple joint, called a halving joint. It is used when you want to make a T-shaped join between two pieces of timber.

1 *Measure and mark the joint* ▷
In this example, the rebate to be cut is 25mm×25mm, set into a 50mm square batten. Using a try square, mark round three sides of the batten, 25mm from the top. Mark across the top and down the sides, 25mm from the front.

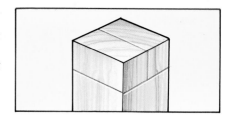

2 *Make the first cut* ▷
Set the batten upright in a workbench and use a tenon saw to saw down from the top, following the marked line, until you reach the line marked round the batten. It is very important that both the pencil marks and the saw cut are accurate, to get a good fit and a perfect right angle.

3 *Make the second cut*
Turn the batten on its side, so it protrudes from the end of the workbench and saw downwards, following the line marked across the batten, until you meet the previous cut and the waste block of wood comes out.

4 *Screwing the joint together* ▷ ▷
Offer up the batten to be set into the joint you have made, and check the fit. Chisel or saw away any surfaces which stand proud. Mark screw positions so they are staggered (to avoid splitting the wood). Remove the batten and drill clearance holes through the batten, plus countersunk holes for

the heads of the screws. Offer up the batten again, and use a bradawl to mark the other half of the joints. Use a fine drill to make pilot holes a few millimetres into the cut half of the joint. Apply woodworking adhesive to all parts of the joint which meet. Position the batten and screw firmly in place.

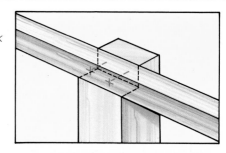

SKEW NAILING

This is a useful technique for making a T-shaped joint between fairly substantial battens (in this case 25×50mm and 50mm square). It is a quick and easy fixing method, but should only be used where the joint is to be covered (inside a stud wall, or behind a bath panel, for example). Also, it is only suitable if the other end of the upright part of the T is to be firmly fixed. In the situation where skew nailing is used here (under the bath) the cross bar of the T-joint is fixed firmly to the floor first.

1 *Position the upright* ▷
Set the upright on the cross bar and use a pencil to mark its position (so you can ensure it is still in the right place when the nailing is finished). Temporarily nail an offcut of wood so that one edge of it butts up to the upright. (Cramp it in place rather than nailing, if this is possible.)
Using a 75mm oval wire nail, drive it in at an angle through the upright, into the cross piece, positioning it about a third of the way across the width of the battens – in this case, about 15mm in from the front edges of the two battens to be joined. (Oval nails are used to prevent the wood from splitting.)

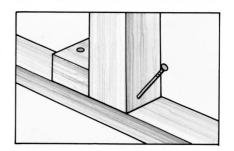

2 *Nail in the other direction*
Remove the offcut of wood, and re-nail it on the other side of the joint. Drive in a second nail from the other side, positioning it so that it is two-thirds of the way across the joint (ie the nails are evenly spaced across the joint).

FITTING A BATH PANEL

The framework can be made of sawn timber (rather than better-looking and more expensive planed all round [par] type). As with all carpentry work, it is important to plan the work carefully before you start and make accurate measurements at each stage. These instructions are for fitting a side *and* end panel, with adjustments for fitting a side panel where appropriate.

1 Measure round the bath
Start by measuring the length of each panel, and decide on the positions of the support battens. Check that there will be no problems fixing them in place (poor plasterwork, missing floorboards, etc) and make good if necessary. You will probably need a batten fixed to the wall at each end of the area to be panelled, two battens down the side and one at the corner (if appropriate).

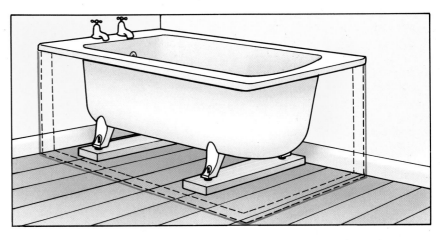

2 Cut timber for bottom rails △
Calculate the exact length of each of the bottom rails: subtract the thickness of the cladding material, plus any decorative finish, from each measurement, and subtract 50mm from the width of the bath to give the measurement of the end rail (to accommodate the width of the side rail). (There is no need to subtract anything from the measurement of the length of the bath if you are fitting a side panel only.) Cut two pieces of 50 × 25mm softwood for bottom rails.

3 Fix bottom rails ▷
Lay the rails on the floor directly beneath (and parallel to) the lip of the bath, checking their alignment with a spirit level if necessary. Mark their positions with pencil lines. Now set them back from the marked lines by the thickness of cladding material plus any decorative finish (eg tiles), to allow the panel to finish neatly below the bath lip. Nail the battens to a wooden floor (beware of pipes running too close to the surface), or plug and screw them in place if the bath is on a solid floor.

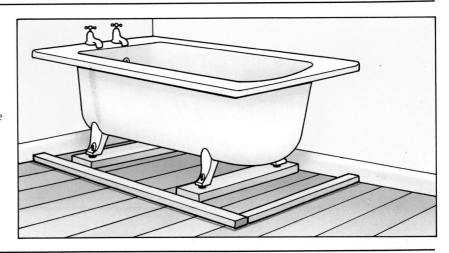

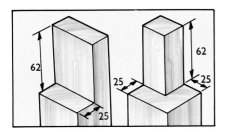

4 Measure and cut uprights △
Then measure the distance between the underside of the bath, up underneath the lip, and the top edge of the floor battens. Cut pieces of 50mm square wood to this length plus 2mm for the uprights; you'll need four to panel in a bath side, or five if you are panelling an end as well. Following the instructions opposite, use your tenon saw to cut out a 62mm × 25mm halving joint at one end of each post, ready to accept the 50 × 25mm top rail later (the extra 12mm is to allow for any overhang of the bath lip). Cut the halving both ways on the corner post if you are also doing the end of the bath.

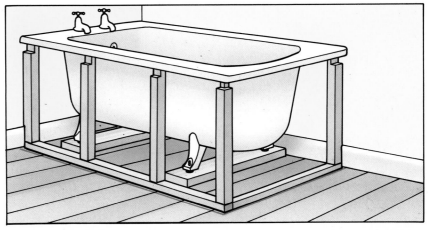

5 Fit the uprights △
Wedge the posts into place between the floor battens and the bath lip, with the halvings at the top, facing out into the room. For two panels, position one post against each wall at the ends of the long and short panels, one at the corner and two more equally spaced down the long side of the bath. (For a single panel you should position one upright against the wall at each end, with the other two equally spaced between.) Scribe the end posts to fit round the skirting if necessary. The extra 2mm in length should ensure that they are a tight fit. Check that they are vertical in each direction using your spirit level. Then skew-nail their feet to the floor battens, and screw the two end battens to the walls.

6 *Position top rails*
Measure and cut to length the 50×25mm top rail(s) to match the bottom rail(s). Offer them up into the halvings you cut in the tops of the posts, drill clearance and countersinking holes, and glue and screw them to the tops of the posts. If you try to nail them, you risk knocking the posts out of alignment.

7 *Fit cladding panels ▷*
Measure up for each cladding panel and cut it to size. If you are fitting two panels, remember to add the thickness of the cladding to the lengthwise measurement to get a neat finish at the corner. You may need to divide the side panel into two sections to get access to the waste trap: this will depend on the nature of the cladding material. A single mahogany panel, for example, can be fitted with six mirror screws, so that the whole panel is removed for access. On the other hand, if the panel is to be tiled, you only want a small access panel, so split the side panel into two parts, one to fit the 'bay' between the first two posts at the tap end of the bath, the other to fit the rest of the bath side. Then offer up each

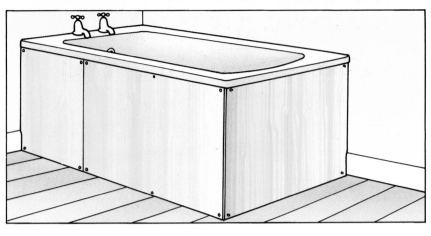

panel to the framework and scribe the ends to fit round skirtings if necessary. Drill pilot and countersinking holes along each edge of the larger panel at around 400-500mm intervals and screw the panel to the framework. Fix the smaller panel with mirror screws drilling pilot holes first. Do not fit the decorative heads on mirror screws at this point, and do not tighten them if you are planning to tile the panels.

8 *Apply finish*
If the cladding is to be decorated, seal it with a coat of size ready for papering (a vinyl wallcovering is best in a bathroom), or with a coat of diluted PVA adhesive if you plan to tile it. Paper over mirror screws, then replace their decorative heads. If you are tiling the removable access panel, remove each corner screw and drill through the tile that will cover it at the appropriate point with a masonry drill. Then fix the tile in position, drive the screws back in and fit the decorative heads.

◁ *Building the framework*
The framework for a panelled bath with a shelf surrounding the edge of the bath has to be slightly more substantial than for a straight panel. Use 50mm square timber with halving joints as indicated. Measure and cut all the joints first. All the uprights are the same length as the finished height of the box, less the thickness of the cladding material (see inset, top right). Halving joints are cut at each end of the uprights, facing inwards to make fixing easier. Cut halving recesses in the horizontal elements of the framework to accept the uprights and the cross struts at the top used to support the cladding. At the corner, the two inner horizontal struts interlock to make a firm joint (see inset, bottom right).

FITTING A PANEL AND SURROUND

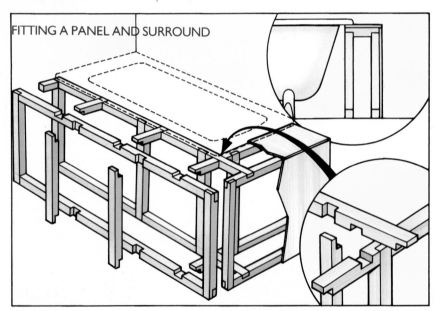

▷ *Bathroom luxury*
If you can spare the room, a 'peninsular' bath with a wide surround creates a really luxurious effect. In a less spacious room, you can still add the surround on two sides to provide a shelf for ornaments and toiletries, without having to move the bath itself. Note how a panelled effect has been created by applying extra wooden strips round the edge of the panels, tacking and gluing it in place. Fit mouldings inside the recess created in this way to give a traditional air. The panels will have to be thoroughly sanded and primed before applying under- and topcoats of paint.

CREATING A GARDEN MOOD

A ground floor room and a glass-roofed lean-to have been knocked together to create a bathroom/dressing room with a look of luxury. The sloping glazed roof makes the room seem open and light and gives it a conservatory atmosphere. The room theme stems from this.

The colour scheme is green and white and a trellis pattern is repeated throughout the room on the walls and curtains to reflect the garden theme. Old-fashioned fixtures and fittings are more suited to the relaxed mood of this room than more modern ones.

Panels and border
Painting the wall panels and border green and covering them with white trellis gives a distinct impression of a pergola. To achieve this you could use garden trellis.

Climbing flowers
When these pretty flower-strewn patterned curtains are drawn the look of the garden is still retained in the bathroom. .

Unfitted look
An old-fashioned roll-top bath, free-standing towel horse, brass taps and brass fittings make the bathroom look and feel cosy and 'lived-in'.

Reflections
Two large mirrors, framed by trellis, add to the feeling of space and light and appear to give glimpses of a whole suite of other garden rooms.

Washstand look
Marble top and brass taps give this vanity unit something of the look of a washstand, which works well with the old-style bath and accessories. With its roomy cupboard underneath it is also a practical choice. The basin is sunk below the worktop surface so there is no lip

surround under which soap and dirt can collect. It is important, however, to make sure the basin is fitted and sealed properly.

Floor tiles
Unpolished terracotta floor tiles work well with the room's conservatory theme. Their old-fashioned look complements the Victorian bath and towel horse.

Painted bath
Painting the outside of the bath in a light terracotta colour with a matt, marble-effect finish is in perfect harmony with the earthy shades of the floor tiles.

A STREAMLINED BATHROOM

A windowless bathroom could be dark and rather oppressive. In this room the problem has been overcome by the careful choice of an almost all-white scheme so that fittings blend in with the walls, floor and ceiling. Because white gives maximum light reflection, the bathroom looks light and everything seems much bigger and more spacious than it actually is.

Small amounts of strong red in contrast to the white and clever use of mirrors and glass all help to add more interest to the room scheme.

Hairdryer
This modern wall-mounted hairdryer is conveniently placed for use. It fits in with the slightly futuristic look of the whole room.

Mirror trickery
There are two narrow strips of mirror: on the wall and at the bottom of the bath panel. These help make the room look longer and lighter and reflect maximum light.

White background
Colouring the whole shell of the room in light-reflecting white and choosing white sanitary fittings helps to make the room look light and spacious.

Glass shelves
Floor-to-ceiling open glass shelves house a supply of towels, flannels and toiletries. These shelves offer as much storage as a tall cupboard and blend well with the rest of the room.

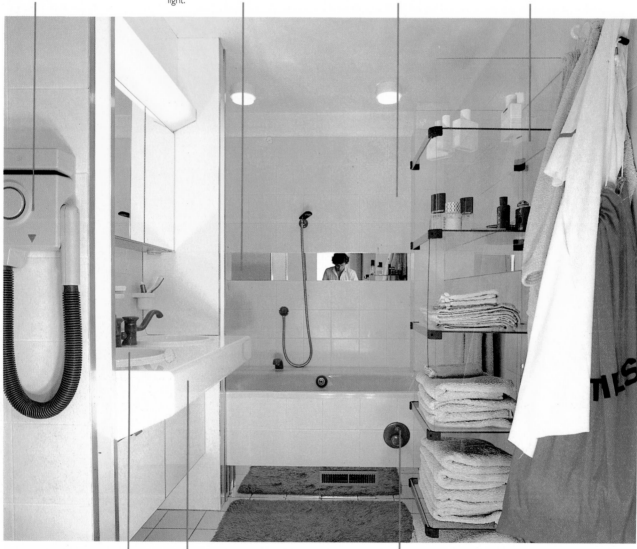

Wall-mounted basin
This hand basin is wall-mounted and cantilevered, which means the plumbing is hidden behind panelling. This gives you maximum floor space.

Modular bathroom furniture
This neat wall unit has been bought as a complete package to include double basins, mirrored wall cabinet, and overhead light. It packs maximum activities into minimum space.

Stark contrast
Splashes of red add dramatic interest to an otherwise monochromatic colour scheme. This only works well if the splashes of red are all the same shade like the laundry bag, bathmat, taps and fittings.

ON A MARINE THEME

In this bathroom the feeling of sea and shore has been created around a modern sand coloured suite.

The walls are lined with tongued-and-grooved boards which have been painted a soft greeny-blue to represent the sea. The carpet has been chosen to pick up the goldy-beige of the suite.

Stencils play a prominent part in this scheme, creating a border of foaming waves around ceiling and skirting and decorating walls with shells and fishes.

Shells and fishes
Stencils in the shape of scallop shells, fishes and waves relieve the solid expanse of colour on the walls.

Colours as well as motifs evoke the sea and shore. Shells and fishes are in a similar sandy shade to that of the bathroom fittings and carpet; the waves are the dark blue-green of a rather stormy sea.

Wooden pelmet
The deep wooden pelmet, made of tongued and grooved boards and painted to match the walls, lines up with the built-in cupboards and the edge of the bath. It gives the room a finished look and makes the bath seem much more private.

Round mirror
The white porthole-shaped mirror has a deep outline made of a delicate looking plastic which has a shell-like colour.

Shower screen
A fixed screen is an efficient choice and more in keeping than a shower curtain which could look fussy in this room.

Wood panelling
Tongued and grooved boards, fixed to a framework of battens, give the walls an interesting texture and have a nautical appeal.

The aquamarine colour suggests the sea in summer with sunlight filtering through.

Fixtures and flooring
The bathroom suite and the carpet are in closely related goldy-beige tones which bring to mind a warm sandy beach.

Lace curtain
The choice of a plain glass window, with its cream lace half-curtain and the view of foliage outside, prevents the room from becoming too austere.

A BATHROOM IN A NOSTALGIC MOOD

The atmosphere of times past is re-created here but given a new slant with a light and airy scheme which suits modern tastes. A traditional cast-iron bath, brass reproduction taps, an old bamboo folding table and chair are complemented by a pastel scheme.

Display board
A collection of postcards and memorabilia displayed on a pinboard looks just as good in a bathroom as it does in a kitchen, where it is usually found. Colouring the board to match the bath and adding a ribbon trellis in keeping with the room scheme turns a utilitarian idea into an attractive and witty 'picture'.

Brass taps
Choose antique-style taps for a roll-top bath. It is still possible to get old taps from architectural salvage companies. There are also numerous reproductions of period designs on the market.

Posters
Posters are a cheap way to decorate walls and the wide range of designs available makes it possible to find something to suit most situations. Here they are linked to the scheme by their subject and because they have been mounted to match the display board. Ribbon corners give a feeling of a holiday album.

Border detail
Softly patterned walls are an excellent foil for posters and are made more interesting by adding a wallpaper border. Positioning this some way above the bath visually separates the 'business' area of the room from the wall decoration of pinboard and posters.

Furniture and floor
An old lightweight bamboo table and chair, coir matting and a cotton rug give an air of informality which suits the relaxed mood of this light and breezy room.

Stylised shell
The simple single-colour stencilled design on the bath continues the seaside theme set by the travel posters. The fan motif on the border has been modified into a fan-shaped shell.

Old-style bath
You can give an old-fashioned roll-top bath up-to-date chic by painting the outside to fit in with your colour scheme. Add a stencilled design for an individual touch.

Cushions
Cushions are a simple device for giving the finishing touch to a scheme by adding colour, pattern or style accents. Here the stencil motif appears again in satin cushions shaped and quilted to represent shells.

BATHROOM ACCESSORIES

A bathroom wouldn't function properly without the simple accessories that make bath times so much easier.

As well as being attractive, bathroom accessories should be practical additions to your bathroom, for keeping a whole host of bits and pieces tidy and easily accessible.

Most items can be selected from large ranges and are usually made from easy-clean materials – choose from plastic, glass, china, wood, brass, stainless steel and chrome. Some accessories even come with gold plating. There are prices to suit everyone, from a few pounds to thousands of pounds.

The biggest choice of accessories comes in the wall-mounted ranges. You'll find toilet roll holders, toothbrush holders, flannel and robe hooks, towel rails and rings, shelves, soap dishes and wall cabinets. In addition, there are freestanding accessories such as toilet brushes, waste bins and towel racks.

STORAGE ACCESSORIES

Toiletries, spare toilet rolls, medicines and cleaning equipment can either be displayed on wall-mounted shelving or stored away inside a cupboard. A good sized bathroom cabinet with a mirror on the front is invaluable – especially if it has an integral light and a shaver point.

Cheaper models are moulded plastic bath bars made especially to hang on the wall above the bath or basin. Most have shelves, but some also incorporate useful additions such as toothbrush holders and a cupboard.

TOILET ACCESSORIES

Give your toilet a new look by swopping the old seat for a new one, or top it with a fluffy fabric cover. Most covers come as a set with a shaped pedestal mat, and optional bath mat.

MATERIALS

Plastic accessories come in a range of pastel, primary and neutral shades to co-ordinate with the most popular sanitaryware colours.

Wood accessories tend to come in just two shades: pine to match light, country style rooms, and dark mahogany which is often teamed with china and brass for a traditional feel.

Metal Cheapest of all is chrome but you can choose from bronze, brass and stainless steel (as well as gold plate).

Ceramic If made by a sanitaryware manufacturer, ceramic accessories should match your suite exactly. If you are planning to tile your walls, there are some pretty ceramic accessories which are made to insert into a standard tile space; others are simply surface-mounted.

TYPES OF ACCESSORIES

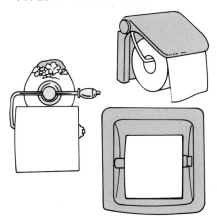

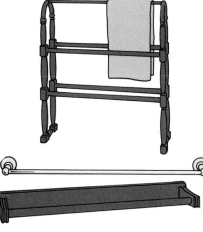

TOWEL RING
Style A round or semi-circular ring made of wood, metal or plastic which is always wall-mounted.
In use Ideal to use where space is limited. Place close to the basin or on a door.
Watchpoint Towels which are not hung flat tend to dry more slowly.

TOILET ROLL HOLDER
Style A metal, plastic or wooden dowel that slips through the centre of the toilet roll. Some are recessed into the wall and others come with musical chimes!
In use Check that the holder allows the toilet roll to run freely – some designs need two hands to use them.

TOWEL RAIL
Style Can be wall-mounted, freestanding or attached to a radiator. They come in plastic, wood or a range of different metals. Heated versions are also available.
In use It's a good idea to place the rail over a radiator so that wet towels can dry while they are hanging – cheaper than a heated rail.

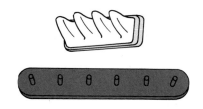

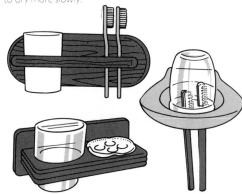

ROBE HOOK
Style Small hook, usually made of wood, metal or plastic, attached to the wall on a bracket.
In use For hanging dressing gowns or robes while in the bathroom.

FLANNEL RACK
Style A small bank of hooks or knobs.
In use Position the rack over the basin or bath to catch drips from wet flannels – over the radiator is a viable alternative.

TOOTHBRUSH HOLDER
Style A small slotted rack to hold toothbrushes. Many holders incorporate a space for a glass or mug and a tube of toothpaste.
In use A handy way of keeping toothbrushes clean and ready to use.

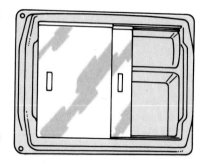

SOAP DISH

Style A shallow, bowl-shaped shelf for holding one or two bars of soap. Some come attached to a wall tile and others can be recessed into a wall.

In use Position within easy reach beside the bath or basin where wet soap will not fall on to the floor.

Watchpoint Look for a mesh design or one with a ridged base that will stop the soap from becoming soft.

CABINETS

Style Moulded from plastic or wood-framed, most cabinets have one or more interior shelves. Some have mirrored doors, built-in lights and a shaving socket. Corner models are available.

In use Position the cabinet where it won't be in the way – in a corner or above the basin are practical.

Watchpoint When storing medicines or cleaning products, choose a cabinet with a childproof lock.

SHELVES

Style Glass, plastic, metal or wooden storage shelves with an ornate or discreetly hidden fixing bracket.

In use Position shelves below a mirror but above the basin, at the back of the bath or in a corner to hold bottles and jars.

SHOWER CADDIES

Style Made in a wire mesh or from plastic with drainage holes, these cabinets are designed for use in a shower since water can drain straight through them.

In use For holding soap, shampoo and flannels while using the shower. Position so that you can easily reach it when showering: next to the shower unit is preferable to below it so that water doesn't soften the soap.

BATH SHELVES/CUPBOARDS

Style Moulded in one piece from plastic, these rigid storage holders are made in colours to match sanitaryware and to fit alongside standard size baths.

In use Tall units can be fitted at the end of a bath or over a basin with space to hold toothbrushes and soap, as well as a shelf and a mirror. Long, thin versions are made to fit along the length of your bath to hold toiletries.

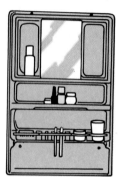

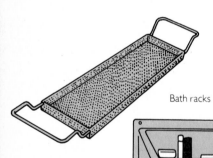

Bath racks

Bath bar

BATH RACK

Style Usually made of metal, often plastic-coated, the rack sits across the width of the bath and is used to hold bath sponges and toiletries.

In use Make sure your rack has holes punched in the base to allow water to drain away freely and stop the soap becoming soggy.

BATH BAR

Style Long plastic unit designed to hang on the wall alongside the bath. For holding accessories such as toiletries, nail brushes and sponges. Many designs also incorporate a small mirror.

In use Position on the wall next to the bath. Directly above is the most suitable place.

Watchpoint Not intended for freestanding baths.

TOILET BRUSH

Style A pot or stand with a detachable brush that is used for cleaning the loo.

In use Some pots can be filled with disinfectant so that the brush can be sterilised when it is not in use. As toilet brushes are usually placed next to the toilet, it is a good idea to choose a co-ordinating style and colour.

TOILET SEAT

Style Many different styles of toilet seats are available in plastic, ceramic or wood. There is a huge range of colours and finishes to select from.

In use Each seat comes complete with fixings so it's an easy job to remove the old one and fit the new.

Watchpoint Not all seats fit all WCs, so measure up carefully or be sure to take a paper template with you when choosing a replacement.

SLIP MAT

Style A square, oblong or oval rubber mat with suction pads on the underside to hold it firmly in place on the bath or shower tray surface.

In use Lay a mat in a bath or shower tray to produce a safe and completely non-slip surface – especially useful for the very young or the elderly.

Watchpoint In a shower, make sure the mat doesn't cover the waste hole of the shower tray.

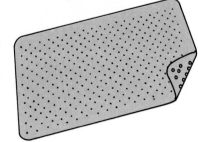

INDEX

ACKNOWLEDGEMENTS

Photographs: 6-7 Elizabeth Whiting Associates, 8 Habitat, 13 Arthur Sanderson and Son, 14-15 Biggie Best, 16(t) Habitat, 17(b), 18(t) Camera Press, (c) National Magazine Co., (b) Syndication International/IPC Magazines, 19 Elizabeth Whiting and Associates/Michael Dunne, 20 Syndication International/IPC Magazines , 21 Elizabeth Whiting and Associates/Michael Dunne, 22 The Picture Library, 23(t) Sunway Blinds, (b) London Door Company, 24 Elizabeth Whiting and Associates/Michael Nicholson, 25 Jahres Zeiten Verlag, 26(t) Syndication International/IPC Magazines, (b) Dulux, 28(t) SIC/MMC/Pataut/Ardouin, (b) Elizabeth Whiting and Associates/Michael Dunne, 30(t) Hulsta, (b) Jahres Zeiten Verlag, 31 Elizabeth Whiting and Associates/Michael Nicholson, 32 Mondadori Press, 33(t) Faber, (b) Bosch, 34(t) Syndication International/IPC Magazines, (b) Elizabeth Whiting and Associates/Michael Dunne, 35 Guy Bouchet, 36,38 Dulux, 39 Jahres Zeiten Verlag, 40(t) Eurostudio, (b) Dulux, 41 Habitat, 42-3 National Magazine Co., 43(b) The Picture Library, 44(t) SIC/MMC/Chabaneix/Mahé, (b) SIC/MMC/Pataut/Bayle, 51 Syndication International/IPC Magazines, 52 Elizabeth Whiting and Associates/Tom Leighton, 54 Elizabeth Whiting and Associates, 55(t) Elizabeth Whiting and Associates/Jerry Tubby, (b) Elizabeth Whiting and Associates, 56(tl) Eaglemoss/Jerry Tubby, (tr) Jahres Zeiten Verlag, (b) Elizabeth Whiting and Associates/Jerry Tubby, 57 National Magazine Co., 59, 60 PWA, 61 Elizabeth Whiting and Associates/Rodney Hyett, 62(t) Dulux, (b) Stag, 69(t) Elizabeth Whiting and Associates/Tim Street-Porter, 70 Elizabeth Whiting and Associates/Di Lewis, 71 Dulux, 72 Martyn Goddard, 73 Elizabeth Whiting and Associates/Michael Crockett, 74(t) Elizabeth Whiting and Associates/Michael Nicholson, (b) Elizabeth Whiting and Associates/Gary Chowanetz, 82-3 IPC Magazines/Robert Harding Syndication, 84 Syndication International/IPC Magazines/Robert Harding Syndication, 87 Elizabeth Whiting and Associates/Michael Dunne, 88(t) Dulux, (b) Bo Appeltoft, 89(t) National Magazine Co., (b) Ken Kirkwood, 90 Nathan, 92(t) Dorma, (bl) Anaglypta, (br) Elizabeth Whiting and Associates/Michael Nicholson, 93 Habitat, 94(l) Swish, 94-5(t) Syndication International/IPC Magazines, 95(b) Elizabeth Whiting and Associates/Tim Street-Porter, 96 Elizabeth Whiting and Associates, 97 Junkers, 98(t) Elizabeth Whiting and Associates/Michael Dunne, (b) Elizabeth Whiting and Associates/Neil Lorimer, 99 Elizabeth Whiting and Associates/Dennis Stone, 100 Elizabeth Whiting and Associates/Michael Dunne, 101 Elizabeth Whiting and Associates/Michael Nicholson, 102 Elizabeth Whiting and Associates/Michael Dunne, 103(tl) Elizabeth Whiting and Associates/Spike Powell, (b) Elizabeth Whiting and Associates/Michael Nicholson, 104(t) Syndication International/IPC Magazines, (b) Jean-Paul Bonhommet, 105 SIC/MMC, 106(t) Jahres Zeiten Verlag, 108(tr) Jahres Zeiten Verlag, (b) Perrings, 109 PWA, 110(t) Elizabeth Whiting and Associates/Michael Nicholson, (b) National Magazine Co., 111 National Magazine Co., 112-3 Richard Paul, 112(b) Elizabeth Whiting and Associates/Frank Herholdt, 113 Elizabeth Whiting and Associates/Spike Powell, 114 National Magazine Co., 115(tl) Eaglemoss/Di Lewis, (tr) Jahres Zeiten Verlag, (b) Elizabeth Whiting and Associates, 116(t) Richard Paul, (b) Ikea, 123 Elizabeth Whiting and Associates/Michael Dunne, 124 Habitat, 125 Marks and Spencer, (b) Ikea, 126(t,c) Habitat, (b) Elizabeth Whiting and Associates/Michael Dunne, 127(t) Elizabeth Whiting and Associates/Clive Helm, (b) Deidi von Schaewen, 128(t) Smallbone of Devizes, (b) Elizabeth Whiting and Associates/Michael Dunne, 134-5 Leicht Kitchens, 136 Elizabeth Whiting and Associates/Rodney Hyett, 143 Schreiber, 144,145 Jahres Zeiten Verlag, 146 Winchmore, 147(t) Bulthaup, (b) Grenadier, 148(tl) Elizabeth Whiting and Associates/Michael Dunne, (tr) Jahres Zeiten Verlag, (b) Wrighton, 149 National Magazine Co., 150 Elizabeth Whiting and Associates/Spike Powell, 151 PWA 152 Smallbone of Devizes, 153 Elizabeth Whiting and Associates/Rodney Hyett, 154(t) PWA, (b) Bosch, 155 Jahres Zeiten Verlag, 156 Poggenpohl, 158 Elizabeth Whiting and Associates/Tom Leighton, 159(t) Poggenpohl, (b) Cover Plus, 160(t) Stelrad, (b) Elizabeth Whiting and Associates/Spike Powell, 161 Miele, 162 Smallbone of Devizes, 163 B&Q, 164 Elizabeth Whiting and Associates/Michael Crockett, 165 EM/Jerry Tubby, 166 Elizabeth Whiting and Associates/Michael Nicholson, 167(t) Arcaid/Richard Bryant, (b) Wrighton, 168(t) Be Modern Kitchens, (b) Siematic, 169(t) Bosch, (bl) Siematic, (br) Jahres Zeiten Verlag, 170(t) Vymura, (bl) Martyn Goddard, (br) Elizabeth Whiting and Associates/Rodney Hyett, 171 National Magazine Co., 172 Leicht, 173(t) Elizabeth Whiting and Associates/Michael Nicholson, (b) Jahres Zeiten Verlag, 174 Bulthaup, 175(tr) Poggenpohl, (bl) Elizabeth Whiting and Associates/Rodney Hyett, (br) Bulthaup, 176 Elizabeth Whiting and Associates/Rodney Hyett, 181 Elizabeth Whiting and Associates/Spike Powell, 182(t) Cristal Tile, (b) Formica, 183 PWA, 184(t) Jahres Zeiten Verlag, (b) Woodstock, 185(t) Elizabeth Whiting and Associates/Clive Helm, (b) Siematic, 186(tl) Moben, (tr) Woodstock, (b) Syndication International/IPC Magazines, 187,188(t) National Magazine Co., (b) Schreiber, 189(t) Smallbone of Devizes, (b) Richard Paul, 190 Elizabeth Whiting and Associates, 191(tl) Elizabeth Whiting and Associates/Rodney Hyett, (b) Magnet, 192(t) The Picture Library, (b) Elizabeth Whiting and Associates/Michael Dunne, 193(t) Elizabeth Whiting and Associates/Jon Nicholson, (b)Bosch, 194(tl) Be Modern Kitchens, (tr) Bosch, (b) Elizabeth Whiting and Associates, 195 Elizabeth Whiting and Associates/Jerry Tubby, 196-7 Elizabeth Whiting and Associates/Michael Dunne, 198(t) The Original Kitchen Co, (b) Allmilmo, 199 Elizabeth Whiting and Associates/Clive Helm, 200-01 Dorma, 202 Elizabeth Whiting and Associates/Spike Powell, 205 Schreiber, 206 Habitat, 208 Acmetrack, 210(t) PWA, (br) Stag, 211 PWA, 213(t) Dorma, (b) Elizabeth Whiting and Associates/Michael Dunne, 214(t) Dulux, (b) Dorma, 215 Sharps, 216 PWA, 217 Elizabeth Whiting and Associates/Michael Dunne, 218(t) Hulsta, (b) Sharps, 219 Arthur Sanderson and Son, 220 Sharps, 221 Camera Press, 222(t) PWA, (bl) Elizabeth Whiting and Associates/Di Lewis, (br) ICI Fibres, 223 Textra, 224(t) Elizabeth Whiting and Associates/Michael Dunne, (b) Interior Selection, 225, 226(t) Elizabeth Whiting and Associates/Michael Dunne, 226(b) Elizabeth Whiting and Associates/Tim Street-Porter, 227 Elizabeth Whiting and Associates/Michael Dunne, 228 PWA, 229(t) Elizabeth Whiting and Associates/Michael Dunne, (b) Bill McLaughlin, 230(t) Elizabeth Whiting and Associates/Michael Dunne, (b) Syndication International/IPC Magazines, 231Skopos, 232-234 National Magazine Co., 235(t) Jean-Paul Bonhommet, (b) Top Knobs, 236(t) Dorma, (b) Dulux, 237 SIC/MMC/Scotto/Postic, 238 Mothercare, 240 Elizabeth Whiting and Associates/Jerry Tubby, 242(t) Elizabeth Whiting and Associates/Michael Nicholson, (bl) Vymura, (br) SIC/MMC, 243-4 Elizabeth Whiting and Associates/Michael Dunne, 245 Dulux, 246(t) Elizabeth Whiting and Associates/Michael Dunne, (b) Coloroll, 247 Elizabeth Whiting and Associates/Jon Nicholson, 248(t) The Picture Library, (bl) Vymura, (br) Addis, 249 SIC/MMC, 250 PWA, 252(t) Schreiber, (b) PWA, 253 Elizabeth Whiting and Associates/Michael Nicholson, 254(t) Sleepeeze, (cl) PWA, (bl) Elizabeth Whiting and Associates/Jerry Tubby, 255 Hulsta, 256 Jahres Zeiten Verlag, 257 National Magazine Co., 258 Jahres Zeiten Verlag, 259(t) Jahres Zeiten Verlag, (b) Spur, 260 SIC/MMC/Pautaut/HM, 262-3 Boots Bathrooms, 264 Crown, 267 National Magazine Co., 268 Ideal Standard, 270(t) Ideal Standard, (b) Syndication International/IPC Magazines, 271 Mantaleda, 272(t) Cover Plus, (bl) Elizabeth Whiting and Associates/Spike Powell, (br) EM/Jerry Tubby, 273(t) Elizabeth Whiting and Associates/Jon Nicholson, (b) Elizabeth Whiting and Associates/Clive Helm, 274(tl) Syndication International/IPC Magazines, 274-5 Syndication International/IPC Magazines, 276-7 Elizabeth Whiting and Associates, 276(bl) Syndication International/IPC Magazines, 277 H&R Johnson, 278 Cover Plus, 279 Elizabeth Whiting and Associates/Michael Nicholson, 280 Dulux, 281(t) PWA, (b) Elizabeth Whiting and Associates/Clive Helm, 282(t) Ken Kirkwood, (b) Grub Street, 283 Tilemart, 284(t) Cover Plus, (b) Next Interiors, 285 Richard Paul, 286(t) Bernard J Arnull, (b) Original Bathrooms, 287(t) Cristal, (b) CP Hart, 288(tr) Allia, (b) Bernard J Arnull, 289 Syndication International/IPC Magazines, 292 Dulux, 293 Elizabeth Whiting and Associates/Michael Dunne, 294 Elizabeth Whiting and Associates, 295 B&Q, 296 PWA, 299 Elizabeth Whiting Associates/Rodney Hyett.

Illustrations: 9-10 Coral Mula, 15-18 Ross Wardle/Portland Artists, 22 Trevor Lawrence, 24 Craig Austin, 27, 29(b) Trevor Lawrence, 29(tr) Ludmilla Pavel, 33-39 Colin McCallum, 45-46 Coral Mula, 53-54 Ross Wardle/Portland Artists, 58, 61 Rob Garrard, 60 Craig Austin, 67-68 Hayward and Martin, 71, 73 Trevor Lawrence, 85-86 Peter Bull Art, 89-91 Craig Austin, 100-103 Rob Garrard, 107(t) Craig Austin, (b) Trevor Lawrence, 114 Colin McCullum, 139 Stan Midson, 144 Coral Mula, 145 Trevor Lawrence, 146 Terry Evans, 150 Craig Austin, 151-153 Trevor Lawrence, 157 Trevor Lawrence, 158, 160 Craig Austin, 163, 164 Rob Garrard, 168-169 Rob Garrard, 174, 176 Coral Muola, 191 Craig Austin, 203-204 Coral Mula, 207 Ross Wardle/Portland Artists, 211, 213 Craig Austin, 214 Sharon Finmark, 216, 217 Trevor Lawrence, 221 Trevor Lawrence, 220-223 Stan North, 227-228 Colin McCullum, 233-235 Colin McCullum, 239, 241(t) Sharon Finmark, 241(b) Craig Austin, 245-247 Rob Garrard, 251(t) Coral Mula, (b) Trevor Lawrence, 266 Peter Bull Artists, 268-271 Ross Wardle/Portland Artists, 275 Coral Mula, 279 Dee McLean/Linden Artists, 285-288 Chris Lyon, 290-292 Stan North.